PINCH ME

How Following The Signals Changed My Life

Bernadette Logue

Other title in this series:
*Going Out On A Limb—How Signals Led Me
Beyond My Limits & Into Truth*

Brought to you by:
www.pinchmeliving.com

First Edition published in 2012 by Pinch Me Publishing
Cover images by iStockphoto.com
Cover design by Dexter Fry
Editing by Sarajoy Porter Bonebright
Design and layout by Elizabeth Gauthier

Also by the Author:
Going Out On A Limb
Unleash Your Life

The content of this book is a personal story intended to provide inspiration and information to assist you in creating a life you love. If you should decide to apply any of the information provided in this book, the author and publisher assume no responsibility for your actions.

Although this is a non-fiction account, most names used throughout this book are fictitious for the purpose of privacy for individuals.

ISBN 978-0-473-20612-3 (Paperback)

ISBN 978-0-473-20613-0 (E-Book)

A copy of this publication is available from the National Library of New Zealand.

Contents

Acknowledgements

I am grateful to many people who knowingly and unknowingly contributed to my journey and, therefore, this book. My interactions and conversations with people, and advice given to me by family, friends and people I've met along the way, have formed a collaborative effort in creating this book.

In particular, I would like to thank Aaron and Charlotte for their guidance and unwavering support. Never once did I see a furrowed brow, a screwed up nose or a raised eyebrow. There was only ever a listening ear and a bear hug when I needed support and reassurance that I wasn't going mad. Without you I would not have come this far; I would have shrunk back and buried my head in the sand. You are both well versed in tap maintenance.

To Stephen, thank you for being supportive of my new direction and seeing the possibility of my continued contribution to your business while I went on a life-changing journey. Thank you for giving me the logistical means with which to explore my life and chase my dreams.

To Jacquie, Joan and all those who offered support, advice and their time when I first embarked on the exciting and sometimes scary adventure of publishing this book. To share my manuscript with people was a leap into the unknown, made all the easier by people who could see the possibility and understood what I was seeking to achieve.

My gratitude to the visionary authors and talented musical artists whose words I have quoted throughout this story. These words acted as very important signals leading me forward in my life-changing journey. All quotes have been cited in the References & Resources section.

My experiences and the information in this book came to me from many sources here in the physical world we live in and from the spiritual realm. Others showed me the way; now it's time to pay it forward.

Introduction

Pinch Me is an appropriate title for this book, as it encapsulates the way I felt in hundreds of moments during a period of major change in my life.

When you think you're dreaming, things seem too good to be true, too coincidental or too far-fetched for you to get your head around, you wonder: *Was that real? Did that just happen? Pinch me. I must be dreaming!*

This book is an uncensored account of an 18 month period in my life when things took a seriously unexpected turn. It is about the odd, sometimes bizarre, and often hilarious occurrences I encountered as I stumbled upon and then adventured deeper and deeper into that 'other side'—the spiritual world. It is a straight-up account in my own words. There is no research behind this, no academia involved. It is just what happened to me, how I interpreted it and where it led me—laid out for you to read.

You can make up your own mind about what it means and what the possible implications could be for your life, if what happened to me seems feasible to you.

The 'Half Life' Syndrome

My life-changing rollercoaster ride started off in early 2010 when I fully awoke to the fact that I was living a 'half life'—a life where I stayed inside a box, valuing safety, security and stereotypical pathways, doing the usual things that society expects of us. There was no doubt in my heart that I was in the middle of a life half lived, with half happiness. I tried to ignore it and focus on being grateful for what I had. The truth was that I had everything I could really ask for, except one thing: joy. Surrounded by all the things one should want in life, I questioned why my heart was songless, seeking and longing for something. I was longing for a sense of freedom to create the life I really wanted. I was longing for the courage to do it. I didn't want to come to the end of my life wondering... what if?

Born out of a quest for answers and a desire to break out of the box I felt trapped in, I went on a search for greater meaning in my life. This search subsequently saw my life changing on a momentous scale. Within 18 months everything turned upside down. Life changed on the outside, but it also changed internally for me as a person. I was unrecognisable to myself. Where had the searching, seeking, longing, half-happy and trapped woman gone? She had released herself and transformed. I found joy and my life has never been the same since.

Are you feeling trapped in a box? Do you feel burdened or blocked? What proverbial sack of potatoes are you carrying around on your shoulders, weighing you down? What worries you? What fears lurk in the shadows? Are you experiencing half happiness or, worse, no happiness? What do you wish was different? What do you want your life to be like? What do you want to create? What did you used to dream of doing with your life? What does your version of joy look like?

These were all questions I asked myself. Throughout my life-changing journey I discovered a whole new way of living; beliefs, thoughts and feelings create one's reality, and most importantly, beyond the physical world is a spiritual realm that is constantly beckoning for your attention to show you HOW to achieve what you desire.

It all started with a just-for-fun session with a spirit channeler, and what followed was an Alice-in-Wonderland-style adventure. I was a normal thirty-something, semi-sceptical, career-driven type, who was guided toward, and convinced of, the existence of a spiritual dimension. Many times I crossed the bridge between the 'here and now' physical plane and the spiritual realm. Having unknowingly started a journey, I got far more than I bargained for.

I still feel like a deer in the headlights at times. Did this really happen to me? By learning how to access an Energy Source that we are all part of, and acting on signals from the spiritual realm, I dramatically changed my life. I'm still an average person, but I transformed my entire 'being' in 18 months: my beliefs, thoughts, feelings, career, lifestyle, health, relationships, financial situation, location, my past, my present, my future and my happiness.

At the time I started writing this book I was not a writer—never had been and never wanted to be. I was certainly no author, that's for sure, and I had no desire to be one. I considered myself creatively challenged, often verbose and certainly nowhere near eloquent or poetic enough to take on a book. This book was effectively born out of this period of craziness, and it came out of nowhere. I just picked up a pen and a notebook, and I metaphorically vomited up a written account of what was happening to me. I was guided to write it, as the information contained in this book is meant to be shared—to give other people the opportunity to reflect, question and consider... what if?

You have a choice in life, just like I did. You can ignore the other side and explain away the strange things that happen, or you can keep an open mind, enquire, learn and harness this other side, to live the best possible life you can.

As you read this book, I want you to keep this one question in mind:

This life will only happen for you once.
What do you want to do with it?

The Natural Flow of Life

So, I had these strange experiences, so what? What's so special about me? As I've already alluded to, the answer is nothing. I'm just an ordinary person. That's the point. I wasn't born with a special gift. I'm not a psychic. I don't see dead people and I was not abducted by aliens! Until recently I had a normal life, just like everyone else, but then I stumbled upon something.

After having hundreds of 'pinch me' moments, I realised that everyone has the ability to get into a natural flow of life. You are either in the flow, where life works for and with you, or you are out of the flow, where it might feel like life is working against you.

How do you get into the natural flow of life?

You can do this by turning on a tap—a tap that allows you to access the Energy Source. You can draw on this Energy Source to transform your life in whatever way you want. Anyone can do this. I did it, and I am no different than you.

> ***Did you know that you have a tap?***
> ***Did you know there is an Energy Source?***

As you focus on what you want in your life the Energy Source responds, creating the circumstances that are necessary to bring about your goals, guiding you forward. Behind the scenes, things silently co-operate towards your desired outcome. You may think... so what?

What Do You Want?

Once your tap is turned on you can direct everything around you, all the energy, towards whatever goal you set. Do you want amazing relationships? Do you want good health? Do you want security? Do you want adventure? Do you want peace and quiet? Do you want a successful career? Do you want to contribute to your community? Do you want to make enough money so that you can roll around in it? Do you want to resolve past issues? Do you want to create the future you've always dreamed of?

What do you want in your life?

When I say *want*, I don't mean something you flippantly say you want but underneath you don't really believe, think or feel it's possible. I'm talking about full-blown, unfettered commitment to what you want. How do you think extraordinary people became extraordinary? Were they born that way, or have they found the potent combination of passion mixed with commitment. Maybe a little bit of the former, but I would say a lot of the latter.

It is important that you don't confuse the Energy Source by being Jekyll and Hyde about what you desire; it will give you what you want if you show it clearly and consistently in belief, thought, feeling and action. It can't be tricked; it knows if you say and act like you want something but underneath you neither believe nor feel it is yours, that it is possible, or that you deserve it. You have beliefs, whether you realise it or not, and those beliefs shape your life. Once you align your beliefs with your thoughts, feelings and actions, something powerful happens.

Right now, look closely at what you say you want in your life. Do you believe, think and feel it is possible? Do you believe, think and feel you deserve it?

What I discovered when I was trying really hard to be and have all the things I wanted in my life— trying to be the best me I could be but failing miserably on several accounts (mainly due to what I commonly joke to be my undiagnosed Obsessive Compulsive Disorder)—was that something was missing. I was full of the philosophy that anything is possible, yet I struggled to really to believe that whatever I wanted I could actually make happen. Surely, there are limits to that?

Then I accidentally fell head first into discovering my tap. I turned it on and a flow of things started happening to me and for me, all working perfectly towards my dreams. When you discover first-hand that you can actively make your dreams happen by tapping into the Energy Source, then you believe. Then they cease to be dreams and they become reality. Then you say... pinch me.

Pinch-Me Moments

If you consider your own life so far, you may have had moments when you felt like things were going really well; people and things showed up when you needed them most, life seemed easy and joyful. You were on top of the world. Perhaps you've had that experience for a fleeting moment or for a day, weeks or months. What was that? How can you recreate that experience and hold it for a lifetime?

This, my friends, is what I discovered. I found my tap and used it to transform my life. I thought life was good before, but now I can see it's on a whole other level. Believe me, it's amazing; you want to find your tap, turn it on and let it flow! *But*—and it's a very small yet important 'but'—life is all about freewill. You have a choice.

Let's say all this pinching and tap talk sounds like nonsense to you. Let's say you opt out right now. Then I'd say to you, "Have fun with your life and I hold no judgment on your decision. I wish you well. You will live a life that is full of the fun and challenges that occur when your tap is hidden, and there is nothing wrong with that. It's awesome."

Let's say instead that you like the sound of all this pinching and tap talk. Let's say that you opt in, going on to find your tap and turning it on. What will be the difference? You will have the option of creating your life and making life happen for you, instead of responding as life happens to you. This is the space where you can turn awesome into awesome-er! This is the space where you design the life you want and live it, instead of accepting your lot.

With your tap turned on life becomes unparalleled, and although you can't physically see what is happening and how it happens, it just does. Once you start to believe it from first-hand experience and every fibre of you resonates with that belief, then your tap will start pouring forth coincidences and happenings, helping you towards your goals with such immense speed that you will get dizzy with excitement.

It is at this point that I should advise you that this book comes with a health warning. You may go on to transform your own life, and you may end up bruised from head to toe... from all the pinching.

Be advised in advance that holding this state of being, with your tap pouring forth full tilt, is tricky. You're human, and as a result you can easily get caught up in life, babbling away to yourself in your head, full of life's challenges and problems, busy doing the things you *have* to do and busy focusing on what you don't want. However, I'll share with you from my own experience how to keep yourself on track.

Breaking Out of the Box

You might wonder: Will this work for me?
My answer is... why wouldn't it?

Considering your own life and whatever change you desire, perhaps I could analyse you and your situation, and ask questions like:

- Where are you at in your life right now?
- How big are the changes you want to make?
- What are your current circumstances?

We could pick it all to pieces and decide how probable and feasible it is to truly create the life you want. But does any of that really matter—whoever you are, wherever you are, whatever your situation?

In a world where anything is possible, it is just that...anything is possible. There are no 'buts' that follow. There are no catches. You have as much capacity and right to live this pinch-me way of life as the next person.

Maybe you're a 45-year-old New York taxi driver with three young sons, and you dream of taking them on fishing trips to a lake, with neither the time nor means to make that possible.

Maybe you're a 16-year-old girl from London who dreams of being an actress, but your parents have you enrolled in law school to follow in the path of your siblings.

Maybe you're a 39-year-old single mother living in Sydney, running a busy insurance firm, and although you have no idea what you really want to do with your life, you know *this* is not it.

Maybe you're an 82-year-old retiree from Canada who is plagued with ill health, and you regret not ticking off a few items on your bucket list due to being too old, too ill and not having enough money.

The first feedback I got from a publisher about this book was this: "Be clear about your reader. Who is your reader?" I wanted to answer in a full-booming passionate voice, "Humans!" However, I appreciated such a response was not going to win me any favours with potential publishers, so I promptly kept my trap shut.

And so the advice carried on... "Speak to your reader. Who are they? Are they mums and dads? Are they young people? Are they old people? Are they corporate professionals?"

My real answer was that my readers are people who ask *how*? My readers are people who want to live a life of joy, whatever that looks like for them. They are people who feel stopped, stuck, trapped or unsure. My readers are people who dreamt of one day doing something, but underneath they wonder if they will take that dream to the grave with them. My readers are people who have a niggling feeling that never leaves them—a niggle that pesters them each morning when they wake to face another day of the same, a niggle that tells them what they are doing with their lives isn't *it*. My readers are all these people who want to connect with some form of guidance on *how* to move forward.

For people who want something, no matter how big or how small. For people who don't know *how*. For anyone who has ever been told something isn't possible, told by someone else, or worse yet, told by themselves. This book is for *you*.

Now tell me, how do I fit you all into a neat little category, a tidy box, to clearly define you as a demographic of readers? So when they ask me to box you, I say, "NO!"

Life and mankind has boxed you in enough already. You are not defined by your age, ethnicity, gender, occupation, country of residence, by your circumstances, your means, your past or your present. You are instead defined by your beliefs, thoughts and feelings.

This book is for people who want to break out of the box and would like to get a helping hand along the way. It is not me that will give you that helping hand;

it is the Energy Source and the signals it is sending you right now—the signals that you are quite possibly not recognising. I simply want to open your eyes to another realm.

Going from a half-happy, trapped and lost person to now being a vibrant, passionate and inspired woman living the life of her dreams, I'm going to tell you what happened, and I'm going to propose that *how* this happened to me could have as easily happened to you. I'm going to suggest that if you open up your thinking, you can have power over your own life in much the same way.

To be clear up front, this is an account of where I started and ended up. This is not a self-help guide; rather, it is a tale of my own adventure. I learned many things during this time, including discovering first-hand that falling over as you progress towards your dream is more than okay. Whereas in the past I thought I was doing something wrong if I faltered, I hope you will see that stumbling is a valuable part of the learning process that propels you forward on your journey of change.

I am sharing this story with you for the purpose of opening up thinking and hopefully inspiring others to design and create their own lives by following signals.

Chapter 1

Stark Realisation

I looked at the number on my phone. She told me that calling this number could change my life. Is that what I want? Am I ready for that? I stared at the phone, willing it to tell me what to do, but I could feel that it was right and that somehow I needed to do this. I wanted to do this, but right then my heart was thudding. The sound was deafening. Fear was rearing up. It was rushing through my body, and part of me just wanted to hide. I looked around, sure that those in my vicinity must have been able to hear the drums beating inside me.

I held the phone in my hand with a feeling halfway between fear and anticipation. I dialled. God, no! I hung up. I dialled again and hung up.

There I sat, staring at my computer screen. I looked around my workplace. All of my colleagues were busy—busy helping clients, doing deals, processing paperwork, tapping on keyboards, talking on phones. There we all were, super industrious worker bees at our workstations, doing our corporate roles, situated in our lovely office with wonderful views of the harbour, nestled in the centre of a concrete jungle.

Perching on the edge of my office chair, swivelling nervously, I glanced around at the place where I had spent most of my waking hours for the last four years, and I experienced a life-changing moment—a moment when all of a sudden I could see my life for what it really was. It was like someone had turned on the lights and I could more clearly see what was going on.

Scanning my familiar surroundings, I saw the work desk and computer I had been sitting at for 40 hours a week for the last four years. It felt like an extension of my body. The 3x3 metre space had been my little corner of success. I had helped many people from that little corner, but I realised something that seemed pretty profound to me at the time. I had dreams for myself, for my life, for my future, and what I saw before me wasn't part of that. What I currently knew as 'my life' wasn't my dream.

I dreamt of a particular lifestyle and a life I wanted to live 'when I grow up'. As a child I was raised in the countryside; riding horses through long grass and along river banks, playing with a tribe of pets in the wide-open paddocks, fresh air, slow and quiet living, country lanes, no traffic lights or exhaust fumes, warm climate with sunshine, swimming and endless summer days. That was now nothing more than a memory. I longed for that way of life again—a longing that had been with me for some time.

I asked myself: *How come, if that is what I love, am I not living that life? How did I end up here? Is my being here, in this place of half-happiness in my life, a mistake? Is this an accidental blunder because*

I took a wrong turn somewhere along the way? Am I just on a detour to my destination?

In my little corner of success, amidst the corporate hub, I was the ultimate type of worker bee, the Queen B no less. Typing a million miles an hour (I had typed so much and so quickly that there were no markings left on my keyboard), talking a million miles an hour, doing deals a million miles an hour, making money and more money and never allowing myself the time to stop and enjoy any of that. I was so diligently focused on the stereotypical pathway, one that had become a default setting for me, because I had failed to create my life any other way. My default setting went like this: strive, have a good career, make good money, save it, get secure, have a family, retire safe with money, play lawn bowls, grow a garden, spoil my grandchildren, die.

I felt lost in a world of 'follow the pack, have the best of everything, be the best this, wear the best that, try to win (at anything), get a good career, and judge each other by the size of our house, car or bank account'. This was all in the attempt to get to some place where happiness resides, before I ended up dead—FOREVER! I'm no rocket scientist, but I'm also no dumb ass. The whole equation didn't add up for me.

Shouldn't I have some greater purpose? Shouldn't I at least try to figure out what that is before my time comes?

I freely admit that the type of corporate work and environment I found myself in, whether it was at odds with my inner self or not, was certainly most worthy and valuable. I also freely admit that the default-setting life path that I found myself facing is an amazing life for some, and for many, it would fit their version of a dream or adventure. However, the prospect of facing that life path myself did not fill me with joy. It was not my adventure. I felt soul-less and empty.

I had looked myself in the mirror many mornings and nights knowing this. But who was I to profess myself unhappy when I had recognition in my work, I had reward, I was valued by others and I had success. I had everything you could ask for in life—from love and health to wonderful family and friends, from career success and money to comfort and security. Who was I to selfishly claim this was not enough?

Now, hypothetically, let's say I stayed exactly as I was and carried on to find myself in that same life for another four years. I'd be more financially secure, older, probably a little more frustrated and tired of corporate and city life, and possibly with a child or two (or three if I was super quick about it). On paper it would look socially acceptable and sensible. However, I would put a lot of money on the fact that I still wouldn't be fulfilled. Why? My heart doesn't sing at the prospect of that future.

A Songless Heart

I had always known what would make my heart sing (well, at least some things), yet I had done nothing truly tangible (action) to bring that into fruition. Sure, I thought about it, dreamt about it and visualised it, but inaction is the death to all dreams. I was waiting for the sun, stars and moon to align on various fronts before I would take action. Once I make this much money, once I pay the mortgage down to this level, once this business takes off, once we've had kids, once I've travelled some more... once, once, once, once...

While I thought about my dream-life happening one day, I realised two things:

> ***Targeted action is required if you want your life to be all it can be. There is no right time.***

For some people, the life I was living could have been their dream. It is entirely feasible that people would dream of living in a safe, clean and cultured city, in a nice house, with a nice job, with good networks, good income and sound investments, in a mildly temperate (albeit very windy) climate. So, I had reasoned, this would make me ungrateful or completely stupid to walk away from it. One shouldn't risk things unnecessarily, should one? The old saying goes, 'If it ain't broke, don't fix it'. The question I had to ask myself was: *Is my current life broken?*

More questions followed: *What if I give it away, go for a simpler life and regret it? Can I get it all back? Should I keep my high heels and daily lipstick application, and pound the pavements to keep bringing in the cash, all in order to accumulate as much as I can while it's possible? But what if I get hit by a bus tomorrow and die with money and security, but no real joy?*

Now when I say 'joy', I'm not talking about fun times, laughing at a good joke, having a nice evening, catching up with friends, watching an interesting movie or enjoying a lovely view. I'm talking about deep down in your gut, right down where your heart pounds, right inside your soul where heartfelt, undeniable joy comes from. It's the kind of joy that when you feel it your eyes well with tears from the emotion it evokes and the gratitude you feel for having access to such joy. If you have never felt that way, consider...

Do you want to know that type of joy?

Back at this time, I thought I had to be all or nothing about my decisions. If I wanted the life I dreamed of, simplicity and the things that made me truly happy, I would have to give up everything I had and run away to live in the countryside. This may sound ludicrous, but this was the blinkered reality I found myself facing. I was looking at life too narrowly; I had honed my vision in on the only option I saw as possible, to the exclusion of all else.

It was a shocking horror to me, at 32 years old, to realise that the old saying 'when I grow up' had suddenly become 'I am grown up!' I realised that, in all likelihood, unless I started to make my dreams happen, I would blink and still be right there in another four years, staring at the same computer screen, at the very same desk, with what would be a very broken and exhausted keyboard. More importantly, without change, what would happen to the already soul-less and empty feeling inside of me? I didn't want to know what it felt like to be more soul-less and more empty.

My little corner of success had served me well; it had brought me to that point. I was grateful. But it was time for change. The time had come for me to be able to look the girl in the mirror squarely in the eyes without feeling a pang of longing for something else.

That day in the office, as my life and future flashed before my eyes, I finally got the courage to dial and book in.

Chapter 2

The Edge of Discovery

Leading up to this early-thirties stark realisation, my twenties had been littered with attempts to further improve my life. I was always seeking more and better. I had achieved a lot. I had set goals and reached them. I wanted love and found it. I sought happiness and captured momentary but never lasting contentment. I was always questioning, reading and learning in the hopes of finding that.

I started to realise that some people seemed to be in that place of lasting contentment; they seemed to have found what they were looking for. I didn't know if it was down to finding the right job for me, living in the right place, doing or having the right things, thinking a certain way, or a combination of all of the above. I didn't know what they had that I didn't— inside or outside. I didn't know how to get to that happy place they seemed to have found, but it seemed like they were living on this higher plane, like they had all the answers or were blessed with luck.

I felt like I was on the edge of this space in my late twenties, like all that personal development material was somehow going to pay off. It was like there were magical qualities available just ahead, but I couldn't quite put my finger on it. I was poised on the edge of discovery. I had some pieces to the jigsaw, but something was still missing. It seemed to me that if I kept alert, met the right people or read the right books, then I might catch a glimpse of what I needed to know to help me get *there*. You know 'there', that place where happiness resides (the blissful happy you read about). I'm sure you've felt this way: *If I do this or get that or move here or change this, then I'll be happy.*

As it turned out, there was nowhere to go, no place to get to, no things to accumulate in order to be truly happy. The answers lay much closer to home than I had anticipated. Following the all important phone call, I had no idea how very close I was to discovering what I had been seeking.

The Meeting

She had been waiting for me inside the café where we regularly met. I spotted her in the corner by the window, steam rising off her peppermint tea as she looked up and beamed at me. Jessie had seemed particularly eager to catch up that day. As always, my morning had been hectic at work. I was a whirlwind of busy, busy, busy, doing, doing, doing. I had dashed to meet her, running in my high heels all the way from the office, so as not to keep her waiting. She has the patience of a saint, my Jessie. I know this well after eight years of friendship.

After covering the usual topics of gossip (status of weekend, work, love life and other such salient points), she earnestly leaned forward over the café table and told me she had recently been to see someone—not just any someone but a someone who channels a spirit.

"Okay," I said supportively, with a slightly hesitant but nevertheless intrigued tone. A friend had told her about this channeler. Jessie, like me, was also seeking—seeking answers, guidance and certainty about the *right* path forward, looking for her happy place in life.

She regaled me with how amazing her session with him was. I could feel her excitement. She had my attention. However, while I was equally looking for answers, I still felt inside like I knew best. I thought: *I must have the answers. I must be smart enough to work this out for myself.* I had a niggling feeling that the answers lay within me, not externally, but I didn't know what on earth to do with that.

The Spirit Channeler

Jessie told me, "David looks about 35 years old, but by all accounts he's much older than that. It's hard to tell his exact age," she said, "because he literally glows with peace and tranquillity! He's been channeling a specific spirit, Augustus, for many years." She shared all about her experience and encouraged me to see him. "This could be exactly what you need!"

I was hesitant. I wasn't afraid he would tell me bad things. I was more concerned that I wouldn't get my money's worth. I thought: *What can he tell me that I don't already know? After all, I've spent a lot of time navel-gazing through the years of personal development. Surely, I must be clued up enough to help myself by now?*

Here is where coincidence came into play, or was it really coincidence? Don't things happen and come into life when you need them most? Well, they seem to for me, and over recent times it has become even clearer that what I need shows up every single time... if I keep my eyes and ears open.

Jessie described a session with Augustus as having someone reflect back to you what you know of yourself and your life, at times to accurate and personal detail, pointing out areas that you need to focus on more if you wish to break new ground and live to your full potential. He could shed light on how to play to your strengths and which of your challenging personality traits (weaknesses) to balance out. She assured me that all of this came mixed in with a little serenity, a lot of wisdom, and a calm and caring approach.

It sounded okay, intriguing even. I took the number for David and dutifully programmed it into my phone. At the time, it felt like I took his number more to avoid offending her kind suggestion that I give it a go. While I felt strangely compelled to see what this spirit had to say, something inside of me continued to resist. Was it cynicism? Fear? Perhaps it didn't help that I researched channeling, and

Wikipedia told me, "... the channeler goes into a trance, or 'leaves their body'. He or she becomes 'possessed' by a specific spirit... who then talks through them."[1]

If I went to see him, would it be weird? Almost certainly.

Would he look like he was possessed by the devil? Quite possibly.

Would he tell me stuff I didn't want to hear? I hoped not.

If I wasn't willing to seek guidance, dismissing an opportunity to find answers, perhaps I was unconsciously revelling in a place of indecision in my life. Was I secretly taking pleasure in being metaphorically lost? There I was, feeling like a buoy lolling around in the ocean, drifting, and someone was throwing me a possible anchor line. Why was I not grabbing it? I doubted that I was too lazy to do it, as I'd set many goals and achieved a lot in my life. However, I knew that I could continue setting goals and achieving them forever and a day, and I'd keep getting the same result: half happiness. Something was missing.

When I sat in the office later that day, I had argued with myself, battling back and forth inside my head. *Really, what harm can it do? I'm clearly having trouble figuring out how to change my life by myself. But I can't really justify throwing money at an appointment that I don't need. If I was sick, then sure, going to the doctor could be justified, but this is a frivolous way to spend money, to have a spirit tell me what I should do!*

I was confident any advice would be generic—something the astrology column in the newspaper would tell me.

The answers would come soon enough. The date and time had been confirmed.

Chapter 3

Decisions, Decisions

At the time, I had no idea how poignant that catch up with Jessie would be. However, I should have remembered back to the time when she led me down another questionable path. Some years earlier, Jessie had convinced me to go with her to a palm reader, a woman called Ava.

Wikipedia informed me, "[Palmistry] is the art of characterization and foretelling the future through the study of the palm..."[2]

The Palm Reader

I went along just for a bit of fun. I had never done anything like it before. Jessie, my new boyfriend and I met up at a quirky market one Saturday morning. We sat shoulder to shoulder on a tiny wooden bench seat, patiently waiting in front of an odd looking gypsy cubicle.

I felt a little awkward sitting on the bench. I quite liked the fact my new boyfriend was so open-minded. I tried to act cool, calm and collected, like I was really open-minded too. In reality, inside my head, I was thinking this was pretty weird and probably a solid waste of my $20.

My turn came. I walked in, crossed my arms, and eyed her up and down. I decided beforehand that I would not be saying a word to this woman. She was going to work for her $20. *You can try your best, lady, but you're not prying anything out of me.*

I had hardly settled onto the 3-legged stool, when she leaned forward and grabbed my hand—an awkward moment of uninvited physical contact with a stranger.

"Ah-ha!" she said. "A piano player who loves to sing and dance, but you stopped. You stopped singing, you stopped dancing and you stopped playing piano too." Before I could get a word in, she was on to the next thing that came to her. She didn't wait for confirmation.

Gob smacked would accurately describe how I felt, because it was true. I had played piano all through childhood, and when I left home for University, I never played again, more for lack of a piano than anything. I used to play loud and fast as a child, and I loved every minute of it. My piano teacher threatened to discontinue lessons because I wouldn't abide by the 'correct' timing, pace and volume. I refused to practice for piano examinations. BORING! I just loved playing loud, fast and to my own rules.

At times, the deafening tones of my playing would force my family to slide the piano room doors closed to lessen the noise reverberating around the house. I loved playing for them, but they loved peace and quiet. You can see how the two combined became somewhat disastrous. This is a long-standing family joke.

And I used to sing. I was in the choir until I was 12. I often wish I had been born a Broadway singer and dancer. It's a damn shame I'm not very good at singing. My mother says I have a wonderful voice. Don't you love how mothers tell you things like that? Granted, as I child I could chortle out a good old church hymn no problem, but who is really going to say you're average when you're singing in church. "Sorry, love, you're a bit crap." That would be most un-Christian!

I stopped singing when I got to high school. It wasn't the cool thing to do anymore, unless you were amazing at it. I self-assessed that I was never going to be *really* good, so why bother? It was one of those moments when your childhood joy gives way to self-imposed limitations—one of many such moments for me.

I also loved dancing. As a child, I made up endless dance routines to songs, rehearsing at home in the living room to Billy Joel blaring from the cassette tape. I coerced my siblings to be in on the act too, creating routines for my parents' viewing pleasure. I rocked the school talent show with a choreographed routine at ten, with my best friends in tow.

Although I didn't do much dancing in high school, other than attempting to look cool while dancing the typical teenage two-step at the discos, I took up several types of dancing as an adult. It makes my heart sing when I dance, and I feel like I am meant to dance as a way of self-expression. However, you'll see a pattern here, I stopped dancing too. I met a guy who was into dancing, and he broke my heart. However, fear not, for I rebounded by falling for another guy who was into dancing. Then, he broke my heart. After two broken hearts (or one very, very broken heart), I gave dancing away too.

This slightly flaky looking lady had picked up that I had given up three things I loved. She also stated with certainty that my relatively new boyfriend, this open-minded character, would be *the one*. I'm not sure how she picked that chalk and cheese would end up like two peas in a pod, but eight years on, two very happy peas we are.

Crossroads

It seems Jessie has a habit of pointing me in the direction of 'helpers'. She had now brought David and Augustus into my life at a time when numerous major decisions lay ahead of me. These decisions were all culminating into what felt like a mountain too high and treacherous to climb. These were quite significant decisions that would shape my future, decisions that had been niggling at me for a long time, lingering and calling me to action. These decisions involved major financial and investment changes, a potentially significant career and income change, lifestyle decisions that would impact my family and social network, the sale and purchase of property, and moving locations.

The changes, while potentially life altering for the better (all part of my master plan to find joy), were also completely nerve wracking and were filling me with a laboured and heavy sense of uncertainty and indecision. My mind was in chaos.

Giving up a fair chunk of our financial security didn't seem like a very sensible decision at all! Although we could have waited another five or ten years to have it all ('all' being our dreams) by saving, paying down debt, shuffling investments and working harder, I was plagued by the sense that life is just too short to wait for 'one day'. For once in my life, I wanted to live for the moment.

> *If you want a different output,*
> *you have to change your input.*
> *Some factor in the equation of life has to alter*
> *if you want a different result.*

But, I didn't know *how* to make it all happen. I was paralysed by fear of doing the wrong thing. I'm a pretty confident and action-oriented person, and I *usually* make decisions without concern or heartache. However, I am also extremely conservative and risk averse.

Enter Aaron, my husband, the fearless risk taker who is happy to throw caution to the wind at any time of the day or night in pursuit of opportunity and adventure. He balances out my worry. My father used to call me a worrywart, and I recall him telling me years ago:

> **Worry is wasted energy.**
> **Things turn out the same whether**
> **you worry or not.**

I was truly conflicted. The chaos in my mind continued, questions churned around and around like a whirlpool. *Do I stay in the highly paid job in the concrete jungle, in a life that while entirely comfortable and blessed, is not fulfilling? Do I continue to make 'sensible' choices, focus on the path ahead and whatever carries on from there? Or, do I give away what most people would kill for, throw caution to the wind, make my dream life happen and be selfishly free to enjoy everything I've always wanted, and see where the adventure will lead me?*

Although this was what my version of adventure looked like, your version of adventure could be something completely different and equally as exciting.

> **What does your version of adventure look like?**

Chapter 4

May the Force Be with You

It's now time to talk about the Energy Source I mentioned earlier. It's a deal maker and a deal breaker. It's important to get your head around it if you want to create a life that you love, and if you want to know the secret to *how* to do that. The Energy Source holds the answers.

For centuries mankind has framed, in different forms, the concept that there is something out there that is bigger than us all—a universal intelligence, a greater being, a force, something we can't see. It has been called things like The Universe, God, The Creator, The Source and The Matrix. I call it the Energy Source.

If you want to call it The Universe, go for it. If you want to call it God, call it that. If you prefer Energy Source, so be it. Labels are just a way of making meaning. Label or no label, it's there, it exists.

The Energy Source is not a concept. It is a very real, silent and invisible field of energy that permeates everything in our world. To understand and access the Energy Source does not require you to have any particular beliefs; this is not about religion. In fact, it is not even about spirituality alone. Modern science, quantum physics and leading-edge minds that are bridging the science and spirituality divide, are providing more and more insights and proof into the existence of this field of energy.

We are told that by recognising we are part of this all-pervasive energy field, and by interacting positively with it, we can change our lives. Apparently, it can help us bring to fruition all the things we want in life, like this Energy Source has some type of mystical power.

I've read many very eloquent descriptions of what this Energy Source is and how it works. In my fumbling attempt to describe my experience of it, someone asked me, "Do you mean it's like in Star Wars, when they say 'May the Force be with you'?" Yes, I guess it is. 'The Force' is an unseen and intangible essence that pervades everyone, everything, everywhere. It is a universal intelligence that silently operates behind the scenes.

Funnily enough, 'May the Force be with you' is very similar to 'May God be with you', which is a commonly used phrase in some religions. So whether you're a Luke Skywalker fan, a regular at Sunday church or someone (like me) who is neither (I'm the Catholic sheep that strayed from the flock), the words may be different, but the meaning is the same.

By recognising that the Energy Source exists, that you are part of it, and that it is an unseen force behind what happens in our world, you can learn how to use it in your own life, to your benefit. As mentioned already, *anyone* can do this.

What is the Energy Source?

Let me share three critical concepts with you to explain the Energy Source further, as they underpin much of how I later interpreted my experiences. While this is my take on it, these concepts are not new and they are not my own. They are well known and well written about by many experts, of which I am not one. I had come across this sort of information years earlier when I started practising Law of Attraction techniques. I sort of understood it theoretically, but I had never understood how it practically worked. I also couldn't see how it played out in reality, in my own life.

Firstly, I will need to get a tiny bit scientific with you, which is humorous as I'm not at all scientific myself. I almost vomited in the high school science lab when the teacher enforced frog dissection on us. What is that meant to teach you as a teenager anyway?!

The first point to make is this: everything we know is made up of energy. The planet, every human, every animal, every physical object, every living and non-living thing consists of energy. Your own body is a mass of energy. This, as I understand it, is a proven scientific fact. Additionally, there is an unseen fabric of energy that pervades everything we know—an invisible energy field that is made up of the same 'stuff'.

Secondly, despite 'things' seeming separate and independent of each other, because we are all made up of the same energy, we are actually all connected.

We all came from and belong to the same thing: the all-pervasive energy.

Consider this analogy: imagine a drop of water. You can see an individual drop of water. It has a clear shape, it is finite and it has a volume and mass. It appears independent as one single drop. If that drop of water is put into the ocean, then the drop of water is still there. We know that logically, but it is now completely and utterly connected to the rest of the ocean in a way that we can't explain. Now we can no longer see the single drop of water as independent, finite and with its own volume and mass. It is now clearly part of one interconnected mass of water: the ocean.

Thirdly, because everything is connected, one shift in energy at any level has an effect on everything else. For example, a move in the earth's tectonic plates can cause an earthquake. That earthquake can cause the ocean to move. That move in the ocean can cause large waves to form. Those large waves can cause water currents throughout the ocean. That one event, that one shake, creates waves and water currents that cause movement and change to all the billions of drops of water that make up the whole ocean. This is an example of how things play out in the physical, tangible environment in which we live.

Let's relate that to life now, to the intangible aspect of our reality. Because you are energy and because everything is connected, one shift in you (your beliefs, thoughts, feelings and/or actions) flows on to affect everything else and creates change in your life as a result.

> *Everything is energy.*
> *Everything is connected.*
> *Change in any one thing impacts everything else.*

If all you are hearing is blah, blah, blah, 'scientificy-psycho-spiritual' babble, I understand. That is what I used to think too. It all sounds great in theory, but really?

Using the Energy Source to actively create your life does take some degree of enthusiasm and attention like anything. I, like everyone else, have plenty of moments where I think it would be easier just to sit still and let life happen to me, rather than make my life happen. I've had my share of life's cesspool moments—losses, heartache, ill health, fear and the list goes on. However, I've only felt those moments (you know the ones, when you moan and think: *Why did this happen to me?*) when I've been trapped in the clouded belief that life happens *to* me, when in reality I make life happen.

Life really does create around you in reaction to your energy (your beliefs, thoughts, feelings and actions) and attracts the things that resonate with your own outlook and energy. This concept was not a revelation to me. I had read it many times. However, it was a rollercoaster revelation to experience it consistently first-hand and realise it was true.

Harnessing the Energy Source

Surely you want to direct your life in a certain way, in a way that gives you everything you dream of. Why wouldn't you want that? So, what if you could harness the world around you, effortlessly creating a life where things happen for your benefit, bringing about all you desire? You can.

I know for some people that this may sound a lot like motivational crap, airy-fairy, tapping into this unseen and supposed Energy Source somewhere 'out there'. The problem—and the reason I propose that many people don't experience life this way—is that people often spend the majority of their day being completely unaware of what they are harnessing, what they are creating and what they are bringing about in life because they pay no attention to their own energy.

Most people pay no attention to what they truly believe and what they are thinking and feeling, and so they unconsciously create their lives and then wonder why they don't like the outcome.

Your own energy is responsible for your outcomes. What you put in is what you get out. How many times have you heard that before? How hard you train for sport will determine how successful an athlete you will be. How committed you are to your job will determine how far you go in your career. How and what you eat will determine how healthy you are. What you believe and how you think, feel and act will determine what sort of life you create around you.

Like-minded people attract to each other. Good thoughts attract good things. Negative thoughts attract negative things. Moreover, a thought fuelled by strong emotion is a powerful change agent. This is the message of Law of Attraction, a universal law that was phenomenally shared in *The Secret* by Rhonda Byrne.3

Having experienced the reality of my own positive thoughts and feelings creating more positive things in my life, and my own negative thoughts and feelings creating more negative things in my life, I can promise you from first-hand experience that this is not self-help propaganda. This is not a construct of the minds of crazy spiritual people, who smoke too much happy herb in the commune. This is not just the experience of people who you may think have been lucky, blessed or born into the life they have.

Question & Answer Time

When I say anyone can access the Energy Source, you may disagree. When I say anyone can create their lives around them by accessing guidance from the spiritual realm, you may disbelieve. It may sound a bit paranormal and kooky. It may seem to you like only super spiritual, 'connected' people do this type of thing.

Some people may say...

"Aren't weird spiritual people born weird and spiritual?
I'm not like them."

Those spiritual people are not weird. You just don't see what they see. You just don't hear what they hear. You just don't sense what they sense. You simply haven't experienced it yourself... yet.

"But how can they see, hear and sense things that I don't?"

Everyone is born different. Something in each person's wiring gives unique personalities, unique abilities and unique ways of perceiving the world. You don't need to hear, see or sense things beyond your physical world in order to harness the Energy Source and to access the answers as to *how* to change your life. But for a moment, let's consider this separation between 'us and them' with regards to the perceived divide between spiritually connected people and the rest of the world.

Before you discredit people who claim to see, hear or sense things that you don't, let's think about this example. In World War II, colour-blind people were utilised for their special ability to more clearly see things that others couldn't. According to the Encyclopedia of Nursing & Allied Health,[4] colour-blind people "...may even discover instances in which they can discern details and images that would escape normal-sighted persons. Colour-blind people tend to look for outlines, not colours. Consequently, they are not easily confused by camouflage." Colour-blind people were utilised in planes to spot camouflaged enemy sites. The colour-blind people could see something that the others couldn't.

If a deaf person conveyed to you that they couldn't hear, would you claim they were lying? It's more likely you would have sympathy for them. If a blind person told you that they couldn't see, would you attempt to discredit them? Their experience of reality may be different to yours. Something in the way their body is wired is different to yours, but you accept this. However, if someone tells you that they see and hear things that you don't, that they've got something you don't, that they know something you don't, mmm... this seems unbelievable, and you automatically ask for proof of validity.

Just because you don't personally register experiences that these spiritually connected people do, doesn't mean it isn't real. Here is where everyone differs based on their personalities. Is it true until proven false, or false until proven true? Sure, there are probably things out there in the genre of mind, body and spirit that purport to be real, which have been fabricated. But generally speaking, many people tend to be cynical and close-minded unless they see pure, irrefutable evidence to prove otherwise. There is one fatal flaw to this way of living, and that is you miss half of what's offered to you in life if you only operate in the physical dimension.

If I ask you what you can't see, your answer should be, "I don't know what I can't see because I can't see it." Precisely! You can't judge that which you can't see and don't know, because you have no knowledge or basis on which to make such a judgment.

Some people may say...

"This Energy Source isn't accessible to the average person,
is it?"

Yes, it is. Everyone is born with the ability to access the Energy Source; it's just that we are all born with varying degrees of that ability. Some people are born with a natural ability, while other people will have to learn and practice to develop their ability.

Some people may say...

"Aren't palm readers and psychics born with special
powers?"

"Aren't spirit channelers, energy healers and
mediums born with a gift?"

These are just some well-known forms of connecting to the spiritual realm. Do they have special powers or special gifts? Yes and no. Some people are born with something, but it's a highly developed ability, not a special power. Others have learned to develop the ability, perhaps to the limits of their individual capability, through discovering it and then training and practising.

Let's use sport as an analogy. Some people are born with extraordinary sporting talent that seems to come naturally and propels them to the top of their chosen sport. Others will study, practice and train for a lifetime, and while they will develop their sporting ability, they may never reach the top level to which others seem to naturally rise.

Most importantly though...

Spiritual or Not—It Makes No Difference

The fact of the matter is this: everyone is connected to the Energy Source; it's impossible not to be! You are part of it. It's simply a case of how you harness that connection.

You don't have to be one of these 'spiritual' people, whatever you perceive that to be, and you certainly don't have to *want* to be one of these people in order to access the Energy Source. Many people are just like you or I: wonderful people going about their daily lives with no interest in delving into spirituality or any interest in things such as psychics, mediums and channelers.

Accessing the Energy Source doesn't have to have anything to do with these things. These are just forms of connecting to the spiritual realm that are well known.

If you choose to, you can simply harness the Energy Source for your own personal application in day-to-day living to improve your quality of life, to create what you want. It is private and it is just for you. It's a learned skill.

What Are You Interested In?

I'm not interested in dabbling in this stuff so I can read the future with a crystal ball or so that I can see dead people (crikey, I think I'd die of fright on the spot!) However, I respect that other people have that honest and real ability, and that they harness it.

So if I'm not interested in that, what am I interested in? If there is a greater being—a universal intelligence, that has something to offer me that will make my life better, then damn straight I want a piece of that action. That is what I'm interested in. That is what I discovered. Why make life a struggle when it doesn't have to be one?

What are *you* interested in? Are you interested in reaching your own true potential, following guidance from the Energy Source? Or are you interested in denying that you have the ability to do, be and have anything you want in life?

Let me be clear: I am not a fatalist. I do not believe my life is determined by a greater intelligence. I believe that everyone has freewill and that life can take an infinite number of potential turns and paths based on day-to-day decisions.

The Energy Source, in my view, is guiding us through our lives, whether we know it or not, on whatever path we take. It acts like a compass that recalibrates every time we make decisions and change direction. It responds to what we say we want in life (consciously or unconsciously). You tell it what you want by what you believe, what you think, how you feel and how you act. It then delivers signals to show you the way.

Chapter 5

Insights from the Other Side

Sitting at work I looked at the clock, counting down until it was time to leave. I felt sick to my stomach, nervous. I fixed my hair up and applied lipstick. I was quietly amused at myself for beautifying for an appointment with a spirit. Really, there is no excuse for poor grooming, no matter where you're going.

The taxi dropped me off and I wandered up and down the road, trying to find the house. I must have gone too far. I turned to walk back, fidgeting with my bag. My throat was dry and my stomach was churning with butterflies.

Across the road, some distance away, I could see him standing in front of his house, like he was waiting for me. David boisterously and warmly greeted me from across the road with a loud, "Hello, Bernadette!" He waved me in.

I remember thinking: *What if I wasn't Bernadette? Or did he already know I was Bernadette? Ooooh, the mind tricks have begun already!*

I followed him inside. He was chattering away as he walked through the house. I was looking left, right, behind, nodding and answering with vacant responses as my eyes and mind were busy analysing his house, his décor, and scanning the environment looking for evidence that I had made the right or wrong decision coming here.

I settled into a comfortable chair. He sat opposite me. I could tell he was trying to put me at ease with smiles and chitchat. I was grateful. He then explained that he would be leaving, and Augustus would be 'coming out'.

Like with the palm reader, I went to this session with Augustus with a slightly sceptical mindset. I admit that I was open and intrigued enough to go in the first place; I was just unsure that he would be able to give me any clear advice or direction unique and specific to me. I decided to remain mute, to wait and see what would happen.

I sat poised, holding my breath, avoiding looking at him as he left and Augustus arrived.

It took less than five minutes of the one-hour session to realise that David really was channeling a spirit. Augustus knew things about me, my life and my relationships in accurate and personal detail, in a way that even the best researcher would never have been able to establish. He knew the specific dynamics of my marriage that only Aaron and I would know. He knew things about our interests, investments, the decisions we were facing, my personality traits, my family and on the list goes. He named specific people and issues in my life without being prompted.

Part way through the session, Augustus told me that a spirit had just arrived. He then said other spirits were coming forward; several of my family members that had passed were "pushing their way to the front" to have their chance to share messages with me. The information he shared about them and the messages from them left me speechless. And, let me tell you, it takes quite something to leave me at a loss for words!

The spirits of my family members passed challenged me to think about what my life would be like if I didn't make the tough decisions at hand. They encouraged me to take the leap of faith that I was so afraid of. Augustus shared insights from my grandmother and things she wanted me to know. She said I was living my life like I was walking around in a full suit of armour, overly cautious and trying to protect myself. She said, "It must be exhausting. What are you so afraid of?" She insisted, "This move is going to be the making of you."

Then Augustus became distracted, talking quietly to someone at his side. Sarah had arrived. Emotion overcame me at the mention of her name. It had been almost 19 years of missing her and feeling the never-ending ache inside from the gap she left. Sarah is my eldest sister, and she died when I was 13. The experience turned me into a teenager who asked more questions than most, like, "Why did you leave me?"

Raised in a wonderful, large Irish Catholic family, I asked, "God, why did you take her from us? What kind of God would do that?" And over time, "God can't really be what they say God is to have done this to me." I felt empty, cheated, confused and full of questions.

For many years, it caused me to look at life with cold, hard, staring eyes, and later when the raw pain subsided, with eyes full of curiosity and seeking. I felt sure there had to be a reason why she had gone and left us, but I could not figure it out.

Yet here she was, and after all this time she had only one question for me, one very simple question. I hung on to every word. Augustus said, "She wants to ask you what your life will be like if you don't make these changes?"

That was all I needed. In a flash, I saw myself in the future living the same life, and one thing was missing: true joy. My answer to her question, which I quietly but categorically said aloud, was, "It won't be the life I've dreamed of, and I don't want to settle for less." Tears streamed down my face as I mouthed the words to Augustus, with the image of Sarah's face in my mind.

I had made a decision when I reached the age of 25, the age Sarah had died, that she didn't have a chance to go on and experience other things but that I could. I had the opportunity to experience life, and I knew it was important to do so, at least to honour her memory by living life as fully as I could.

Yet sitting there in my thirties, why was I hesitating about taking the bull by the horns?

Balanced Advice

If you're thinking that Augustus gave me a happy, clappy spiel about chasing dreams and 'doing whatever you have to in order to make it happen,' you'd be wrong. When asked, he gave me advice on what decisions to consider now, what to give more time and thought to, what risks to be wary of and what to pay heed to. He didn't once tell me what to do. He didn't even allude to what he thought I should do, but he acted like a trusted advisor and gave me prompts around the pros and cons.

It's all well and good listening to your banker, your accountant, your financial advisor, your lawyer, your family, your friends or your work colleagues. For that matter even your partner or spouse. They all come at it from their own perspective. They all have something vested in your decision, whether they or you admit it or not. But you are the one and only person living in your skin, experiencing your life and your reality. You are the one who must live with your decisions—or lack thereof.

When a wise old spirit who seems to know everything about you tells you all of the above, wrapped up with a reminder about why you're alive, how and why souls come to have 'human experiences,' and what things really matter, it feels like you've been struck by lightning. Things suddenly seemed crystal clear.

I can't explain how I went from being so uncertain about this whole spirit channeling thing to being so certain about my path ahead. All I know is that I left that session with no doubt about what I had to do. Something clicked. I left knowing that I wasn't prepared to waste away my days and years accepting mediocrity.

I thought: *I want my one shot at this lifetime to be all it can be, and I want joy. I want that for myself. I deserve it.*

Leadership

I had zoned in on the parts of my session with Augustus that resonated with me—the things he said which answered my longing questions. These were the things that made me say, "YES, YES, YES! That's how I feel!"

I pretended not to hear the things that hit a nerve. My session with Augustus yielded one particular piece of advice that didn't sit well with me. It made me squirm. I wanted to tell him to shhhhhh. I wanted to say, "You've got it wrong. Your spiritual radar is off target."

He said to me, "I want you to consider ways you can use your leadership skills..."

My ears heard, "Working closely with people in a corporate setting and dealing with problems." I wanted to scream back at him, "But you don't understand! My heart is songless in a corporate career; it's not my joy! Don't make me do it!"

I automatically assumed leadership in the workplace, which was a natural conclusion for me to jump to in my blinkered view of the world. The thought of leadership in this context didn't excite me; it didn't feel like my passion. It didn't appear to be the path to my bliss. I thought life would be simplest and happiest if I operated in my own bubble like a lone ranger, avoiding problems, keeping to myself and preferably running away to do that in the countryside!

The humorous thing about this, in retrospect, is that while in my head I thought of myself as a lone ranger, in reality I tended to jump in to fix problems at any given opportunity. People who know me will attest to this. I have this inability to be around a problem or question without fixing it or finding an answer, and I'm always right in there giving advice to others and leading the way.

As it turned out, the leadership question from Augustus came at the perfect time. Several things were about to happen that would shed light on this.

What Will People Think?

Plagued by paranoia that people would think I was a weirdo, I slunk back to work and acted like I had just been out for a standard lunch break. I checked for mascara streaks before returning to my desk, worried people would see I'd been crying.

I told only my close family about my session with the spirit channeler. At that time, the start of my journey, other people's opinions mattered greatly to me. However, as time wore on and 'things' started happening, I slowly and selectively started sharing with others. This book is, I guess, the ultimate form of sharing—a way to have my message reach beyond my personal networks and beyond where my spoken word can be heard.

What I have written in this book could end up labelling me with many people, including people I know and respect, as 'a bit out there', or a hippie, or worse... full of crap. I'm actually a reasonably private person, and I have the same underlying fears that most people have. Ultimately, no matter what we say and do, at some level and to some degree we do care what others think of us. But you know what? I've learned in the last 18 months that playing your life safe won't get you anywhere. And I genuinely, wholeheartedly believe in what I have to say, so there is little hesitation in me laying bare these experiences and my interpretations of them.

Chapter 6

The Holy Grail

For some time I had known that the key to creating your life was to focus on what you want—be positive, visualise, believe and affirm. However, my questioning mind would never stop at this. You can be positive, visualise, believe and affirm all you like. If you lock yourself in a cupboard and consistently do these things for the rest of your life, guess what happens? NOTHING! You'll probably die in that cupboard.

Action is required. When you align strong desire, belief, thoughts, feelings and focused action, then you become *very* powerful in creating your life. It was this focused action bit that seemed elusive to me. I could take action—no problem. But what action should I take? What path should I take? What direction should I choose? What should I do, and when should I do it? Show me how!

When you're trying diligently to create your life and you hit a wall or shit happens, and you think you've taken a wrong turn or somehow misinterpreted all of the self-help material available, how do you make sense of what to do next?

The Holy Grail

Here is the holy grail of creating your life. The bit I had been missing all along—the bit I had never been told, never read about, never understood and never looked for. I found the key to unlocking my joy.

I started to realise that there were signals—a broad and endless array of peaceful, ever beckoning, ever present signals to show us all *how* to move forward, like clues in a crossword puzzle. They are there just for you, and they are unique to you.

This realisation tipped my world upside down. I always got the front-end bit—the focus on what you want bit. But without the signals it was never powerful. It was never consistent. It was never unstoppable. It was never life changing.

Was my catch up with Jessie and her suggestion to see Augustus a signal?

Was the content of my session with Augustus and the prompts he gave me, including what would become repeating references to leadership, a signal?

It got me thinking: *What if these actually are signals. What if they're not just coincidences, and what if this is actually how life works?*

I had read about how—through the right believing, thinking, feeling and action—an increasing number of beneficial coincidences can start happening to a person.

In his book, *A New Earth*, Eckhart Tolle shares with us, "When you become aligned with the whole, you become a conscious part of the interconnectedness of the whole and its purpose: the emergence of consciousness into this world. As a result, spontaneous helpful occurrences, chance encounters, coincidences, and synchronistic events happen much more frequently."[5]

Beneficial coincidences are wonderful, but what if it's more than that? What if these events are more than useful occurrences and these happenings are actually trying to guide us forward, showing us what direction to go, showing us how to achieve our goals?

Every day we are bombarded with visual signals everywhere. Signs, signposts, directions...

EXIT

ENTER

UNAUTHORISED ACCESS PROHIBITED

WALK NOW

STOP

TRAIN PLATFORM THIS WAY ⇒

GIVE WAY

GO

SHARP BEND 50m AHEAD

SLOW DOWN

⇐ PARKING

In the modern age we even have the GPS or Navman guiding us. We programme in the destination and follow the on-screen and audio signals all the way to our desired location. "Turn left. Turn right. At the next intersection, go straight ahead." We arrive happily, after trusting implicitly in the guidance from this wonder of technology.

These are the signals that guide us in our day-to-day lives. We trust them because very sensible people erected those signposts, and very smart people designed those GPS and Navman systems, to make our lives easier. These are the signals you see and hear. What about the ones you don't? What if there are less recognisable, more helpful signals that not only guide you day to day, but actually show you *how* to reach your big goals and your dreams.

There were still more questions I asked myself, and ones you might also now be asking yourself, such as:

If this is the case, that signals exist, that spiritual things beyond our understanding happen in order to signal us forward on our path, then how do people not know about this? How come I've never read about this as an actual philosophy? Why isn't everybody aware of this? What could this mean for life? What could this mean for not just my life, but for the lives of others?

This is seriously big!

I'd certainly read and learned a lot about helpful coincidences and how things flow to you according to the natural laws of the Universe, but I saw something in this concept of signals. Like if I put some effort into looking for and deciphering these signals, perhaps they could propel me forward to my happy place. The signals could be my ticket...JOYVILLE THIS WAY ⇒

Birds, Fish, Rivers and Bicycles

You may still be thinking: *Does it really make a difference if I'm in the flow or out of the flow? Does it really matter if I get signals or don't get signals, see them or don't see them? Life just happens anyway, doesn't it?*

Here are a few practical examples to show you why you might want to consciously choose life in the flow.

Migratory birds are known to find the wind currents that circle the earth, flying into and along the wind currents, going with the force of nature to help them on their migratory journey. In this instance it is easier for the birds to travel this way than to battle their way to their destination outside of these natural currents. If you were a bird would you want to join all the other smart birds and get into the wind current, or would you prefer to flap your wings harder for longer?

For anyone who has seen the movie *Finding Nemo*, think of it like the experience Nemo's Dad had when he found the great ocean current that he swam into on his quest to find his son. He saw all the other sea creatures racing along at an incredible speed in this invisible ocean current that seemed to propel them forward at great pace, a strong force of nature helping them on their way. If you haven't seen *Finding Nemo,* then consider this following example:

There is a raging river. The river is flowing fast. Effortlessly, nature carries the water along, and anything in the river flows with it. Next to the river is a muddy and grassy bank. You have two options. You can follow the path of the river by stumbling along the grassy bank, tripping over clumps of weeds, with your feet sinking into the muddy ground. Or, you can reach your destination by jumping in the river and being taken along with the current, the tremendous flow of the water. The river is where you are if you are in the flow of life, accessing the Energy Source and recognising signals. The grassy and muddy bank is where many people live their lives.

Don't you think it would make sense to jump in the water? If you're not a good swimmer, just work with me here, it's an analogy. Just pretend for a moment that you can swim or that you're in the river on a sturdy inflatable raft. For anyone having flashbacks to school camp and being made to go rafting on crazy river rapids with a genuine fear you might drown in the process, you may now be reliving a childhood trauma. (I can relate!)

Let's try one more example, just to cement the explanation. In road cycling there's a term called drafting. Drafting is when a cyclist rides at the back of another moving object (e.g. another cyclist or a vehicle). The reason for this is that the moving object creates a slipstream behind it, where if a cyclist gets in the slipstream they can ride with ease, with little wind resistance, saving themselves time and energy.

Living life with your tap turned on, accessing the Energy Source, might sound like a kooky, crazy, unexplainable way to live, but I challenge you to see for yourself. Put yourself in this space where things happen easily, where there is little if any resistance, where you will get to your desired outcome quicker than if you cycle along fighting the elements and burning all your energy and determination trying to get there. Let the natural laws of life help you on your way. The Energy Source is constructed to do this for you, so why not make the most of it?

The catch up with Jessie and the session with Augustus had brought me right to the water's edge, and while at that time I couldn't yet fully see the raging river, I could hear the water rushing past close by. Soon I would be wading in knee deep. Soon the current would sweep me away.

Signals

The unusual experiences, strange happenings and supposed coincidences that I have alluded to, which I will share with you in detail, were signals. These signals could have been missed or misinterpreted by me as seemingly meaningless. They could have been explained away in any number of ways. However, when I started to recognise them, they started to happen more frequently and obviously. When I not only recognised the signals but also followed them, positive changes in my life amplified and fast forwarded.

Signals may, in some instances, seem like random happenings. However, they are *not* unrelated things that occur by accident. It appears that way to you because you are not engineering them with your own hand. However, you are engineering them with your beliefs, thoughts, feelings and actions.

If you can learn to recognise these seemingly random happenings for what they really are, signals, you then have access to a powerful part of life, and the hardship of working out *how* to achieve your goals becomes free and easy, with the signals pointing you in the right direction.

You may think you are not receiving any signals, but I beg to differ. You are. You just don't interpret them as signals; you may be missing them or interpreting them as something else. There are no limits to the type of signals that you can receive. They can be tiny and seemingly insignificant, or they can be large, bold and 'in your face'.

Signals can be things that you read, see or hear. They can be people that you meet and/or situations that you find yourself in. Perhaps you had a strange dream; maybe the lyrics of a song unexpectedly run through your mind over and over again; or maybe you experienced a strange incident or a funny coincidence. Perhaps you had a gut feeling or an inspired idea; perhaps you crossed paths with someone who suggested something to you; or maybe you read a book or an article at an opportune time. These things all seem like quite normal everyday occurrences, which is why they can be so easy to miss. While these are things you might easily relate to, believe me, it gets more bizarre than this! I'm just warming you up.

As these moments happen to everyone every day, in thousands of different ways, the question is this: do these moments pass you by unrecognised or misinterpreted, or do you see them for what they really are? Beyond that, if you recognise them for what they are, then are you really willing to do something about it? Will you listen and follow the guidance?

At first I didn't know I was getting signals. Then, I realised I was and I started to recognise the signals. Then, I started following the signals. The latter was a very, very big step for this self-confessed control freak. To surrender to a greater intelligence and trust that perhaps something out there is looking after you and is guiding you in the right direction? Big freaking ask! I resisted and resisted, and then, well, you'll see what happened...

The Tap

The only difference between people who know about this and use it and those who don't is that they are aware of it and awake to it. That's the only difference. There is no magical ability that you are born with that allows you to receive, recognise and follow signals.

Let's talk about the tap. The tap is your access to the Energy Source and the signals it is sending you. The tap allows you to see these signals for what they are. Some people are born with their tap proudly displayed, and it's turned on full force. Others are born with their tap visible and slightly turned on, so it's dribbling a bit but not really enough to notice. Finally, others (I'll estimate a large proportion of people, which included me) are born with not only their tap tightly turned off, but their tap is hidden from sight.

Now if you're in this latter category, you'll be wandering around with a hidden tap, wondering where all those strange people got their funny taps from with the spiritual water pouring out. You may be thinking...

Where is my tap? How do I find my tap? Moreover, do I even want to find my tap? What is going to happen if I find my tap and turn it on?

When we talk about your tap and I say 'find it and turn it on', we are of course talking metaphorically. I don't literally mean that you should look for your tap. You don't physically have a hidden tap (and if you did you should be in the Guinness Book of World Records for the weirdest body appendage!) This tap, this opportunity for you to consciously connect yourself with the Energy Source, is not anywhere to be found. It's not hiding from you.

The tap is an analogy. While this analogy is fairly simple, please take a moment to reflect on what it actually means.

> ### The tap symbolises awareness.

We all have a tap (i.e. we all have awareness or, more accurately, the ability to be aware).

We all receive mysterious signals from the Energy Source that are there to guide us through life, to show us *how* to achieve our desires.

You are either aware of the signals or you are not. Regardless, they are *always* there. If you are aware of them, then your tap is clearly turned on. You are awake to this aspect of life and your life is in full flow. If you are not aware of them, then your tap is clearly turned off. You are 'asleep'. Your awareness is non-existent or has dried up, and you are missing the ability to make life happen freely and easily for yourself.

Just as the analogy of the tap suggests, awareness can be turned on and off. You'd think that once you are aware of something that it would be hard to forget about it, to turn it off. You'd be dead wrong there! You're only human and you can easily lose your awareness. In fact, from first-hand experience, you can lose it as quickly as you can click your fingers. When this happens you sideline your ability to direct your life, to recognise signals, and to subsequently make life happen freely and easily for yourself.

If that happens, how do you turn your tap (awareness) back on? You bring attention to the fact that you lost your awareness in the first place, thereby becoming aware again. It's that simple and it's that hard—both at the same time.

I speak from experience. My tap has been on, off, on, off, flowing, dripping, rusted, repaired and on again. My awareness has been constant and then missing. I have been in full flight and then grounded like a busted up bird with a broken wing. Later, you will hear about what it was like at the times when I was flying and what it was like when I crashed.

Interestingly, just after writing this little busted-up bird example, I had a week where things got very difficult for me, and my tap was clearly rusty. I was sitting at home and a bird literally flew straight into the window in front of me, dropped and hit the ground. It was flying one minute and busted up and flightless the next—a signal. The Energy Source obviously decided to show me I was out of the flow by using my very own analogy to get my attention.

Awareness is seemingly such a simple thing, but it has such a massive impact on how our lives play out. With a bit of maintenance (your attention), you can keep your tap on and working effectively most of the time. This correspondingly results to life in the flow, where things happen freely and easily, or more freely and more easily depending on what your life is already like.

> *Awareness gives you access to the Energy Source and the signals it is sending you.*

People, whether they know it or not, are designing and creating their lives every moment of the day. By accessing the Energy Source, using your awareness, you can participate actively and consciously in creating the life you want.

Consider your life and be honest with yourself... are you along for the ride or are you designing your life?

Choosing My Direction

After seeing Augustus, I thought to myself: *Where do I head now with all this information, these new insights, and these new questions posed? What should I do? What's the answer?*

Look for signals!

Chapter 7

Spirituality 101

Aside from my heart to heart with Augustus, one other thing really jump-started this journey for me: a short course I went on. It was actually more like an adventure, but I suppose the technical term for something you pay money for which happens every Tuesday night for five weeks at 7pm is 'a course'.

I was diligently punishing the gym treadmill, listening to music on full volume. Aaron, unbeknownst to me, was loitering around the water cooler, and something on a noticeboard in the far corner of the gym caught his eye. He wandered over. A little notice, nestled between many others, called for his attention. An advertisement for a course called 'Introduction to Spirituality'. It had little tear-off phone numbers on the bottom. There was one tear-off left. Then there were none. He pocketed the number.

Aaron is very open and has a curious nature, living by the philosophy 'try everything in life at least once'. He believed that his happening upon that advertisement was not a mistake. Having just seen Augustus himself, he registered for the course without hesitation. Aaron asked me to go with him. I was full of, "Um, ah, I'm not sure". However, curiosity got the better of me. I decided I didn't want to miss out, so I tentatively registered too.

As it turned out, two people we know well (who had also been to see Augustus) decided to register for the course once they heard we were going. These two people, both thirty-somethings, are also your average mainstream type of people. They were interested in finding out more about this newly discovered realm of spirituality too.

Coincidentally, all the other attendees that were registered for the course pulled out just days before it started. The teacher offered to refund our registration fees or to continue as planned but to instead meet at her home. It would only be the four of us attending. The course had turned into private tuition.

Enter Meredith. Meredith the Teacher or 'Meredith the Wise' as I like to call her. She was kind of like Gandalf in a way, but female and minus the grey hair and beard!

Every Tuesday night, over five weeks, the four of us met up at Meredith's house, for what I refer to as the ITS course. On the first night we were edgy and full of anticipation, wondering what this was going to be like.

As we hurtled along the motorway heading to Meredith's house, I sat pensively in the passenger seat. I silently hoped that we wouldn't be chanting, swaying or undertaking any other such awkward group activities that would put me outside my comfort zone. I wondered if her house would be a kooky cottage with black cats, crystal balls and dark creepy trees draped over murky windows. Aaron was excited.

We arrived. Knock, knock, knock was followed with a big smile and a warm greeting, inviting us inside a beautifully renovated villa in a trendy area of town. No dark creepy trees, no murky windows, no crystal balls were insight. There was one cat, not black.

The Teacher

A fascinating woman, formerly an owner of a very successful corporate business, Meredith had travelled extensively and was very drawn to places of spiritual significance around the world. She was fond of indigenous people and their cultures, healing practices and beliefs. While running her corporate business and managing a large team of staff, she explored her personal interest in many things spiritual, including numerology, astrology, crystals, animal totems, meditation, spirit guides, healing, feng shui and more.

Widely read and well trained, she was fascinating to listen to as she shared her own personal experiences and views in a forum designed to encourage open discussion. My ears perked up when she mentioned a stage in her life when she realised her calling. She sold her corporate business and took a leap of faith, creating a business around her passion for all things spiritual, including leading tours overseas to spiritual landmarks. She left her very lucrative corporate career to follow her dream, to live in her joy. It did not escape my notice that she had done just what I was thinking of doing at the time, which was leaving my corporate career to follow my passions. One small yet critical issue was that I wasn't entirely sure what those passions were!

Meredith seemed to have a knack for picking up on how at ease we each were with being there and with what was being discussed. With her gentle and warm nature, she would quietly shine her attention on anyone who seemed unsure. She didn't launch into the depths of spirituality with any heavy and profound statements, and thankfully, there was no group hugging. I am sure Aaron would have run a mile if we'd started holding hands and incanting life-affirming statements. (He wouldn't have been the only one.)

It was pretty clear that Meredith had some type of psychic ability, whether it was the way she looked at each of us, how she spoke with such insight, or whether that was just a natural assumption for us to make about someone doing this for a living. As it turned out, Meredith was what many people refer to as 'intuitive', very connected with the spiritual realm.

The coming weeks were going to include some very eye opening discussions. Many of the topics we were about to discuss were currently filed in my 'complete rubbish' and 'fictional fantasy' categories, to be scoffed at if talked about in any serious way. That was until I experienced a few things first-hand.

Cataloguing

What happened from the day I met Jessie in the cafe, through the ITS course, continuing on for 18 months, was so spooky and bizarre to me that I literally catalogued the occurrences in notebooks. Regularly going to the stationery shop to buy stocks, I filled the notebooks with dated entries, descriptions of what happened, scrawls, scribbles, question marks and exclamation marks. I didn't really know why I was cataloguing the rollercoaster, other than perhaps as evidence to remind myself that I was not going crazy or proof in case anyone else thought I was.

My sister Charlotte later pointed out that it was quite odd for me to have done that. It was odd because I diligently catalogued every single unusual thing that happened for an 18-month period, every day without fail. She proposed, "Don't you think that it's strange? Don't you think something was drawing you in to do that, guiding you to do so? Why else would you have done it?"

I just thought any person would have done the same. But then I started to get clearer and clearer signals that my notes were going to end up forming a book and that the book was going to end up being published for others to read, to facilitate other people finding their tap. And here we are.

Person B

Aside from the signals I received to write this book, there was one other thing that kept me cataloguing and writing: a thought that sat patiently but persistently in the back of my mind. When it came to understanding the spiritual realm and how to manifest change in my life, I always felt that I was different than the people who I followed. The books I read, the courses I attended, were all written and delivered by people who seemed to be a part of that group of calm, serene, glowing, celestial-like spiritual people. You know—the ones who seem to meditate with ease and live perfect lives in peace, like experts and gurus (a.k.a. not like me and perhaps not like you either). I saw an opportunity to say to readers, "Here it is—the views, facts and examples from an average Joe."

Let me refer to some extremely absurd and polarising spiritual stereotypes for a moment. True or not, they will allow me to make a point.

- I don't wear crystals. I have crystals and use crystals. I just don't wear them. There is nothing wrong with wearing crystals.

- I don't hug trees. I like trees. I just choose not to hug them. There is nothing wrong with hugging trees.

- I don't burn incense. I don't even like incense. I like aromatherapy oils. There is nothing wrong with burning incense.

- I don't wear kaftans or tie-dyed clothing. I don't like them and I choose not to wear them. There is nothing wrong with kaftans and tie-dyed clothing.

- I don't grow armpit, leg or facial hair (luckily for my husband). I choose not to. There is nothing wrong with being hairy.

If I told you something about mind, body and spirit, and our connection to the spiritual realm, strange spiritual experiences and unusual coincidences that happened to me, would you listen?

See how you feel. Which person do you relate more to and who are you more likely to believe?

PERSON A - The crystal-wearing, tree-hugging, incense-burning, kaftan-wearing, hairy, hippie, super-spiritual person, who tells you that we must love ourselves, love each other, think happy thoughts and be good to the planet in order for good things to flow to us.

OR

PERSON B - The corporate career-focused, thirty-something, suit-wearing, average Joe, who discovered something freakishly unusual was going on and decided to tell you about it straight up, relaying what actually happened, proposing to you that perhaps these things are real and accessible to everyone.

I'm purporting to be stereotypical Person B. Please be assured I think Person A is great, but I'm definitely a Person B—at least I am now and have been for some time.

I believe a lot of people who perhaps don't 'get' spirituality, who don't believe in the Energy Source or this pinch-me way of living, might just pay attention and subsequently improve their own lives if the information comes from someone they can relate to.

My Life Number

The course took off with a hiss and a roar as Meredith raised numerology. I tried to hide my disinterest. I thought: *Can we please get to the good stuff?* That was until she gave me a book, *The Life You Were Born to Live* by Dan Millman, and she asked me to read my life number aloud. Life numbers are derived from your birth date and are indicators as to the purpose of your life, the lessons that your soul is here to learn in this life.

My life number is 8. Millman shares that, "Individuals working 8 as their life purpose are here to work with abundance, power, and recognition, and to apply their success in service of the common good. However, since our life purpose offers inherent challenges, those with 8... have to work through issues related to money, power, authority, control, and recognition."[6]

The following questions arose in my mind: *What is my version of service for the common good? From this, will further abundance flow? From this, will I feel deep down joy on a level never felt before?*

The traits of 8 are very amusing to read for anyone who knows me well; it's very accurate. Money is the one thing that has always made me anxious and worried. I am a self-confessed control freak. Everything has to be in its place, and I must plan for and control all situations and happenings towards the outcome that I want. I do this to ensure nothing goes wrong. I have a fear of things going wrong.

8 Resonates

Two things about 8 resonated strongly with me, resulting in poignant realisations. These realisations happened in a flash, as I sat there on Meredith's couch, with the book in hand and reading aloud.

Firstly, Millman went on to describe that as an 8, I may feel an internal tug of war between my drive to succeed and my fears and impulses to avoid material success. I could see it clearly; my city-living, highly driven, career-oriented self was battling internally between striving for more and wanting to run away from it all, to find a simple life. This was the cause of my indecision and turmoil.

Secondly, "in service of the common good" sounded a bit like the leadership signal I was trying to avoid. A raft of thoughts flew through my mind simultaneously: *Augustus told me to look at ways I can use my leadership skills. Leadership is a form of service to others; that seems like doing something for the common good. Is leadership my version of service to others? Does serving the common good mean I have to do voluntary work? I have a mortgage and a busy job. How can I fit in voluntary work alongside everything else? It's all well and good being fulfilled and achieving inner joy from my service to others, but what good is that if I can't pay the bills or I'm exhausted from juggling too many things?*

And the real clincher was that I'd previously discussed a potential leadership role with my boss Stephen. He was keen for me to take on a managerial and coaching role with long-term prospects. I was not feeling fulfilled in the consulting work I was doing, so this leadership role was another option.

While I showed interest (for lack of courage to say otherwise), I was still internally shying away from it. My interpretation was that it would mean more responsibility, tying me down further to corporate life and burdening me with issues. Surely that couldn't be a good thing. My heart kept saying, "RUN AWAY, RUN AWAY!" My head kept saying, "BE SENSIBLE AND DO IT!" Why did he want to entrust in me the position of guiding and mentoring the staff? I at once felt lucky and grateful, but in the next heart beat I was filled with dread that I was doomed to forever play out the role of corporate Queen B.

Was it a coincidence that Augustus asked me to consider using my leadership skills, that Meredith entered the scene with my 'service to others' life number in hand, and that my employer was prodding me towards a leadership role? Was this the Energy Source telling me to step up to the plate and great things would follow? Were these signals, all part of this unseen flow, working for my benefit and calling me to action?

I was very keen to pretend this wasn't happening and that there was no correlation. However, no matter how hard I tried, it nagged at me incessantly. Perhaps good things come from the places we least expect them to.

My struggle was as a direct result of my desire to accumulate money. I ignored my countryside dream in order to diligently play out my corporate life for one reason: money. It wasn't just for the money, but rather for what I felt money would eventually give me: freedom. I deemed money to be the access to freedom on many levels: choices, time and flexibility. I thought that these things, once I had them, would help me find my passion.

In my self-created vicious cycle, I felt too scared to throw it all away. *It* being the highly paid job and the fact I could continue on for years and pay off my mortgage, doing something I didn't love (but certainly didn't hate), while at the same time doing the right thing according to society's standard path of 'work, save, retire, die'. I couldn't see a realistic, practical way that I could create a life where I could have the best of everything.

So, I marinated on these concepts, and I said to the Energy Source, "Please send me signals to show me what to do to make this possible." Then, I clearly visualised the day-to-day life I wanted. I visualised it like I was already in the middle of it, creating the feelings inside myself of the joy I would experience with money flowing in from doing something I am good at and love, with the peace and tranquillity of a simple life. This all felt right. This is how you get what you want in your life, right? Visualise it. Believe it. Manifest it. The books say it. The courses say it. The DVDs say it. Enlightened people say it. Augustus said it, and Meredith said it.

How can all these people and self-help materials be wrong? They're not.

Meditation

As the ITS course went on, I was clear on two things. Firstly, I had to make change happen in my life and no one else was going to do it for me. Secondly, something very strange was going on in the world, something spiritual and 'out there', and I needed to figure out what it was. It looked like it might have the answers I had been seeking.

One of the first things that we learned to do with Meredith was a guided meditation, where she talked us through entering a deep meditative state. I used to think it was hard to find time to meditate, and it was hard to stay in meditation, which put me off doing it. I realised that I was right. It is hard to find time, and it is hard to stay focused! *But* what I also realised was that it's well worth the effort. I discovered how effective meditation is and what a difference it can make in one's life.

In a world where we are bombarded with external stimulus, it's amazing what happens when you sit quietly with yourself. Things arise from within your quiet core that you may be astounded by. You are a vessel for answers to your own questions.

It's funny how many people don't question the widely accepted fact that meditation is known to induce a state of relaxation that is scientifically proven to be positive for one's health and wellbeing. It's well known that meditation is commonly used by some of the world's most successful business people. Most people don't seem to question that meditation and visualisation techniques are used in sports psychology and widely accepted as a tangible way to prepare high performance athletes for achieving their goals. However, when there is talk about applying such techniques to achieve our own personal goals and dreams, some people may wonder how effective it is or struggle to make time in their day for it. Perhaps if the simple techniques used by highly successful, healthy and fulfilled people were applied, you may in fact get the same benefits.

Spirit Guides

Meredith then explained we would be calling upon our spirit guides during a meditation. Despite spirits having 'visited' me during my session with Augustus, I was still ready to assert, if asked, that I didn't have any spirit guides. "I'm not intuitive like you, Meredith. I'm fairly confident there are no spirits 'guiding' me. I don't see things, hear things or feel things." However, we were assured that *everyone* has spirit guides.

Your guides might be spirits of people you have known that have since passed away, or they might be spirits with no particular connection to you from this lifetime. Perhaps the spirit guide has a particular area of expertise that they are able to share with you through guidance; perhaps they feel drawn to support you. They are available to you 24/7 to call upon for guidance and support. I can tell you first-hand that they send you this guidance by way of signals.

When you call upon your spirit guides, you are simply in a meditative state, and you are inviting them to come forward to be with you. For those of you screwing up your face, laughing or about to throw this book in the nearest bin, fear not! I have not lost the plot. I am not talking about ghostly figures drifting around the room, making 'ooooohhhhhhh' and 'ahhhhhhhhhhh' noises. It's a little subtler than that.

I was so intrigued by all of this, but I was also concerned that I'd open up some can of worms that I'd never be able to close again. I'm the kind of person that gets a deathly fright if I see my own image passing in a mirror, let alone having first-hand experience of some paranormal activity. I recall thinking to myself: *You don't need to show yourself to me. I'm happy to believe without visual evidence, thank you.* Note: I found the movie *Sixth Sense* very scary; it should have been rated as a horror film.

As it turned out, although I didn't see things, I could feel things. Meredith suggested we pay close attention to any change in the room temperature or any change in temperature directly around our own bodies. We were told to be alert for any feeling of a light wispy breeze blowing on our face, arms or legs and/or a feeling of being tickled on the tops of our head. These, we were told, are common ways of experiencing spirits being present with you.

The room was silent. I sat on the couch with my eyes closed, falling deeper and deeper into meditation. Meredith's gentle voice came from the corner of the room telling us to invite our guides in to be with us. A minute or so passed, and then I felt it. It was cold air on my cheek, but not a draft blowing or a breeze, rather like someone whispering air ever so gently very close to my face. The windows were shut. The room was warm. There was no one physically near me in the group. It stopped. I waited. Then, the hairs on the crown of my head moved, exactly that tickling sensation. The hair was actually moving.

Meredith asked us to relax and just let it be, to see what we could learn from the experience. We were encouraged to speak to our guides (in our heads). I wasn't sure who the guide(s) were, and I couldn't seem to get any messages or clarity, just the physical sensation of something present with me. However, this was not the case for others. One of my friends present had a very specific interaction that left them quite emotionally moved.

As the evening drew to a close and it was time to head home, I could feel the curiosity bubbling inside. I couldn't wait for next week. The four of us fervently spoke to each other over the coming days about what happened when we practised again at home and what questions we had for Meredith. I had to find out more, I had to experience more, this stuff seemed like it was real, and if it was real, then what could this mean for life in general?

The Man I Was

Tuesday rolled around again, and weird doesn't begin to describe it. Meredith knew we had all had sessions with Augustus, so she was aware that we had already been exposed to the topic of past lives. Augustus often refers to past lives and what your soul is here to learn in this life, advising that each human experience (life) your soul has is designed to teach your soul new lessons. Each life is rounding out and balancing your soul, until such time as your soul reaches a level of completeness and enlightenment.

Apparently, your soul chooses the life it is born into, the family it is born into, the environment, good, bad, everything. Souls have to live through all life has to offer and throw at us, in order to become enlightened, and that also involves going through hardship and difficult times, in order for us to learn and grow.

The idea is that if you have/do/be a certain way in one life, you're likely to end up on the other end of the spectrum at some point, so as to discover how to be in all situations, circumstances and relationships. Karma is, apparently, not a far-fetched concept. If you go by the principle that what you put out comes back to you, what goes around comes around, basic Law of Attraction, then both good and bad karma will play out. This is not a reward or punishment process, but they are experiences to learn from. What hadn't occurred to me, until this time, was that it plays out across life times.

We were told we could glimpse one of our own past lives using meditation, accessing hidden knowledge within our being. Seriously?

Listening to her words, we fell into meditation and were guided (in our minds) to a doorway. Standing facing the door, she verbally prepared us for turning the handle and stepping through that door into one of our past lives. We were told to experience whatever came to us—whatever feelings, sights, smells and sounds became apparent.

I struggled to believe that this was going to result in a real insight into a past life. Surely, my imagination would just make something up. However, what happened next was surreal. It was like watching something happen, not participating in it or thinking about it. It is as clear in my mind now as it was during that meditation session. It was like pressing play on some past life DVD, and I was sitting watching it play out. I don't know where past life information comes from or how it works, but this experience was so strong, free flowing and so real for me that I couldn't fathom it being anything but genuine.

I turned the handle and stepped through the door. Instantly, I felt different. Looking out, it was bleak, rural land. There was snow. It was dusk, and I felt cold. The time was centuries ago, the Middle Ages. A feeling of sadness came over me, a sense of resignation almost. When I looked ahead of myself, there was an unsealed, winding road, with a few small shacks set back off the road.

Speaking quietly from her corner of the room, Meredith invited us to pay attention to our hands, feet, clothing and the environment we were in. What do you see? Right away, I smiled, not because I doubted anything she was suggesting, but because I was surprised.

Looking down, I clearly saw large, black, dirty work boots—men's boots. The boots were thick leather, rough, rugged and worn. Then I saw large, dirty, worn and calloused hands—working hands. I was definitely a man (or a really scary woman).

In silence, the scene played out. I still felt really sad and cold, and a kind of hopeless despair swept over me. It felt like the day-to-day trudge of life had worn me down and taken its toll. It seemed like I felt trapped, like I had no other options. This was my life.

In a flash, I was now entering a small shack. It was dim inside, but there was a fireplace. Immediately, I knew I was either very tall or the building was very small with a low ceiling, because I had to stoop to get through the door and walk around inside. I could sense my own size, broad and cumbersome, by the way I moved slowly and lurched around in the small space. Someone was sitting next to the fireplace; it seemed like a woman hunched over.

Meredith said that we could ask questions. In my mind, I asked: *What do I do? What is my occupation?* The images in my mind were gone, immediately replaced with a sense of wielding a long stick-like object and clanging it against something. Lifting something heavy and banging it down. The action and image came to me over and over again, like it was a repetitive task. I wondered if I was using a hammer; however, it was larger than that. I could actually hear the clanging of metal on metal in my mind, over and over, swinging this long object. It was heavy, hard, tiring work. Then, I sensed fire. It was a hot metal poker of some sort. The next image brought clarity: leather hung over low wooden beams in a dark and damp shed. I could almost smell the environment. Then, I saw it clearly. I was a blacksmith.

The second that it clicked I was shocked. Since as young as five years old, I have been drawn to horses. I am drawn to them like I know them, and I love to be around them. I love the smell of horses. I love riding horses. I love tending to them. I love the smell of the leather saddles and bridles. I always wondered why we are born with strong attractions or aversions to certain things, unexplained as to why we would choose to like or dislike something so much with no previous experience of it. Later, Meredith told us that she had met many people with current life obsessions, aversions, fears or affinities that were in some way linked to past lives.

Despite all the obvious differences between that life and my life now, not least of all I was man then and quite clearly I am a woman now, I felt akin to him, like I hadn't just intruded on someone's private life. I had just glimpsed back on something linked to me.

We had a group discussion after the meditation, each of us relaying our own experience. One saw a young boy, wearing clothes of an early century, working in a tavern in the countryside. He was sneaking out late at night into the forest, meeting others, telling stories and foreseeing things, a Seer. It was secretive and forbidden, and it was dangerous in case he was caught. The person that experienced this is currently a writer of stories and fables in this life.

Another person saw themselves in early English times, writing with scrolls and feather quills in a dark room in the depths of a building, working as a scribe. This person was amazed by what they saw. At a very early age in this lifetime, they loved calligraphy. It is hard to understand why a child so young would be so drawn to something like calligraphy to the extent they would ask their parents for a calligraphy set for Christmas. No Barbie or pony, no skateboard or football—so adored was the calligraphy set that it is still stored away in a box in their attic.

Past lives interested me so much that I obtained a copy of *Many Lives, Many Masters* by Dr. Brian Weiss[7] and devoured the book. If you doubt past lives, I encourage you to read this real life account with an open mind. I challenge you to read it from the perspective, what if? The book swayed me. Before all of this, I would never have entertained such an idea. It is a personal account by Dr. Weiss, a psychiatrist, and it documents the work he did with a patient to address particular issues she was experiencing in her adult years.

He regressed her back as far as early childhood, dealing with any occurrences and disturbances that could be linked to her current day problems. What happened was nothing short of astounding. He was as bewildered as you may be when you read what happened. He regressed the patient to 2-3 years of age, at which point she started recalling experiences of being other ages, with different names, in different places, in different centuries—male, female, different ethnicities, young, old, wealthy, poor. She recalled countless past lives under hypnosis.

My eyes were opened to new possibilities.

Chapter 8

The Mighty Animal Kingdom

Animal totems—yes, I am talking about animals acting as totems. Animals have particular meanings, and apparently, they come to us to share their meaning as a way to guide us. Animals are another way that the Energy Source alerts us, sending us signals, trying to get our attention to guide us in a direction that will aid us in learning, growing and reaching our goals.

Meredith touched on this subject, but as Aaron and I were particularly interested, we spent our own time finding out more. Aaron has a real affinity with animals. He bought *Animal Speak* by Ted Andrews, a guide to animal totems.

Totems show up in our lives in many different ways: actual live animals, animal images, animals in dreams and so on. If a particular animal shows up in your life multiple times or in unusual situations and circumstances, then this may have meaning for you. The meaning may be something for you to be aware of at that particular time in your life, something relevant to your current circumstance or a reminder for you. Keep your eyes and ears open to see if you are being given a signal by way of an animal totem.

What's Green and Looks Like a Stick?

After reading about totems in-depth, you'd think we would have been highly attuned to animals, waiting for the signals. However, Aaron and I thought nothing of it when a multitude of stick insects started showing up in our courtyard at home—big ones, baby ones, on the paved ground, on the fence, in the garden. It was a garden. It was summer. Of course insects would be there. Granted, there were a lot of these stick insects, and we had lived there several years and never seen any before—let alone this many.

Okay, so we had an infestation. Kind of like you get with ants perhaps, just cuter and more tolerable, given they don't crawl into anything remotely looking like food. We didn't really pay them much attention, until they started sitting on the windows downstairs. "Oh, they must like being in the sunshine," I said.

Until a week later, when they started appearing on the 2nd story windows, "Wow, they really are climbers."

One day, I came home to find one on the inside of the bedroom window upstairs. The window was not open; it was hooked closed with the security latches. *How strange,* I thought. "Aaron, look! They're crawling into the house now." I opened the window, and (sorry, animal lovers) I picked it up and dropped it out the window into the garden far below. You'd think after what we had just learned at the course that we might have clicked to what was going on. Perhaps I didn't really believe in totems.

During that night, something crawled on my arm. Being a stereotypical girl, I reacted like a giant tarantula had attacked me. Arm flung up, light flicked on, shrieking. There on the carpet next to the bed was a tiny, cute green stick insect.

It was then that I clicked. The proverbial light came on. *I wasn't paying attention, so you literally had to crawl on me to make me notice.* Dutifully, I researched stick insects as totems. The family of stick insects signify patience and the ability to remain focused and very still, yet prepared and able to move/strike at exactly the right time.

I had no doubt what this was about. We have a foreign currency trading business. Aaron trades FX. He had been passionately and religiously studying, learning and devoting his time to FX for the past four years outside of working a 9-5 job. It had been a rollercoaster ride of ups and downs. Still, we had faith that our commitment to it and Aaron's thousands of hours of learning and trading would pay consistent dividends for our future. Absolutely fundamental and critical to successful FX trading is psychological/emotional control (read: focus) and patience. It is a well known fact that traders need to learn the inbuilt 'knowing' of when to trade (read: move/strike), when to wait (read: be still and patient) and when to withdraw.

Not long after our totem discovery, we experienced a reasonably significant setback in our trading business. It was not the first, and potentially not the last, as trading is a challenging thing to learn how to do well consistently. Many people try, fail and quit as a result. Others try, fail, try, fail, try and eventually succeed, going on to have great success with trading long term. It takes a genuine love and passion for it, in order to stick with it and commit the sort of hours required to master it. That love and passion is what Aaron has. However, setbacks still take their toll.

The next morning, after this particularly tough night of trading, I opened the door to go to work. What should I find in front of me on the doormat? A very poorly, sick-looking stick insect. In fact, it looked pretty damn dead to me! Now you can imagine my reaction. *If the stick insect symbolises focus and patience, and the stick insect is dead, does that mean our patience is dead, caput, gone? Or does it mean that last night the patience was gone, and this is a reminder to be focused and patient again? Know when to strike and when to retreat?*

I moved the stick insect and put it on a bush, peering at it, hoping it would survive the playful blackbirds swooping above. There I was, wearing high heels, dress, make up on, hair done, handbag slung over shoulder, head down in the bush, arse up in the air, wondering about the fate of this convalescing insect. Well, I couldn't stand there all day like an insect-watching weirdo; I had work to do. So off to the office I went.

It was a busy day, and I hadn't relayed what happened to Aaron, until the next morning, when... he was back (not Aaron, the stick insect). But, wait, it was worse; this time he was dead—dead as a dodo, dead on our front door step. I prodded him several times with my finger to confirm that he was in fact gone. There was no movement, no life, nothing. That's right; the little blighter, or one just like it, had crawled out of the garden, across the patio, onto our front door step, centred themselves in the middle of the doormat, lay down and died right there. *What does this mean?!*

I promptly convened a meeting with my husband and stated, "We need to give CPR to our patience."

He was very confused. "Explain yourself woman!"

I leapt in to explain, and I asserted, "It's okay. All is not lost. We just need to remain focused and patient. The stick insects have shown up to tell us this; it's a signal to show us the way forward."

The old B would previously have seen nothing more than a dead insect. More accurately, she would not have even seen the insect at all. Rather, she would have stood on it with her shiny high heel shoe. But I did see it, and I did pay attention.

We refocused and remained patient with trading. Sure enough, the curve swung back up again so to speak, and it kept us from wallowing in the recent setback. Self-pity never won any awards for most loved personality trait, and it sure as hell doesn't do any good.

Although we are both positive people, we take setbacks just like everyone else. We strive for big goals, and when something occurs that makes that goal look impossible or much further away, we want to curl up in a ball and have a good old cry. But, there is something that keeps the strong going in these situations. That something is dogged determination, and total faith and belief in what is possible.

Manifesting and achieving really big goals in life takes some serious resilience, commitment and willingness to risk. "Risk what?" you ask. Risk anything—big, small, some, all, risk trying and failing, risk reputation, money, relationships and/or your sanity. Although some goals and dreams take a few weeks or months to manifest in your life, others take years. Perhaps it takes years because the challenge of getting there is teaching you life lessons that you are meant to learn. Perhaps our trading goal was teaching me life lessons; perhaps it was teaching Aaron life lessons. Perhaps it was about taking the journey together and not at all about the end result.

Looking back now, the journey we have been on has tested every aspect of our personalities and every aspect of our patience, commitment and determination. It has tested our relationship and communication, our faith and trust in each other, our ability to manifest what we want in our life, and our faith and trust in the Energy Source and the signals.

We made a conscious choice to never give up on our goals and dreams. We want to create greatness in our lives and to always strive for that. We know that the Energy Source brought us together for a reason; we have something to teach each other and something to learn from being together. My control and planning, underpinned by a conservative approach, balances out his dynamic, entrepreneurial, high risk approach—and vice versa.

If we didn't skip gleefully through this journey together, we'd be two separate entities, operating like trains going off the rails. I'd have played into my obsessive and controlled way of living to the point of insanity, I'm sure, and he would have haphazardly attacked opportunities before planning the path forward. We balance each other.

The Pigeon

This animal totem experience wasn't the first, and it wouldn't be the last. Aaron had an encounter with a pigeon. Working at home on his computer, he was busy researching and analysing trading patterns when he noticed something outside the door in the courtyard. A pure white pigeon was sitting on the patio looking in at him. Aaron stared back. It paced back and forth in front of the door, looking in for several minutes. We had seen plenty of little sparrows and blackbirds in our time living there, but we had never seen pigeons.

It was such an unnerving thing, like the pigeon was trying to get his attention. A few minutes on the internet soon revealed that pigeons were originally used for carrying foreign exchange between countries.

The Chrysalis

Once the Energy Source knows you are paying attention, it makes it so much easier to send you the signals you ask for or the signals you so desperately need to help you move forward. As big decisions weighed heavily on me, I started to notice a new totem.

Chrysalises started appearing at our house, which wasn't that odd, I suppose. Although in previous years, we hadn't had any. The first chrysalis we saw was hanging at eye level from the garage entry way. The next one appeared inside our letterbox, hanging in there where the mail gets delivered. Then, it got a little more 'in your face'. After leaving for work one morning, with no chrysalis in sight, we returned home later that day to find a chrysalis fully formed hanging from the front door handle. The next chrysalis turned up at eye level on the frame of the front door.

I was ready for this signal. I looked up chrysalis and butterfly totems immediately. The results? Transformation, metamorphosis, change and new beginnings. It made me carefully consider the timing of this totem with respect to the changes that lay ahead of me. I was still resisting change. Aaron was rearing and ready to go, but I was not. I was clinging on to the safety blanket of my current job, my income, my home, my familiar surroundings and my network of family and friends. I desperately wanted change, but I was not willing to risk anything to get it.

I felt sick in my stomach about the reality that I would have to step out into the unknown if I wanted to move towards the life I dreamed of.

Although my tap was turned on and I was recognising the signals, I was still standing on the muddy, grassy riverbank, saying, "Oh, hey there, nice signals! But I think I'll just pretend I didn't see them and hope for the best."

I was seriously considering trudging along that rough, old riverbank, hoping it would get me to my desired destination the safer way. I was holding on to my current life, regardless of the fact that it wasn't fulfilling me. I was willing to live in half happiness if it was safe, versus taking a leap for true joy with risks that could end up ruining everything. I'm sure you can relate to some extent; it felt like potential Armageddon. However, the chrysalises came for a reason.

The change ahead was what I needed; it was the natural progression for me. I knew this deep down and was simply paralysed with fear. My head kept trying to override my heart.

What if it isn't right? What if it goes wrong? What if I don't like it? What if I don't like a new job? What if we don't like the new place we move to? What if I miss all my friends? What if I miss all my family? What if my income isn't enough? What if we can't sell our house? What if we can't find a tenant? What if, what if, what if, what if...?! And so it went on, around and around in circles; my risk averse profile was in full swing.

The chrysalis hung peacefully from the door handle beckoning my attention, while I raged in debate with myself inside my head. It called to me, encouraging me to recognise that I was cocooned in a comfy little space that was familiar and safe. It showed me that true transformation, where I could spread my wings and take life to the next level, would require me to break out of my comfy little space and explore new areas, new ways of being and new experiences.

Now, scoff if you will at such a subtle sign, and cry out, "B, it's a coincidence! That's all it is!" Well, I beg to differ. Life is full of these small and subtle signs, calling for our attention. They are there to prod and point us in a direction that will benefit us. The Energy Source is guiding you, even if you haven't specifically asked for help. However, for many of us, life has become so fast paced and we are so in our own heads that it literally takes a freight train to stop us and make us open our eyes.

Get Out of Your Head

Augustus had said to me, "Get out of your head." I asked him why Sarah, if she was really around me in spirit, had never made her presence obvious. I said to him, "If she is really there, why isn't she trying to make contact with me?" His response, and apparently her response also, was this: "You are always in your head. You're always thinking, talking to yourself, gabbing away, with no stillness, no listening, and no way to connect with you because you are so much in your own head."

This wasn't the first time I'd heard this comment or thought this myself. It's true of most people, isn't it? We all spend too much time in our heads and not enough time being truly present and *aware*.

If you don't want your life to be controlled by the incessant babble that occurs in your mind every waking moment of the day, then start to watch your thoughts. I encourage you to read *The Power of Now* by Eckhart Tolle.[8] It's the first book I ever read in this genre that had a massive impact on me. When I started observing my mind, I would find myself laughing at some of the self-defeating rubbish that was going on. How could I be attempting to sabotage myself? Why be concerned about other people doing harm to you or impacting your dreams when your own worst enemy lurks inside your head?!

My journey had only just begun. I had a strong feeling that I would soon be jumping into the abyss, the vast unknown stretching out in front of me. The only way for me to do this was to trust in the signals and have faith that I would end up at my desired destination. For once in my life, I was going to have to listen to my heart instead of my head.

My awakening had been kick started. This is how I often refer to this period of my life: an awakening. I feel less labelled by this word than if I went all the way and called it 'the year I discovered my inner hippie.' See? Now you're imagining me running around barefoot, wearing tie-dyed skirts and hugging trees. Granted I do go around barefoot now that I have created the life of my dreams, living in the sunshine, on the tropical beaches of an idyllic, semi-rural island paradise, but so far I have avoided tie-dyed clothing. Additionally, although I love trees, you already know that I have no desire to hug them.

Are you wondering how the heck I ended up in my version of paradise? Read on.

Chapter 9

Miscellaneous Messages

Crossed Wires

Matt and Trina popped into our house for coffee one Sunday afternoon. As trusted friends, we shared with them all about what we had been learning and our excitement about where it was leading us. Our thirst for more was tangible.

For the first time, sitting there chatting and laughing, I saw energy fields—their energy fields. Meredith had spoken about it and suggested we practice looking for energy around people. Typically, this looks like a haze of colour around a person's body. First I saw a blue haze around Trina, a definite field of something around her body. Then I saw Matt's. I was very excited, but with poker face on, I said nothing as I didn't want to appear distracted from the actual conversation or obsessed by all these new things I was learning. In all honesty, I didn't want them to think I was strange.

As soon as they left, I was so excited to tell Aaron about this. We immediately googled 'seeing energy fields' to find more information. We clicked on a website from the search results and started reading.

Perched on the arm of the couch, I peered over Aaron's shoulder as he scrolled through the information while we read and chatted. All of a sudden, static noise came out of the computer speakers.

I looked at him; neither of us had touched anything. The static noise was like an untuned radio, and then, it changed to what sounded like crossed wires or telephone lines. We could vaguely hear voices, but it was barely audible. It didn't even sound like English. Somehow, our computer must have crossed frequency with a radio station, phone conversation or something of the like. It was all very odd but understandable—sort of!

Then, strange, ethereal music played from the speakers. I thought Aaron was playing a joke on me, but he hadn't touched anything. The music played for about ten seconds, just long enough for us to look at the computer and check if any internet pop-ups had caused it. Nothing. It must have been the music on the web page, inbuilt into the site.

Then, the music stopped and something happened that sent chills up my spine. It was the most vivid and freaky thing that had happened since all of these unusual situations started occurring, and we were left speechless.

After seconds of silence, a deep clear voice came from the speakers and said, "I love you." Slow and deliberate. Then, again, "I love you." Another pause, and then for a third and final time, "I love you." It was followed by silence.

What the BLEEP was that?! Where did that haunting voice come from? We looked behind the PC. We checked the speakers. We checked the computer programmes. Nothing.

We recreated the same set up on the PC. We opened the search engine and visited the same website. We sat waiting, but we heard nothing—no static, no crossed wires, no music, no voice. We did it over and over again, but we heard nothing.

We searched the internet for sound viruses, for viruses that say "I love you," for viruses that say anything and for voices coming out of a computer. Could it have been a virus? Quite possibly. An online forum for sound viruses said, "First scan for viruses. If there is no virus, see your doctor." We scanned for viruses, but we found nothing. So, mmm, see a doctor?

Could it have been an elaborate prank? Possibly. Could it have been a real, unusual, paranormal incident? Possibly. Am I concerned by the myriad of logical explanations that exist to explain what happened? No. I could have left this example out of this book and saved myself the hassle of being challenged and/or told to 'get a grip'.

Perhaps what happened was logical. Perhaps it was beyond logic. Maybe it was nothing, just an undetectable computer virus.

The interesting point is that it happened in my life at a time where I was experiencing all sorts of odd things and at a time where I needed one last massive push forward to make me sit up and take notice. I needed to be tipped over the edge so that I would action my new life plan. It was enough to make me ask, "Could that have been real?"

Regardless of whether it was or not, it was still a signal. If it was a virus that hid itself away from us, I'm glad it was a virus that said, "I love you." It made me think that the Energy Source was encouraging me forward. I'm glad it wasn't a virus that said, "Stop being so bloody stupid. Go back to your cynical, old way of being. Accept your lot. Grow old half fulfilled, and die. That's just how life goes."

Readings

Aaron and I both knew we were verging on making *the* decisions to start the change. I knew this was going to get uncomfortable, while I pushed outside my comfort zone. I was excited about what lay ahead; it gave me that funny feeling in your stomach when adrenaline mixes with fear mixes with anticipation mixes with worry mixes with thrill.

I spoke to my sisters and mother about my fear, and they shared their thoughts. Apparently, it was natural to feel scared of making the wrong decisions. Something would be wrong with me if I didn't feel nervous and scared by the thought of making all these major decisions at once. They said, "These feelings show you are human. Fear of the unknown is natural. Fear of losing control is natural."

It was no major surprise to me that I received such a relevant signal during a 'reading' session. What is a reading? That was precisely my question when

Meredith had announced one evening that we were going to learn how to do one.

This sounded suspiciously like something a very spiritually connected person would be doing (i.e. not me). But, by now I had learned one very important lesson: don't judge what you don't know. So armed with the one necessary tool, an open mind, I launched myself head first into learning how to do a reading.

Imagine this: two average people who had never heard of or tried this 'reading' thing before, asking ourselves, "Can it be this easy?" The process was to have someone meditate and hover their hands over me, around my energy field, and images, thoughts and words would come into their mind as messages relating to me and for me. Really? It's that easy? Yes, is the short answer, as we discovered.

Practising at home, Aaron got several clear images in his mind when he did a reading for me. One was a rabbit. *Animal Speak* explains, "Those with rabbit totems will see movement occur in their life in varying degrees of leaps and hops. It won't be a steady step-by-step movement. The leaps and hops do not usually take more than the cycle of one moon (28 days) to occur."9 *Crikey, that's a short time to make big hops. Will my hops be made that quickly?*

Another rabbit totem meaning is about moving in balance, not to be doubtful, as fear paralyses growth and movement. It teaches not to dash for safety at the sign of new things.

Although it is human nature to feel fear, as the old saying goes, feel the fear and do it anyway. Nothing is gained from giving into fear. The greatest successes, joy and personal growth occur when you break through fear and take action, despite that feeling.

I had applied and shared this theory in my workplace. When you feel uncomfortable and fearful of a task at hand, then push through and step over that invisible line of fear you have drawn in front of you. Your greatest achievements lie on the other side. There is a sense of fulfilment and personal power over your own life when you make decisions and take action, despite the almost paralysing fear that is twisting knots in your stomach.

Note: I believe there is an inherent knowing in each person of the difference between the feeling of foreboding warning that something isn't right and isn't good for you versus the fearful, nervous butterflies or the 'I need to go nervous pee every five minutes' feeling.

Next, Aaron saw an archer's target, with coloured circles and a bullseye at centre stage. I thought: *Surely, it must mean something about hitting the target.* It was fair to say that my greatest fear was that all these changes we were about to make would not actually help me fulfil my goals. I worried: *I might not hit the bullseye. What if I go to all this effort and end up in the same situation? What if it doesn't bring me the happiness and type of life I am seeking?*

The final signal Aaron received for me during the reading topped it all off: an image of a wolf standing next to a path. I referred to *Animal Speak* for the meaning of wolf and found, "Breathe new life into your life rituals. Find a new path, take a new journey, take control of your life. You are the governor of your life. You create it and you direct it. Do so with harmony and discipline, and then you will know the true spirit of freedom."[10]

Freedom was what I was seeking.

You may well say that any animal totem could have related in some way to my situation. However, I debate that you'd be wrong. I devoured information about totems, and the meanings of animals are wide and varied, and often very specific.

Musical Innuendo

Music is another way that the Energy Source garners our attention. Songs, more importantly lyrics, are signals. Meredith had suggested we pay particular attention to songs that popped into our heads and the exact lyrics that were playing over and over in our minds.

With this, she was not referring to how that catchy Britney Spears number you heard in the elevator sticks in your head all day. We are talking about songs that pop into your mind from nowhere. You didn't hear it on the radio that morning. You didn't decide to whistle or sing it because you love that tune. It is the random humming of a song for no reason, the random 'why does this song keep going over and over in my mind' situation. It is likely you don't even realise it is happening. It may be the moment when you first wake up in the morning and a few lines of a song repeat as you drift out of sleep.

I started to pay close attention to what songs were running through my mind like a broken record. I awoke one morning after a dream about an eagle. There was nothing exciting about the dream; the eagle wasn't doing anything notable, just the head of an eagle sitting static in my mind. Then, I entered that semi-awake, semi-asleep state when you're conscious enough to wonder what day it is and how long before you have to get up. A song came to me—actually, just two lines of a song, over and over. It took me a moment to realise that this was one of those moments I should be paying attention to. It went, "Love lifts us up where we belong, where the eagle flies, on a mountain high..."[11]

I leapt out of bed, scrawling the lyrics in my notebook as I dashed to the bookshelf and laid my hand on what was fast becoming my most frequented book. Eagle as an animal totem means illumination of spirit, healing and creation. The book read, "...to take on the responsibility and the power of becoming so much more than you now appear to be... it reflects that the events will now fly faster... to accept a powerful new dimension to life... only through doing so do you learn how to move between worlds, touch all life with healing, and become the mediator and the bearer of new creative force within the world."[12]

The eagle was guiding me as I faced the prospect of creating massive change in my life at a lightning fast pace. I was a little perplexed about the "touch all life with healing" bit, but that perplexed feeling soon changed to astonishment.

Chapter 10

Healing with Energy

Energy healing, healing with energy—something I had previously scoffed at. (Yes, more ignorant scoffing—how did I find time for anything else?) It seemed like a very small and remote possibility that any of that mumbo jumbo, alternative healing stuff could actually work. Wikipedia enlightened me, "Energy healing is based on the belief that a healer is able to channel healing energy into the person seeking help..."[13]

Heads up. I was your typical hypochondriac. Not surprisingly, due to my love of focusing in on any sign of illness, I was plagued by a wide variety of issues. Occupational Overuse Syndrome; eyesight, knee and hip problems; recurring chest infections and bronchitis; low vitamin levels; asthma, allergies and sinus infections; and a raft of other one off and operable conditions. These saw me swing between GPs, specialists, surgeons, physiotherapists, acupuncturists and osteopaths. I made a significant financial investment in the medical fraternity over a 15+ year period. I also vividly remember a day when I was walking along the street in my early twenties, feeling lost and thinking about all the questions I had about life, and I thought that perhaps I was also depressed. So, I added that to my list.

With a fully paid-up membership to the local medical centre, I'm surprised they fell short of putting a nameplate above a seat in reception for me. First sign of illness? See a doctor and pop a pill. That's what I knew; that's all I knew. I had not seen or believed in anything other than medical forms of treatment.

A Shamanic Husband

During a session about healing, Meredith had said to me that she sensed Aaron had innate healing abilities. She said she felt some connection for him to healing and shamanism in a past life. She didn't know that healing was the one topic Aaron was most interested in.

Back then, I had no idea what healing was all about. When it came to conducting healings, I thought you either had it or you didn't. You either can heal, or you can't. It's something that these spiritually connected people have that I don't.

Repeating references to shamanic healing started to show up everywhere. Sitting down to breakfast one morning, we flicked the TV to the Travel Channel and were faced with an old man. The subtitles ran as he explained the shamanic healing practices of his tribe. It wasn't quite what we were expecting. We usually watched the getaway and luxury travel programmes as we daydreamed about what life could be like. We watched the whole documentary about the Yuhup tribe in Colombia, focusing on the Shamans and their healing work.

Healing Homework

I didn't tell Aaron what Meredith had said to me. I wanted to see what he would do with what we had learned about healing. He came home a few days later with *The Reconnection*, a book by Dr. Eric Pearl.[14] It's about Dr. Pearl's own experience as a chiropractor, where he started to have strange experiences with patients in his clinic during treatments. Out of nowhere, one day, he randomly started to feel and see odd things in the room when he was treating patients. Patients started behaving strangely. He and others he came into contact with started to witness miraculous healings, transcending medical boundaries.

Aaron was excited about the book, which detailed ways to practice experiencing the healing energy and how to tap into and reconnect with the energy. Aaron tried it on me, and I tried it on him. My mind tried to reason out what was happening, logically trying to figure it out. I don't like not understanding something. I know most children ask 'why' a lot, but I think my mother will attest to the fact that I was still asking why every five minutes until... well, I never stopped.

When we practised what we learned, I wanted to be great at it.

Personality Type: Perfectionist
Typical Trait: Only do things one is great at
Typical Behaviour: Ditches anything one is not
great at first time round

And so the healing practice began. There wasn't much to it from what we read, which made it all the more bizarre that from such a simple process we were about to uncover something very unusual. Following the instructions, I closed my eyes. In a meditative state, I was to hover my hands over or on the person (Aaron being my only guinea pig at this point).

There he was, lying on the bed with his eyes closed. There I was, standing over him, meditating and concentrating. I wasn't sure if what I was doing was right. Thoughts began to flow through my mind. *I am doing it correctly? Am I meant to get a reaction, or is Aaron meant to experience something? Are we both meant to? Do I break this lovely silence to ask him what is happening?*

Personality Type: Highly Analytical
Typical Trait: Always questions things
Typical Behaviour: Analyses everything to death,
much to the torment of all around

(Note: I'm the one in the movie theatre whispering a million questions to whomever is the lucky person sitting next to me to ensure I fully understand the plot!)

I wasn't getting any images or messages for Aaron, to share with him. Aaron didn't have anything physically wrong with him that I could really heal as practice, so I was simply experimenting to see what would occur. I don't know how or why, but after five minutes things started happening.

Crazy Eyes

REM (Rapid Eye Movement)—it started very slowly, like a flutter. Then, my eyes uncontrollably shook at lightning speed.

We all have REM at night when we sleep, but experiencing it awake is quite something. It was most definitely not me moving my eyes around, and I assure you I was certainly not asleep. My eyes were spasming at a tremendous rate. It was not pleasant. Something was connecting to me or through me, and I was witnessing it happen quietly as I sat still. It was a little distressing, because I wasn't sure what to do, but inside I felt sure I was in control and could stop if I wanted to.

After wanting to connect to this energy, I was now more than a little freaked out by it and unsure whether I wanted to delve further. But curiosity got the better of me.

I breathed deeply through the REM, as it was physically uncomfortable. I wondered if this whole healing thing was possibly going to be a bit like a baby learning to put a spoon in its mouth for the first time. For a while, the baby keeps poking the spoon in its face (the odd spoon up the nose or spoon in the eye moments), until finally it is coordinated enough to have spoon meet mouth. I wondered: *Perhaps it's just a matter of practice and time until I figure how to do this, until it becomes easier and not so uncomfortable.* I came out of the meditation and decided that was enough for one day—time to give my tired eyes a rest.

Questions lingered. *So I have reacted to this Energy Source, but that is all. What do I do with it now? How do I utilise it? How does it heal?*

Elvis is in the House!

My guinea pig husband was quite happy to take a siesta while I practised again. This time I had REM again, but something new happened. The REM stopped and my facial muscles started twitching and spasming. One can only imagine how bizarre I must have looked, and I am sure, as Aaron lay there with his eyes closed, that he was wondering what all the heavy breathing was about.

In the silence, both of us in meditation, I couldn't share with him vocally what was going on as my face contorted and grimaced all on its own. I'm glad he didn't have his eyes open to see his wife imitating a cross between the Hunchback of Notre Dame and Elvis Presley's curling top lip. That's right; the predominant facial spasm I get is a curling upper lip. Very hot!

I was bewildered, excited and tired by the end of the fifteen minute session. Still no healing, no messages, no actual information came to me for Aaron as the supposed recipient of the healing. *What is happening in these healings? Why am I reacting strangely? Perhaps I am reacting as I connect to the Energy Source, but I haven't yet learned how to use it, to direct it or to ask it to heal something.*

In the days that followed, my eyeballs were bloodshot. *No pain, no gain,* I thought to myself. I read books and researched online in the hope of understanding what was happening to me during these healing practice sessions.

Midnight Message

I headed north from my home in Wellington to visit my sister in Auckland. After a day full of fun and laughter, walks on the beach, playing with my nephew and a sumptuous dinner, I retired to the guest room. I had no idea I was about to be 'signalled'.

In the middle of the night, something happened. Directly outside the bedroom window, a set of wind chimes came to life. I stirred and listened closer. There was not a breath of wind. The chimes didn't clatter and ring out their usual melodic song as they do when the breeze rattles all 4 cylinders. Instead, one note chimed on that still night. It was a clear and crisp sound as the singular tone sounded over and over again.

I was in that semi-awake, semi-asleep state. The chime stopped, and I heard a word loud and clear: "Asara."

I whispered it aloud several times, unsure if I heard it correctly. Asara, Ashara, Asana, Ashana? I was alert enough to realise this was unusual and eerie. I knew I had to pay attention. I felt compelled. As I melted back into sleep, I had a strong feeling all of these strange occurrences were leading me somewhere, and then I heard it like a whisper, "Book." But it seemed too odd to take seriously.

"Am I going to end up writing a book?"

"Yes."

"Did I just say yes to myself?"

"No."

As sleep took over, thoughts tumbled gently in my mind... *I'm no one special. I don't write. I'm not writing. This isn't really happening to me. Did I just hear voices?*

I rang Aaron back home early the next morning. We googled Asara and discussed the results. One of the first matches that came up was www.asara.com, a website run by a woman called Asara Lovejoy. On her website we read, "You learn that by lowering your brain frequency to theta you access unused portions of your brain that can, and will bring you all that you desire."[15]

We read on and then found an audio download of an interview with a woman called Vianna Stibal, the founder of a form of energy healing called ThetaHealing™.[16] *Healing, mmm, signal?*

We listened to the interview and to a guided meditation, guiding us into the theta brainwave. Here is where the true healing journey began for me.

Chapter 11

Life-Changing Healing

ThetaHealing™

From what I could gather, it seemed that this form of healing was based on the premise that you could connect to the healing properties of the Energy Source through putting yourself in the theta brainwave state of meditation. From this state, your brainwaves and focused thought would direct the healing energy to create positive changes. As I researched more, I was intrigued to learn that ThetaHealing™ could be applied as a supplement to medical treatment, for healing any form of physical, psychological or emotional ailment. Apparently, it could be used to transform negative, limiting beliefs and feelings (of which I had many).

Aaron and I had listened to the guided theta meditation several times, and it was interesting, yet I wasn't sure what exactly I was meant to do with the information. Aaron saw something unique in using this meditation technique for manifesting what we wanted in our lives. We decided to find out more about this by visiting Vianna's website, www.thetahealing.com.

We discovered the details of trained ThetaHealing™ teachers all around the world, running courses and teaching people to become trained ThetaHealing™ practitioners.

Driven by Desperation

There is one very important reason that healing interested me. Someone very close to me was sick—sick in a way that no one could help, sick in a way that not even the best doctors in the world could fix. This knowledge ate away at me every time I thought about it. It made my chest constrict and my stomach knot. And here I was hearing words in the middle of the night, happening upon these websites, discovering a form of alternative healing. Let's not pretend it was coincidence. I knew it wasn't. I knew in my gut. It was a signal.

Ryan was very unexpectedly diagnosed with a degenerative medical condition. Through visits with numerous medical specialists, and discussions with geneticists and medical researchers in New Zealand and the USA, we learned that he was severely limited in his options for treatment. In essence, the doctors said they could try one or two things that could possibly slow the condition, but there was no known cure. They were quick to fill us with the clear expectation of no hope.

I refused to accept this. I could not allow this to be the only answer. Driven by my concern for Ryan, my inability to stand by and accept medical opinion, and my desperate feeling of non-acceptance of what we were told would happen as his condition worsened over time, I promptly alerted him to the ThetaHealing™ information. I saw something in this information; potential is what I saw.

In the interim, I mused about how amazing it would be to know how to do healings for myself and those close to me, how much that would add to the quality of our lives if we had access to such a thing on a daily basis. If it worked, then the possibilities would be endless.

What if it was real and readily available to us? My recent reactions to the Energy Source had made me think quite seriously about all this healing business. Aaron and I discussed this at length, and I continued to ponder: *Is this the path I am meant to follow? Are the signals pointing me in this direction?*

I kept wondering if all of this was meant for Aaron. After all, Meredith sensed some healing connection from him. She never said anything to me. I wondered if I should find out about doing the healing course. Aaron was all for me giving it a go. "What have you got to lose?" he said.

I spent many hours, days and weeks thinking about energy healing, feeling drawn and compelled to do it. I felt like I had to try, in case I had stumbled across this information because I was meant to help Ryan.

Inescapable

Leaving home on the way to work one morning, there at the bottom of our road was a new sign erected on a fence. Approximately 3 metres high by 2 metres wide, in capital letters it read, "HEALING." On closer inspection, it was for some sort of healing event being held at a church. Interesting.

On the drive to work, Jessie called me and said, "After you told me about that healing website you saw, I felt compelled to tell you that I saw a poster yesterday for a healing event. It wasn't so much that it was for a healing event, but more about where it's being held. It's being held at St. Bernadette's Church." I felt like the signals were hunting me down.

As we neared the parking building, I had a spooky recollection. Having been raised Catholic, I know a little bit about saints, especially this one, given we share the same name. St. Bernadette of Lourdes saw apparitions of the Virgin Mary above a grotto in Lourdes, France. St. Bernadette was guided by the apparition to drink from a spring of water in the grotto. The water in turn ended up healing people of many illnesses over centuries, as people travelled from around the world to bathe in and drink from the water at Lourdes, renowned for its healing properties.

I researched this to find out more. It was documented in a wide range of cases about people who, over time, were cured of seemingly incurable diseases and disorders by the water at Lourdes. I wondered: *Is this somehow linked to the signals I'm receiving? Is this telling me healing is real and that I*

*should learn how to use it? Is it telling me that Ryan
can be healed or that he should go to Lourdes?*

Surely it wasn't that literal. I was confused. How
was I to interpret these signals?

One thing I did know, I felt strongly that he could
be cured, no matter what the doctors were saying. I
felt it in my gut. I felt like anything was possible.

Doctors are human. I know they're very smart
people, and we need doctors, but they weren't born
doctors. They studied textbooks to learn how to make
medical decisions. Is all reality and truth written in
medical textbooks? No. Have some doctors been
wrong in the past? Yes. Have doctors occasionally said
someone will only live a short time, but they go on to
live years? Yes. Have doctors occasionally said people
will never come out of a coma, and then they do? Yes.
Have people been told they will never walk again, and
then they have walked again? Yes.

Perhaps they had gotten it wrong with Ryan. I
knew that the medical information available all
pointed to one conclusion, but perhaps they didn't
know everything. Perhaps he shouldn't adjust his
reality around what they say will happen. Ryan
shouldn't have to live into the future that they have
created for him, believing that he will either never get
any better or, worse, that it will deteriorate further. If
people believe, think and feel something, then surely
that's what they will get.

I guess what I'm trying to say is that, while I have
the utmost respect for doctors and medical treatment,
having been a regular and very happy customer for 32
years, I also believe in miracles. In a world where

anything is possible, I believe the body and mind can be healed in ways beyond medical explanation.

What is the Meaning of Illness?

For most of my life, I thought illness and disease just happened to you. After reading, learning and discussing this topic with many people, it was enlightening for me to consider the possibility that we attract illness and disease to ourselves, and/or illness and disease come to teach us something. I have heard various opinions on and around this topic, such as:

a) Perhaps if we have negative beliefs, thoughts and feelings, they emit negative energy and attract back, like a magnet, sickness into our bodies;

b) Perhaps we get sick because our bodies are calling out to us, trying to tell us to pay attention to something that needs altering, signalling to us that we are out of balance in our life in some way;

c) Perhaps karmic influence is playing out. This may not mean the sickness is due to something 'bad' done in this lifetime; it may be karmic influence from a past life of which we have no conscious knowledge; or

d) Perhaps sickness comes into our life in order for our souls to learn and grow from the experience.

If you are sick and you are confronted by these ideas, I appreciate why you feel that way. The last thing I would want to hear if I was sick is that I attracted the illness myself. I am not saying anyone deserves to be sick, but I do believe being sick is no mistake. It happens for a reason, even if we can't pinpoint or understand that reason.

In retrospect, when I consider the illness my sister experienced and her subsequent death, I believe it was her time. Perhaps it was karmic influence. Perhaps it was part of her life lesson to experience that illness. Perhaps she had learned all she needed to learn in her life, and it was time for her to go. Perhaps it was my karma to lose her and experience that. However, back then, in the midst of raw pain, if you had told me any of the above statements about why people get sick, I'm pretty sure I would have told you to f@#% off in no uncertain terms.

Birth of a Book

Kneeling in my bedroom, resting my elbows on my bed, I closed my eyes tightly. It was the first time I had knelt on my knees and prayed of my own volition in a very, very, very long time. I meditated, prayed and asked. I said, "Creator, God, Energy Source, The Universe, whatever you are, please cure him. Please!" Tears welled as I pleaded for help. My worry for Ryan made me feel physically sick.

Then, I had what I thought was an inspired idea. *If he is cured, then I will definitely write the book.* It came across with a sort of polite force, like a veiled demand, "You'll only get the book if you cure him."

I don't know what I was thinking! Quid pro quo, healing in return for a book—I quickly realised that it probably wasn't the best idea to try to bargain with the Energy Source. In life, we should do things without expectation of pay back; this is true giving. This is what I'd been taught. This is how I was raised, and this day would be no different.

It would not be long before I knew for sure that this book would be written no matter what happened to Ryan. When something so profound happens to you and your eyes are opened to something that can impact people in such a positive way, something accessible to every single living human being, you cannot ignore it. In my view, there is only one single block in the way of all humans benefiting from their own connection to the Energy Source. That block is themselves or, to be more specific, their minds.

- Is your mind open enough?
- Are you up for exploration and adventure?
- Are you willing to trust?
- Are you willing to see what exists beyond your world?
- Do you want to believe?
- Do you want to experience the Energy Source?

Diving Into Theta

I looked up the dates for the healing course. There was one being run in two weeks time, at a venue next door to Parliament. I felt hesitant to register. I was afraid of what it would entail—afraid of going to something like this, afraid of who would be there, and afraid that people I knew might find out I was doing something like this. It felt taboo.

I was full of 'I'm too busy' and 'I can't take leave from work at short notice' excuses. Then I thought: *What if it works? What I could help myself and other people, and what if I could help Ryan?*

I called the number and spoke to Janine, the teacher. Yes, there were spaces left. Yes, it was not too late to register. Yes, I was more than welcome.

Hesitation persisted. I didn't enjoy the phone conversation with Janine. I wanted to be reassured and told everything was going to be great and that normal people do this. Then, I reflected, it was a telephone conversation about a course, not a counselling session!

Crossing the road on the way to work the next morning, I stepped up onto the footpath and noticed a discarded sticky label trodden into the pavement. I looked twice. It was a Visitor Pass for Parliament. The course was being held next door. Signal? Probably not, but it reminded me again about the damn course. Fear gripped me. Pure and simple, I was afraid.

It was 'practice what you preach' time. I knew it was time to push through and over that invisible fear boundary. I booked annual leave and registered for the course. Within 30 minutes, it was all done and dusted. No turning back.

The course reading material arrived in my letterbox the next day. It said, "Please review before attending if possible." It was a big fat book, and it was now less than a week until the course commenced. I got reading quick smart.

I awoke one morning to hear "...felt the healing in her fingertips, it burned like fire..."[17] These lyrics played over and over in my mind all day.

As I made my way through the reading material, absorbing everything I could before we started, the content started to freak me out. It was 80% interesting and feasible, and 20% completely unnerving. *I'm not like these alternative people. I've given up a whole weekend and a day off work to go to this. What was I thinking?!*

I knew I had to suck it up. It went back to the night when the word Asara came to me. Since that night, there had been too many 'in your face' signals to ignore. If I ignored these, it would be a clear snub to the Energy Source and the signals being given to me.

Here is a really good lesson to learn: Sometimes you don't like where the signals point you, and you don't know why the signals take you in a certain direction. However, as the saying goes, hindsight is a wonderful thing. Hindsight has shown me that if you trust in the repeating signals, you will be led in the direction that serves you best.

Three Days of Surprises

So off I secretly went. Excuses were fabricated about where I was. Only a couple of people close to me knew what I was doing. I was afraid people would ask me questions that I wouldn't know how to answer. I could look like a loony if I tried to defend myself to people who didn't believe in this sort of thing.

On arrival, I scanned the room. There were four chairs in a semi circle. I plastered a big smile on my face to cover how uncomfortable I was. When it came to introductions, I felt like screaming out, "I'm here because Ryan is sick, and I NEED ANSWERS!" Though I knew that would possibly make me sound like a crazy desperate person, so instead I just said, "Hi, I'm B."

As I sat there on the first day listening and practising, I thought to myself: *If only they could see me now. They* being everyone in my life who thought that I was straight laced and mainstream. I could barely believe it myself. I was sitting in this room, experiencing a connection to this Energy Source. And when I say connection, I mean CONNECTION! My practice at home with Aaron had been one thing. This was on a whole other level. R.E.M. and curling lip step aside please; the Big Kahuna has arrived.

I wondered: *Can it really be this easy? It sure seems that way. How come everyone doesn't know about this? I guess those who explore will discover and those who don't won't.*

I do feel like there is one prerequisite: you need to believe (even just a tiny, weeny little bit) that there is, or could be, something greater and bigger than you. If you don't, then I think you are flying blind, coming into it with your mind already set in a different direction. Your compass won't align, and we all know what happens with broken compasses. Does lost and confused ring a bell?

During the course, I was dumbstruck when my body physically reacted when I connected to the Energy Source. Others in the course saw colours, shapes and images. Some heard noises, voices and messages. Others felt strange sensations. My body literally moved of its own accord in reaction to the Energy Source. I felt a strong push on my head, as my forehead and neck fell backwards and down. I tried to resist the push to see if I could move and to challenge if it was just me doing it to myself (still challenging and testing to see if my mind was playing tricks on me). I really tried, but the physical sensation was strong. I was not practised at how to respond and manage my reaction to it, yet.

It was heartening to hear from Janine that this was very normal. Many other participants had also had the same reaction. It seemed to me that it was just a matter of time before I'd work out how to use this technique without having this type of reaction to it.

In addition to these physical reactions, I was shocked to find that when I asked a question, I got an answer. I heard the answer in my mind. I was not giving myself the answer; it was being told to me. I could hear it, but not actually hear it with my ears. I was told this was clairaudience. I received clear responses to my questions, and I had dialogue with the Energy Source when I facilitated a healing for myself or others. At times I received one word answers, and sometimes I received whole sentences. It was the oddest thing.

After the course, I enthusiastically went about practising what I had learned. I believe that in any discipline, 'on the job' training is the best way to improve your performance. All I needed were willing guinea pigs; otherwise, Aaron was going to be perpetually under my microscope.

Firstly, I spent endless hours on myself, clearing negative beliefs and feelings. Like an onion, I peeled back one layer after another, each time feeling lighter, happier, freer and more capable. I then turned to a wide circle of willing family and friends who were only too happy to be the focus of my practice. I realised what I was seeing in myself and others was just the tip of the iceberg as far as the raft of things many of us carry around on our shoulders every day like a heavy sack of potatoes. I found a level of peace and fulfilment that I didn't know existed when I transformed my own beliefs and did this for others. It's inspiring to witness people let go of life-long limitations from regret, resentment and guilt to lack of confidence, low self-worth and loneliness. The list is literally endless, or shall I say the sack is bottomless!

My practice has been tested with healings for a diverse range of physical and psychological ailments, illnesses and injuries—from temporary, fleeting conditions and minor issues that niggle away through to more serious and long-term problems. I am constantly astounded by what energy healing can help with and what blocks people from healing themselves.

I have worked with babies and toddlers through to elderly people, and even pets! These people have all sorts of views on this realm of spirituality, including self-proclaimed sceptics. People are surprised by the results, and many don't even want to know how it works. For some, it has opened up their eyes, just as it did for me.

This newfound knowledge is forever imprinted on me and has enriched my life to no end. I don't live in a euphoric state 24/7, in denial of reality, running around like a peace child. I simply view and process things differently now. I feel like I've come home to the truth and reconnected to something I was disconnected from. It now frames the way I view life. I now understand what I had heard and read about earlier: that all of us are souls, each with our own challenges and life lessons to learn and our own karma to deal with. We're all just running around trying to figure it all out or, to be fair, in some cases, never knowing there is even anything to figure out.

There are many different types of healing modalities and alternative therapies of this nature. It is not a gift you are born with; it's just a case of whether you were born with your tap turned on or off. If you're like me and you were born with your tap turned off, you can turn it on and learn how to harness your connection to the Energy Source if you wish. You can utilise it simply to get guidance, to recognise signals or to give and receive healing. It depends on what lights your fire. Harnessing the Energy Source is a learned process, and everyone has the right to do so.

Traditional Medical Treatment and Energy Healing

For whatever reason people get sick, there are different ways of healing. When I discovered energy healing was real and effective, I thought: *These 'alternative' people have the key!*

Now, ask me if I got a serious life-threatening sickness today, if I would vouch for energy healing alone. I'd mostly likely go with medical treatment and energy healing, hand in hand. Or possibly, I would first try a short period of time with energy healing and monitor the results very closely. If I didn't see a quick enough result, I'd probably zap myself with the full force of medical treatments quick smart. I'm a believer, but I'm not about to die trying to prove it.

I'm guessing that often most people will go for traditional medical treatment first and only revert to energy healing or alternative therapies when all medical options are exhausted and the doctors don't know what to do anymore or say there is no hope. Energy healing can and, in many cases, definitely should go hand in hand with qualified medical and/or psychological treatment. Energy healing is something to supplement what we already know and use in our world today.

Personally, if I have the option and circumstances allow, I will always go for energy healing as a first option before medical treatment; that's my personal choice. With what I now know, if I'm sick, I want to find out why so that I can address the root cause, rather than slapping a sticking plaster over the symptoms.

Chapter 12

Courage vs. Fear

Self-Diagnosed LCP

I was fervently on the lookout for signals relating to my life number 8. I started on the basis that 8's are here to provide a service for the common good.

I began by meditating on the future I wanted. I visualised the lifestyle I wanted, the achievement of all my goals through doing something I love, with a good income, while using any success in service of others and helping the common good. I kept it 'big picture' simply because I didn't know what I wanted in detail. I wanted to be shown the way forward, shown what to do next, *how* to move ahead, and *how* to make it all happen. I asked for signals.

I was haunted by Augustus' comment that I should look at how to use my leadership skills; I coined this aversion LCP (Leadership Commitment Phobia). Stephen had gone silent on the proposed leadership role at work. It had been raised and discussed much earlier, but nothing further had eventuated. The exact definition of the role he intended for me was not clear, nor was the timing. Perhaps the ball was in my court. Perhaps everything was hanging in the air, waiting for me to decide.

Since my eyes had been opened with all this newfound spiritual knowledge, the pull to a simple life was now more intense. This was something I could no longer ignore. I knew I had to find a way to create a life where I would spend my time doing things that were more meaningful to me, things of the mind, body and spirit. I wasn't entirely sure what those things were, but I felt sure that given time and freedom I could discover them.

The signals about leadership rattled around incessantly in my mind. My LCP was like the elephant in the room. It wasn't a quiet elephant hanging out in the corner, but rather, it was an elephant that was stampeding around me, making hooting hollering noises.

In relation to what Augustus had told me, I wanted to apply the very useful skill of selective hearing. Fortunately, on reflection, I realised he was the wise one and I was the student, so I should probably pay close attention to why he was saying it.

On that basis, with regards to leadership and my desire for change, I considered: *How can this serve me in a positive way? How can this help me move forward? Maybe there is some way to use my leadership skills where I would enjoy it—a way I have not thought of, where it would be a service to others and would benefit me in reaching my goals of a more fulfilling life—a win-win scenario.*

I wondered if, perhaps, the way to achieve my end goal was actually down the path I was most resisting. Imagine if what seemed to be the most unlikely place to look for answers was, in fact, the exact place the answers lay. In committing to the one thing I was resisting, I could possibly set myself free. What an oxymoron. Why else was I getting these signals?

Sometimes, we know the end outcome we want, but we also try to define how we will get there. It's important not to self-select from the buffet of signals. That is no different from living a life led solely by your logical mind. Signals work best if you let go of your desire to pick and choose and let them lead you in the direction that serves you best.

I considered that maybe I could be good at this leadership thing, and perhaps a corporate career doing this type of role would in fact give me more flexibility, not less. Was leadership where my joy was hiding?

I swung my legs out of bed one Monday morning, with no inkling at all that the coming hours would change everything. That day, the sparks would fly and change would be ignited.

The Dare

We parked the car and wandered down the terraced alleyway towards the city centre, preparing to robotically say goodbye and walk on to our respective offices, to our respective desks, to do our respective tasks for the coming eight hours before repeating the experience for the following four days of the week.

No matter how outstandingly brilliant the company, colleagues and job were, my passion had left the building. I was faced with what had become logistical tasks to me. I had tried hard to get my heart singing; I listened carefully every day to see if it was even humming a little.

If I had been light heartedly walking down that alleyway, kissing Aaron goodbye with a twinkle in my eye, skipping to my office, and engaging in eight hours of activity that challenged me, stimulated me and made my heart sing, then things would have been different.

That morning, one step away from turning to say goodbye, I said to him, "Why don't we just do it? Let's just bloody well do it."

"Do what?"

"Go! Go where we want. Live the life we are planning for, dreaming of, conspiring about. Why are we waiting for the right time? There is never a right time! If we do it, things will fall into place; they will have to. If we wait for things to fall into place before we do it, we could be waiting forever!"

It had dawned on me that I could ask a million questions about what to do, whether to move, where to move, whether to give away my career, whether to take on a leadership role, and I would never know the answers. I would never know unless I gave it a go. I had to do something.

Inspired by the events of recent months, we had already started musing about possible locations for us to live, places that would fit our dream lifestyle. Sticking with our love for New Zealand, we asked ourselves: *What places offer slow and quiet living in a rural, coastal setting with a tropical climate, yet are close enough to the amenities of a city for the practicalities of life?* The answer: Waiheke Island.

A little over half an hour by ferry from New Zealand's largest city, Auckland, Waiheke offers all of the above and more—stunning coastline, golden beaches, lush native bush, tropical climate, a slow and peaceful lifestyle, warm and friendly people, dreamy vineyards and summer seems to last forever.

Standing in that alleyway, in a split second decision, Waiheke jumped from being a mere musing to a reality.

I said to Aaron, "I'll ask Stephen if I can transfer to our Auckland office. You quit your job, and we'll just go."

"Okay, I dare you. Do it!"

"Okay," I said. "I'll do it if you promise to resign as soon as I text you."

"Okay, deal!"

With a hug, kiss, grin and goodbye, the dare was on.

How amazing would life be if we could decide just like that, if we could indeed be so bold as to sweep our lives away to paradise in nothing more than a heartbeat?

Self-Imposed Rules

When you're on a roll and you're swept up in adrenaline, it pays not to hesitate. Just take action ASAP before the boring, rational, risk-averse side of your personality grabs back the steering wheel and diverts you on the route back to Safeville.

What had, in fact, been holding us to Wellington was another goal we had set. We agreed that when our trading business could replace one of our incomes in full then Aaron would quit full time work permanently and we'd go after all the things we wanted in our life.

For some reason, we can't even remember why, we decided that we wouldn't go anywhere or do anything else until that goal was achieved. It's not like they didn't have computers and internet access in any other places! The challenge with that somewhat faulty plan being that trading is volatile. We had wins, but we also had losses. It had taken years to master it thus far to get consistency. Although we knew we were on the cusp of creating an income requiring minimal time and effort going forward, we didn't know how long exactly it would be before that would be consistently reliable to replace a pay check.

So we had waited, and waited, and waited, while our other plans sat on the shelf labelled 'when X goal is achieved then Y and Z action plans can be commenced'. We had made self-imposed rules and created an order in which things would happen. We were manifesting something that didn't work for us. We were dictating to the Energy Source *how* we wanted life to go, down to the detail of what order it should happen, and it wasn't in a way that would serve us positively. Of course, the Energy Source obliged and sat by patiently, allowing us to control how everything played out in a neat little order of events. It's no wonder life stalled into a seemingly endless series of groundhog days.

We could have gone on like that for years if we'd stayed bound by self-imposed rules. There is no right time or right way. Don't get me wrong; there is being completely reckless and throwing all reason and common sense out the window. However, in most circumstances there will never be a right time, and it takes courage to take action.

In realising this, we freed ourselves from the commandment of "Thou shalt not pursue more than one major goal at one time." We removed the shackles that were keeping us in jobs we didn't love, in a lifestyle we didn't love, in a location we didn't love. We saw clearly that we were trying hard to manifest what we really wanted, while doing so in a frustrated frame of mind and then foolishly wondering why we weren't getting the results we wanted.

We had decided the end result we wanted, but our mistake had been also deciding how it would happen. We missed a critical law of creating your life: surrender up *how* it will happen and follow the signals you receive.

I felt courage spark somewhere inside me. Out of nowhere it seemed to momentarily roar at me, and most importantly, it was roaring louder than my fear.

Gaining Buy-in

Arriving in the office with a feeling of exhilaration, I booked a meeting with Stephen before I lost my nerve.

Sitting before him I opened my mouth and out fell, "I need to leave Wellington." It was followed by, "I'm probably moving to Waiheke." I made a mental note at this point that I had only visited there twice in my life—once when I was 10 years old on holiday with family friends and again as an adult for a day trip, at which time I was completely hung over with mind and senses not fully operational. Yet somehow I knew we were going to live there, enough to confidently state this to Stephen. I was hearing myself speak and it sounded like a different person—a person who just did what they wanted, whose fear was not holding the reigns anymore. I quite liked the sound of this person.

"If I do move there, can I work out of the Auckland office?"

The answer was a prompt and certain, "Yes, sure."

In a world where you create your reality by what you believe and think is possible, I'm not sure why I was surprised by the answer. We decided that this was what we wanted, and our reality was responding in accordance. I was astounded by how accepting and supportive Stephen was in that conversation with me. He instantly sensed my change in direction and came on board.

If his answer had been no, would I have gotten upset and stayed where I was, doing what I was doing? I don't know. I don't think so. If the answer had been no, it could have led me down any number of different paths. Everything happens for a reason, and life conspires around you to prod you in the right direction. When things don't go the way you planned or thought, when a signal leads you to what looks like a dead end, there is a reason. It is leading you to feel, experience, move and/or think in a different way. This way of living is an equation—nothing more and nothing less. If you follow the process—believe, think, feel and act in accordance—you *will* get to the end result you desire, but you might just get there via a different path to the one you thought you would take. Think of it like an unplanned detour on a road trip, with scenery you would not otherwise have seen.

You decide the WHAT.
Let the signals show you HOW.

Vanilla, Mango, or Boysenberry?

On realising we could now go and live in our dream destination, I didn't stop there.

Although I didn't dislike my job, I didn't love it. I certainly didn't hate going to work. In fact, it's the only job I'd ever had where I never felt like taking a 'mental health' day. I was certainly more than willing to do what I was paid to do, and I did it with a smile on my face. I enjoyed my work environment and professional relationships with colleagues and clients alike, but I kept coming back to, "I don't love it." I was neutral. My job was vanilla ice cream. I much prefer mango or boysenberry. I needed to find my mango job or my boysenberry career move.

Smiling and staring at Stephen as he said yes to my transfer, Augustus' words rang through my mind. It felt like he was there on my shoulder, whispering in my ear, "It's time."

Then, it came pouring out, "I don't want to do this role anymore. I need to change my path. Is there a leadership role I could do in Auckland?"

The answer was, of course, "Yes, sure."

A Different Future

Instead of feeling dread, the feeling I thought would arise if I committed myself further to corporate life and to a leadership role, I somehow felt lighter, freer, happier. I had just created a new future for myself, in a different place, doing different things—all within the space of several hours and all created through thoughts and words alone. The confusing minefield of interwoven goals was gone. Clarity had arrived. I had removed my own obstacles, and I felt enabled.

It is amazing how you feel in the present moment when, with mere thoughts and words, you instantly transform the future you are living into. I dare you to create a different future outlook and plan for yourself, one that inspires you. Although in this present moment nothing has tangibly changed around you, your thoughts and feelings have. When your thoughts and feelings change, you start emitting a different energy, attracting to yourself the very things you desire.

Chapter 13

The Move

As days passed, my mind spun. *Surely people don't just up and leave their entire life and move somewhere remote on a whim!* We weren't going for a little break, to see what it was like or to rent for a while. We were going to do it full on—all or nothing.

Waiheke Island is a dreamy place where people visit for summer getaways, vineyards, private coves and corporate retreats. Do average people like us just move there to live permanently for no other reason than we feel like it? Not very often. Why? There is the commute to town for a start, the ferry each morning to the mainland, and then transportation on the mainland to wherever you work. This is then repeated on the trip home each night. There is the lack of accessibility on the Island to the conveniences one is used to when living on the mainland. It is perceived to be an expensive place in terms of living costs and commuting costs, but mostly due to real estate prices.

Still, this was the location of our dreams, and we were going to make it happen.

Reconnaissance Weekend

A wise idea cropped up. How about we actually visit the Island together? After booking flights, signals for Waiheke popped up everywhere. We laughed each day as TV programmes, news articles, and magazine and book references shouted 'WAIHEKE' at us. Perhaps such references were always there, but we just became *aware* of them. Our taps were on, and the signals were now being recognised.

Just seeing the Island as the ferry drew closer relaxed me. There was definitely something about this place. Within hours, we had lined up real estate agents to tour us around properties for sale. Three days and fifteen houses later, we stumbled upon it: a home so similar in style to our current house that it was comical.

The kitchen cabinetry was exactly the same—same colour, same handles. The flooring in the kitchen, laundry and bathroom was exactly the same—same tiles, same colour. The carpet in the house was the same as the carpet in my parents' house—same thread, same colour. The furniture in the house was almost identical to ours—similar dining table, exactly the same chairs. I actually felt like I was at home.

This house fit all of our non-negotiable house purchasing criteria. It met the 'dream lifestyle' requirements that we had written on a list many, many years ago. Surprisingly, we could afford it. The market was down; the vendor needed out; and it appeared that we were in the right place at the right time.

One of the key requirements was outdoor living space so that we could enjoy our new climate. It would also have to come with land so that we could create the orchard and sizeable vegetable garden we had dreamed of. This was all part of our semi-rural, self-sufficient dream. Sitting on half an acre with native bush, this house had land that was steep and seemingly unusable, in the eyes of other prospective buyers. When we gazed at the steep grassy bank, we saw a glorious courtyard drenched in sun. When we traipsed through an odd shaped weed ridden area, we saw a vegetable garden like no other. It would take serious landscaping—excavation, retaining, fences, terracing, paving and planting—but we could do it.

Driving away from the property, we didn't even talk about making an offer. I just said, "How much?" Within an hour, we negotiated a purchase price with the seller and were on our way to sign the paperwork at the real estate agency. I'm not sure if it was the fastest deal ever done, but it felt close to it! Although we made a decision that weekend that may have seemed rash to an onlooker, it felt nothing but perfectly right to us.

How did a weekend visit to Waiheke Island result in us just 'knowing' this place was home? How did we make that decision on the spot? We followed the signals. We noticed all the little coincidences; we saw all the correlations between that property and what we had been manifesting and dreaming of for years. We listened to our gut instincts, which were telling us it was right.

We were meant to be scouting property prices and locations, not buying. Consider it crazy, rash or spontaneous, but something pulled at me. I followed the call.

Instantaneous Showing Up

Sitting in the car outside the agency, we chatted about landscapers and how much the job would cost. Heading in to sign the paperwork, a man walked past us. He had just moved away from two people he was chatting to in the carpark. He turned around and called back to them, "If you know anyone who needs some landscaping done..."

Aaron and I looked at each other and laughed. "It's that easy now, B. We just ask and the Universe delivers." *Life has become this easy? It appears so.*

Aaron approached him, "Sorry, but I overheard you. We're in need of a landscaper."

He gave us his contact details and invited us to visit his home if we ever wanted to see an example of his work. There was no doubt we would.

The property deal was done, signed on the bottom line. With time to spare before ferrying back to the city, we drove around a few bays and beaches we hadn't yet visited. We found a gorgeous little cove and parked. And who should come wandering down the road towards us? The landscaper. Waving out, he shouted, "I'm on my way out, but if you want to pop in and see my work, my house is just up the hill on the right-hand side." So we did. Although we thought it prudent to get a few quotes, we knew we would end up choosing this person. He fell into our path for a reason.

Transitioning

The timeframe from the reconnaissance weekend to the date we were due to leave Wellington was 12 weeks. We had the short rabbit hop of 12 weeks to action our dream life transformation.

I began finalising my transfer with work and the creation of my new leadership role. In planning for the daily ferry commute into the city, I was eternally grateful for Stephen's willingness to allow me to work one day a week from home on the Island.

In the quiet moments before I went to sleep each night, after frenetic days preparing for our move, I reflected on how my life was about to become completely extraordinary. My stomach churned with excitement.

Now we needed to sell our Wellington house. This would fund the purchase of our new home and many of the associated moving costs. The property market soon dictated the outcome of that situation. When it didn't sell, we reassessed. *Why is this happening to us? This isn't what we manifested!* After wallowing in frustration, I wondered if perhaps this was happening for a reason. Perhaps we were meant to keep it. Perhaps we hadn't given proper consideration to ways we could keep it. Forced by circumstance, we kept the property and were now lumped with more debt.

Aaron had upheld his end of the earlier dare, resigning from his job. I had a new job, but he did not.

We'd gone from two incomes and one mortgage to two mortgages and one income. It doesn't take a rocket scientist to work out this wasn't good! We both agreed to focus 100% of our attention on what we wanted and needed, thinking about more money flowing to us, feeling the feelings of having all that we needed financially. With a need for more money, not knowing where it would come from or how, we asked for signals.

Having just resigned from his role as an Energy Trader for an electricity company in Wellington, Aaron was highly employable but in a niche profession. In Auckland, there were only a small number of electricity companies, and within those companies, there were literally only a handful of trading roles. Just weeks before our move, a trading role arose in one of the Auckland companies—not just any trading role but a senior, more interesting and better paying trading role. One of the 10-15 people who held that unique job in a city of approximately one million people decided to leave their job at just the right time. We felt sure the job had arisen for him.

He signed the contract within the week.

Settling

You could think this all sounds dreamy and easy the way I paint the picture. Let me put this into real life terms for those of you that think I live in a Disney movie. Everyone has challenges, and life often throws curve balls. That's how life works. Achieving all of this within 12 weeks was pretty chaotic, but then, I knew that if I wanted to create greatness, I would have to be up for the challenge!

The following months were so much fun and also exhausting. It seemed like everything at our new property that could break did break—broken kitchen tap and bench, broken showers, septic system needing servicing, water tank overhaul required, flood in the laundry, broken toilet seat, broken garage door, and a carpet problem. Although I thought I was going to explode from doing a full time job, coordinating a zillion tradespeople and landscaping the section—the outcome of six months of work crammed into three months: dream home, dream property, dream lifestyle.

Having made friends with one of the tradespeople who helped us, we were invited to lunch to meet other locals. Then, the questions started, "Why did you come here? Did you know people here?"

"No."

"Did your jobs bring you here?"

"No."

"Had you spent much time here before?"

"No."

"Why did you move here?"

"We wanted our dream lifestyle. The Island ticked all the boxes, and we just knew."

"Knew what?"

"We just knew it was where we were meant to be. We weren't sure why, but we knew it was home. In our hearts it felt right."

"You seem like you are people who make quite big decisions quickly and easily, but you are guided by some sort of knowing."

Yes, I thought, *I guess we are people like that. Well, we are now.* A moment of truth.

From the first day in our new home, in our new life, we felt completely at ease. It was like we were always meant to be on the Island, and it was just waiting for us to arrive.

Chapter 14

Reflecting on Progress

Progress in the Physical Realm

Some years ago, during a period of stagnancy, I created a scrapbook of all the things I wanted in life and filled it with photos downloaded from the internet—places I wanted to go, things I wanted to buy, experiences I wanted to have, and pictures depicting the type of relationships and lifestyle I wanted. This was an aid to help me visualise my future. It was a book version of a dream board, which is a commonly used tool for visualising goals.

I then decided the scrapbook wasn't enough. I needed to reinvent myself immediately to help speed things along. So, I got myself a new hairstyle. Every woman knows a great new hairstyle goes a long way to perking you up if you're feeling below par. Following the change of hairstyle, I then enlisted my sisters to help me change my look and style with new clothes. Looking back, this makes me laugh; thinking that cutting my hair and putting on new clothes would somehow make things different. I was trying to fill the void I was feeling inside with a bandaid on a gaping open wound.

I had headed home that afternoon with a little less cash and a lot more clothes, shopping bags slung over both arms. The bags contained the new me. On arrival home, I tried them all on and looked in the mirror. I did not like the new me. This wasn't helping! I felt too embarrassed to tell my sisters that I'd changed my mind. The new me in the bags was going back. I secretly returned everything and got my money back, feeling worse than before my ridiculous reinvention process began.

I told them a few days later; it seemed funnier in retrospect. They laughed lovingly at my mini crisis. I jokingly said that with my failed reinvention perhaps I should have also changed my name. I tried to think of the least likely and most inappropriate name given my personality. Being that I am not at all peaceful or flowing, I suggested the name 'River'. It was the first peaceful flowing word I could think of.

Don't get me wrong; extreme makeovers are fantastic. However, my attempt was just a half-arsed effort to mask some level of dissatisfaction that no haircut or new dress was going to fix. My open wound needed more serious attention.

The Marvellous Life

I later came across *The Winner's Bible* by Dr. Kerry Spackman[18], a book I saw as a guide to success, however one defines that, using a formula to get you there. I went about following the instructions, creating my personalised winner's bible: a flip folder version of a dream board. It was time to upgrade my previous scrapbook. Completing all the exercises, I filled my winner's bible with photos, mind maps, words and descriptions. I kept it on my bedside table and looked at the pages daily, helping to create within me the feeling of having what I desired.

The inspirational images told the story of the life I was creating: happy faces, relaxed people, pampering and entertaining, families, exercise, yoga and meditation, pictures of our honeymoon holiday in Thailand, images depicting gratitude, fresh flowers, a baby grand piano, horseback riding on the beach, pictures of people with traits I respect and admire, a gorgeous red Doberman puppy with big floppy ears, rural coastline, a gorgeous large house (why dream of a tiny bach), stunning home interiors and exteriors, an outdoor fireplace and Jacuzzi, wine and tapas, a silver SUV, a boat with people having dinner on the back deck and a myriad of Mediterranean coastlines and villages, representing adventure and new cultures.

Sitting on Waiheke Island, months after our arrival, I reflected back on all of this. I saw all that we had achieved as I looked back at my winner's bible, and surprisingly, most of it hadn't come about through conscious choice to specifically match up outcomes to fit. It's just how life plays out when you focus in on what you want and actively participate in your life, following the signals to show you how.

In full health and loving life, we were enjoying yoga, meditation, running, swimming, tennis, surfing, body boarding, cycling, mountain biking and... I had been cantering down a one kilometre stretch of beach on the Island astride a gorgeous grey horse. Never mind that my new riding boots had been lovingly chewed by... Cash, our handsome puppy—a red Doberman with big floppy ears. As I reclaimed all the things that brought me joy, my piano took pride of place in the living room. I was most excited to exclaim to my family that there were no doors that could be slid shut to dampen the joyous tones of my loud and furiously fast piano playing. At times I could vaguely hear a distant voice coming from the couch saying, "B, I'm trying to watch the cricket." Pondering whether it was my long suffering husband, I continued playing loud and fast in my moment of complete bliss!

Strolling the short distance to the nearby white sand beach for our daily swim, I would often marvel at the beautiful coastline, the semi-rural setting, the native bush, trees and glorious gardens. Relaxing afternoons were spent in our sun-drenched courtyard. On warm summer evenings we sat around the outdoor fireplace, circling it like moths to the flame, with wine and tapas to wile away the hours. Forced to upgrade our vintage car, we found a bargain online. The best deal available was a silver SUV, perfect for island living, as we needed something to tow the boat. Well, okay, it was more of a zippy with an outboard, but it was a start. As we sat on the water, waiting for the fish to bite, I considered that there wasn't quite enough room for dinner on the back deck... yet.

The comparison between what we visualised and focused on, and what turned up in our lives feels to me like living proof that this pinch-me way of living really does work.

If you ask me how this happened, with less income and more mortgage, I will tell you that I have no idea. Really, I have no idea! I am particularly good with money management, and I checked our finances a hundred times to ensure I hadn't missed something. I could not have imagined that this was even remotely possible back when I was in Wellington, in my old house, in my old job, in my old life, with my old perspective on how the world works.

When a fire ignited within me and my tap was turned on, somehow heaven and earth literally moved in my favour. Life became just marvellous.

Progress in the Spiritual Realm

Although my life was clearly progressing in a tangible, physical sense, I seemed to be making progress with my intuitive abilities as well. As I connected to the Energy Source more frequently, I noticed my connection becoming clearer and easier. At times when I was least expecting it, I was experiencing strong physical reactions to the Energy Source, like a message was coming to me, but I wasn't consciously going into a theta level of meditation to ask for it.

At first this came to me via clairaudience, what could have seemed like my own voice in my head. However, you really know when it's guidance and not your own thoughts when the things that you think (or you think that you think) are really things you would *never* think to yourself. That's a mind bender for you!

5%

I was reading *The 4-Hour Workweek* by Timothy Ferriss on the ferry ride home from work. Standing in the queue as we docked at the wharf, I was glued to the pages. The final thing I read just as it was time to disembark was, "Fewer than 5% of the 195,000 books published each year sell more than 5,000 copies."[19]

Up until that point, I'd had no doubt that my book would a) be published, and b) be a success in the sense it would reach the people who would benefit from it. I was guided to write the book, and therefore, it would be successful. Additionally, I had been manifesting it to be so. So, of course it would sell! Despite this confidence, when I read this one line in Ferriss' book, my initial thought was: *Oh no, what if I am one of the 95%?*

Straight away, without time to even finish this thought, let alone time to ponder it, my mind was interrupted mid-sentence by a loud and clear voice, one that was determined and assured. The message was, "Do you want to react with fear, or are you going to go out and grab life by the balls?"

This message certainly got my attention. I thought: *Either the Energy Source is a little crass, like me, or my spirit guides are quite forthright!* I didn't get a chance to feel a sad reaction to my negative thought, as my mind was totally overruled by this message. I actually laughed, very quietly in order to avoid the stares of other commuters in the queue.

Angry Dog with a Bone

One evening, I had a similar uninvited message when I was nagging my husband. Yes, it's true; I nag my husband just like every good wife does. Surely, it's just a case of to what degree and frequency the nagging occurs! There I was 'asking' Aaron to do something, and for some reason (probably PMS), I was like a dog with a bone. I was not a happy dog with a wagging tail lovingly gnawing on its bone; I was more like an angry, mean dog crunching the living daylights out of its bone.

Mid-sentence, as I was berating him for something (bless him for his patience and tolerance), I was told off—and not by Aaron. Loud and clear it came in, "Leave him alone. You are not achieving anything. You need to walk away."

I felt like screaming, "I'm sorry, but I'm actually in the middle of a full swing hissy fit at present. I didn't ask for advice!" Well, apparently, you can't pick and choose when you get guidance. That's how it works when you become 'tuned in'. If you're going to have your tap turned on, beware; it will flow whether you want it to or not. Advice may come any time of the day or night it is needed, even when you don't ask for it and least want it.

I walked away from Aaron and there was silence from 'out there'. Apparently, no further intervention was required.

Business Decision

When I do healing work, I have several ways of communicating with the Energy Source. Sometimes I see images in my mind's eye in response to my questions. Sometimes, via clairaudience, I hear messages in the form of words or sentences. Sometimes my head lurches left or right in the form of a yes or no response.

Aaron was in the midst of making a major decision about buying into another business in the trading arena. He was torn about the decision and unsure of what path to take. On the surface, this opportunity looked to be quite good, but he was also eager to continue with his own business 100%. The signals did not appear clear enough for him to see which path was the right one. We had been discussing this for some time. One afternoon, as I sunned myself on the deck, Aaron marched up and plonked himself down in front of me. He announced, "I've made a decision. I've worked long and hard to get where I am. I like doing my own thing and I have always wanted to be in business for myself. I know I can do it better on my own. I'm not going to invest in their business."

As my head snapped left, Aaron looked at me and said, "What are you doing?!" He thought I was mucking around, not paying attention to what was a very serious conversation.

"I'm not doing anything!" was my response, because I wasn't. It happened involuntarily: a strong yes. Previously, I had been receiving guidance of this nature via theta level meditation, asking questions and receiving answers. Now it appeared that answers were coming to me of their own accord, meditation or not.

For anyone who is wondering, I do not suffer from any health condition that causes my body to behave in this way, in case you're thinking I have a medical problem to explain away these odd spasms! Aaron knew his decision was right as well; his statement was affirmed.

When I realised what had just happened and marvelled at it, I had the full body shivers. Meredith had told me that getting the shivers is a signal something is pure truth. Sometimes, it is referred to as the psychic shivers.

Aaron had earlier emailed David, the spirit channeler, asking for guidance on this decision. Augustus had offered Aaron the opportunity to email him in future with a business question. If he felt stuck and unsure on a business matter, then he should email David, who would then channel Augustus for guidance. A few weeks into the due diligence process regarding this business opportunity, Aaron and I were discussing what to do. Aaron's face changed, and he said, "I'll email Augustus and seek his advice. This may be the moment he was referring to."

Augustus replied. His response arrived just hours after our conversation on the deck. It all pointed to the same answer, the same decision: do your own thing. We later discovered further information that confirmed Aaron's decision not to invest was undeniably the right one.

Crystals

Wandering through the local Saturday morning market, I walked past a stall selling crystals. I glanced in passing, and my eyes were drawn to one particular crystal. I stared at it for a few seconds, and my head snapped to the left. (I pretended I was stretching!) I asked the lady what the crystal was. It was Calcite. I googled this when I got home. Calcite has properties that are beneficial for distance healing. Since moving to Waiheke, almost all of my healing sessions for clients were being conducted as distance healing because the recipients were located elsewhere around the country and overseas. I went back and bought the crystal.

Chapter 15

What It Takes

What does it take to support the change you want to create in your life? I know the answers that have rung true for me...

Having a Laugh

It occurred to me many times (okay hundreds of times) while writing this book that I was laying bare my soul for the world to see. Laying out one's innermost fears, aspirations and personal experiences is not an easy thing to do. This involves taking a risk, putting oneself out there. One could become a little neurotic worrying about what other people might think. But then again, that is only if you take yourself too seriously. Luckily for me, I don't.

Over time, I have cultivated a healthy appetite for self-mockery (all in good jest of course). What I am really trying to say here is that I can laugh at myself. No, this is not laughing at my own jokes (typically, I would be the only one who is), but laughing at things I do. I was born with the ability to do an extraordinary number of silly things, perhaps more so than the average person, and so I've had plenty of opportunities to practice the aforementioned laughing at self.

There was the time I reversed out of the garage, gunning the engine, tyres burning hot rubber, and I wondered why I wasn't moving. To my horror, I turned around to see the roof of the car buckling. The neighbour stifled his laughter as I realised I had accidentally knocked the garage door remote. I cackled as I flew down the road with a slightly concave roof.

There was the time I changed my first tyre, using telephone relayed instructions from my father. Suited up, ready for work, I knelt on the frosty ground, levering off the hubcap... only to find it shattering into small pieces. With frustration, I asserted, "Dad, this doesn't seem right. The hub cap is off, but I can still see the nuts!" Neither of us could speak as laughter erupted when we both realised I had destroyed my hubcap despite the fact the nuts were actually protruding in the first place.

There was the time I should have had a good strong coffee before getting ready for work. At the time, I was the Assistant to a Chief Executive. Note to self: I am meant to act demure and maintain an appropriate level of dignity at all times, so as not to contradict clause 3.1.5.b of my employment contract: "Thou shalt not do anything to bring thyself or thy employer into disrepute." I had walked to the office with not a care in the world, whistling as I went. Standing at the coffee machine, my colleague greeted me, but the usual morning conversation quickly took an unexpected turn.

"B, there's something different about you today. Um... Oh, my god! You have purple eyebrows!"

In a split second, the penny dropped, as I realised I had accidentally used my bright purple lip liner instead of my eyebrow pencil. It was a nightmare of unprecedented proportion. If you are a woman, you will understand.

I raced to the restroom and furiously scrubbed at my eyebrows, smudging the purple lip liner. But, fear not, I had simply removed it enough so that I could then cover it with my trusty concealer. This hell suddenly turned from bad to worse as I discovered my handbag had eaten my concealer. It was nowhere to be seen. Why?! How could this happen when I have my performance review with the new Chief Executive in an hour?!

I could have cried as the joke spread amongst the office floor of 100 people. I hated the wonder of mass email in that moment. I subsequently got an invite from a colleague to her child's birthday party, their clown had pulled out last minute, and she had heard I was proficient in the use of face paint. Cry or laugh? I decided to laugh. The meeting with the Chief Executive commenced with, "I heard you had an eyebrow issue this morning." Oh, god—cry or laugh? Definitely laugh.

In these many self-induced silly situations, as I watched the faces of other people laughing, I could have said that they laughed at me, in which case I would have felt hurt or embarrassed. Instead, I chose to say they laughed with me. However, for the latter to be true, I would, of course, have to be laughing as well.

In the course of creating your life, if things go a bit haywire, then choose laughter instead of crying, give yourself a break instead of a hard time and look for the light side of life.

Doing something silly does not make you silly. Fear of looking silly or failing can paralyse and stagnate your life.

From all my silliness, I learned the following lessons:

1. Not taking yourself too seriously stands you in very good stead for future life challenges; and

2. Purple eyebrows can actually thicken your skin.

Taking a Risk and Making the First Move

Rather than wait for life to create around you so that you can follow its lead, the pinch-me way of life often involves you making the first move. In making the first move, you allow life to follow your lead; you allow the signals to respond to your show of intention, thereby providing a clear direction towards your goal or dream.

I applied this philosophy in my single days in my pursuit of a prince, as I proactively went about ruling out the frogs. To be clear, this means I asked prospective suitors on dates, rather than waiting for

Prince Charming to find me. I did get quite creative with my approach: flowers sent anonymously, questionnaires sent mysteriously, and so on. Although you could consider that stalker-ish or overly confident, you don't necessarily hook Prince Charming by sitting around waiting to be swept off your feet. Statistically speaking, a white horse is probably just as likely to walk past and crap on you, than it is to come galloping by with your Prince Charming aboard. Making the first move and taking a risk meant I heard a few more of the following statements than I might have otherwise encountered: "No", "Thanks, but no thanks", "I'm attached", "I'm unavailable", "Sorry, I'm gay", and other variations of this.

> *Failing at something doesn't make you a failure.*
> *Hearing no doesn't devalue what*
> *you have to offer.*

I reasoned the risk was worth it, and I was right. I was sick and tired of relationships that all had the same thing in common: the wrong bloody guy. I decided to stop leaving my happiness to fate. I manifested the man I wanted by simply telling the world I was ready for love (well, telling my friends and family at least), with a clear list of criteria. Amusingly, the Energy Source responded by literally delivering me a CV to my very desk at work one day, outlining in writing the exact man I had manifested. This 'grab the bull by the horns' approach allowed me to discover the eighth wonder of the world that is my Aaron. By being willing to take a risk and making the first move, the Energy Source was clear on my goals and intention. This led to love.

In relation to your goals in life, why not make the first move. Set the goal, big or small, and make your intention clear by telling the world about it. Stepping out of your comfort zone to declare your goal and your intention to achieve it is a powerful step forward in creating change. Release the fear of not looking good, of being ridiculed, of being told it's not possible, of being scoffed at, of failing and of worrying that people will watch you fail. They will only be watching if they are so stagnated in their own life that they have nothing better to do than watch yours in motion.

If you do not go outside your comfort zone, you will not grow.
Life is about expansion and growth.

Stand in your space with confidence and with unwavering faith that your goals are attainable. You may not know how or when your goals will be achieved, but you know what you desire and simply living into a future that you have clearly defined, and telling the world about it, is enough to start the process.

Be Consciously Conscious

Many of us miss what is going on around us in day-to-day life. We are busy absently thinking and doing all the time.

We all know we're conscious; it's the default setting if we're not unconscious. But how often are you consciously conscious? What I mean is, how often are you actually fully aware of exactly what is happening in each moment of your day? It goes beyond the mere awareness that we have already spoken of, of what you think and feel. It's being present to all your senses.

How many instances can you recall when you were walking along and you really breathed in the air consciously and smelled the smells, really saw the sights and really heard the sounds all around you? Do you sometimes arrive at a destination, perhaps walking to work, dropping the kids at school or driving to visit family or friends, and you realise you don't even recall the trip? This is called living on autopilot.

Imagine if your entire life goes like that. How will you feel when you get to the end and realise that you missed it? Don't let this happen! Soak up every moment, and be consciously conscious.

Consistent Thinking and Feeling

Chopping and changing what you think and how you feel will bring you a mish-mash, hotch-potch, melting pot of results. It took me a while, quite some years in fact, to figure this out. I was up one minute, then down the next. Highs then lows. Optimism then pessimism. The needle on the compass of life was spinning wildly in reaction to my variable outlook and mood.

Your reality will be a mirror image of your beliefs, thoughts and feelings if you send the Energy Source a consistently clear message.

Become aware of your pattern of thinking and feeling. Are you sending a consistent message? When your thoughts and feelings are consistent, your results will be consistent too. The challenge with this simple equation is that we are only human. At first, it's quite hard to monitor all your thoughts and feelings to ensure that you are always directing these towards the manifestation of your goals. It is certainly possible though. It simply takes practice to form new habits.

If you let the spin cycle of life throw you around all the time, your thoughts and feelings can easily be affected, and you can go off on a tangent. On a tangent, you are creating thoughts and feelings that do not reflect what you really want for your future. This can happen momentarily or for prolonged periods of time. Either way, if this happens, you can mistakenly manifest what you don't want, whatever you are busy thinking or obsessing about.

We all have busy lives, which means we are not always 'present' and aware of our thoughts and feelings. At times, I revert back to complaining about something or someone, or focusing on the negative in a situation. I can go hours, sometimes days, without being present and aware. However, the trick is to realise this and get yourself back on track. You're the only one who can do this. You have to 'own' your thoughts, your feelings and your resulting outcomes. You're the master of this situation. Keeping your tap turned on with your awareness flowing is the answer.

It also helps to have others around you that understand your goals and your path. Other people supporting you and caring enough to prod you in the right direction adds weight to your outcomes. Aaron and I live on the same page. He guides me, and I guide him. We reality check each other. We call out to each other when one goes off track. We have actually agreed to do that for each other. At times, this produces a 'stop preaching to me' response, but it still provides an opportunity to wake up and snap out of whatever funk we are in.

Who can be this person for you? Could it be your parents, children or partner, maybe your friends or workmates? Look across your network and see where like-minds exist. When we have someone like-minded to connect with, they help us stay on track, and we can do the same for them. We can give and receive the 'thought and feeling tangent' call-out. If you hear someone trying to save you, don't bark back; take it onboard. Take a moment of 'time out', and refocus your energy towards what you desire.

Action

Yes, beliefs, thoughts and feelings create reality, BUT action is required. If you consistently believe, think and feel to create the exact reality you desire and then consistently take action when signals present themselves, then your life will change. Again, this is an equation.

Does this action bit sound like a lot of hard work to you? If your answer is yes, then I ask you this...

> **How strong is your desire to create the life you want?**
> **What are you willing to do for it?**

It is not hard. Turn on your tap; your awareness is all it takes. There is nothing monotonous or hard about this pinch-me way of living. Doing things that move you towards your dreams is exhilarating; action in this context is nothing short of plain old, good fun. It can seem hard when you think you have to work out *how*, but signals are coming to you frequently to effortlessly guide you.

Push & Pull

If you are only pulled towards your goal because you desire it, but you are already actually quite comfortable and happy, then you are missing the push factor. If you are only pushed away from something, a current circumstance that is not what you desire, then there is nothing pulling you forward. The ideal situation for manifesting and creating change in your life is to have both push and pull factors. It's definitely not the only way, but it's a strong combination to propel you into your new reality.

The push needn't be negative or unsavoury situations, circumstances or people. It can simply be something that does not sit well with you and is just enough to motivate you to be consciously aware of your desire to progress.

For example, my new leadership and coaching role at work was enjoyable, well paid and not in the least bit stressful. However, day in day out, I knew it was *still* not making my heart sing. I was part way there, but my journey was not complete. I wanted to immerse myself in healing, writing about my passions, coaching people in their own life journeys of change, and learning more about spirituality. The fact I was not doing those things consistently and regularly in my day-to-day routine (to the extent I desired) was just enough to create my push and pull factors.

That definition of push and pull had motivated me to be consciously conscious every day, with my tap on, doing incantations and meditating to manifest what it was that I desired. I had actually diarised to do so every day. What better way to keep it on your radar and ensure you are giving time to what really matters than to schedule time for it?

What are your push and pull factors?

Positive Relationships

In relation to creating a life you love and going on a personal journey for positive change, it is worthwhile assessing the relationships in your life, to consider which ones serve you positively and which ones serve you negatively.

Not every relationship you have in life is a good one. Not every relationship serves you well. Perhaps some relationships feed a need for power or control; perhaps some feed a feeling of dependency or negativity. Those relationships still serve a purpose, feeding some form of belief or feeling you have. However, those relationships aren't making a valuable contribution to the attainment of all that you desire.

There is no doubt that you can learn something from the less desirable relationships in your past or present, but surely given the choice you would choose to forgo those lessons hard learned and surround yourself with only positive influences.

One of the best things I did in my life was take stock of who I spent my time with. Previously, I would accept invitations to attend things because I felt I should. I would spend time around people who made me feel uneasy or who I did not feel very connected to. Then, I realised nothing positive was gained for me or for them by doing that, by putting myself in those situations. It wasn't adding anything to me, and often, it was doing worse than that. In some cases, I knew it was detracting from me.

If you come away from an interaction or relationship feeling smaller or like a piece of you is gone, ask yourself: *Why would I do that to myself?*

As I pondered this myself, I thought: *I'm a grown up. I should be able to do what I want, not what I feel like I should do.*

And so, I started making very conscious decisions about who I spent my time with—people I felt added to me and that I added value to in return. I applied this to all areas of my life.

At times, I realised that I had simply grown apart from people. We all grow and develop, and sometimes we grow in different directions. There is no shame or harm in that. It takes more guts to admit it and move on than to live in the memory of a relationship that once used to be good—be it friendship or love.

I have also made career moves in the past for this reason, because I could no longer be in a situation, environment or professional relationship where I felt like there was a very real, negative dynamic. Recalling some instances, it literally felt energy sapping. I'm not talking about having high idealistic values here. I know how to survive being in tough work environments and how to operate in situations where many different people with different views and personalities come together. That makes for a rich and diverse culture. I'm talking about the type of situation where you really feel like it's not okay to be treated a certain way, where particular behaviour or values just don't match your own.

This is sustainable for a period of time, but then you realise you're a square peg in a round hole. Perhaps there's nothing wrong with the round hole, and equally, there's nothing wrong with you being a square peg. The two just don't fit well together. Recognise it and move on. Life is too short to keep hoping your square peg will change shape.

> ### *Do you have relationships that do not serve you well?*

Think about people in your life. After spending time with them, which ones leave you feeling drained, sad, upset or negative? Which ones leave you feeling upbeat, inspired, supported and loved?

Now decide. Choose who you want in your space. If you tell me that circumstances require you to be around difficult people, I understand, because we all have commitments and life is not always straightforward. In some situations, you may well have to spend time with Energy Sappers, but do it on your terms if you must. Stand for who you are and what your values are. Don't be the carpet that someone else treads on.

Avoid the Negativity Vortex

Let's say someone wants to talk negatively around you, about you, running down other people or moaning about something, and you're the lucky person who ends up being around this. It's this kind of repetitive behaviour that can wear you down. Your mission, if you choose to accept it, is to avoid being sucked into the negativity vortex.

You have options when faced with a Negative Nelly:

1) AVOID.
   Exit the conversation. (For example, "Please excuse me. I need to use the bathroom." Or, "I need to finish ironing my socks.")

2) REDIRECT.
   Politely empathise and redirect the attention and conversation. (For example, "Sorry to hear that. Oh, did you hear about the band that is playing next week? And gosh, how about the weather lately?!")

3) ADDRESS.
   Directly take them on. (For example, "Perhaps a better way of looking at this situation would be...")

It can be socially awkward to take any of these approaches. If you EXIT, you may be considered inaccessible or distant. If you REDIRECT, you may be considered insensitive or a bad listener. If you ADDRESS, it gets worse, as you may be considered blunt, rude or righteous. But consider that really only one thing matters: what motivates you to do, say or be a certain way? If it is positive in motivation, your energy will resonate that way, and others (deep down) will know that.

I believe that the biggest disservice you can do for someone else is to feed their cycle of negativity, or better put, the biggest *service* you can do for someone else is to share with them a different way of viewing something, a way that may be of more benefit to them. This doesn't mean preaching or being pious; it's just about gently bringing a new perspective. Doing so doesn't mean you can't be supportive and empathetic. There is a big difference between empathy and sympathy. Humans crave sympathy, and everyone loves it when someone else reflects back their own views. I know this because I used to be the worst type of sympathy craver.

I'm not talking about situations that are genuinely heart breaking, devastating and life changing, where genuine sympathy is completely and utterly called for. Sympathy in those situations is a gift. I'm talking about negative cycles in day-to-day life, when little things are turned into dramatic disasters that are shared with anyone who will listen.

Don't be that for people if it doesn't serve them well. Love people enough to want better for them. Break the cycle, and help them step out of it. If you do this for others, then perhaps you will attract people who will, in turn, do it for you. I still, to this day, find myself occasionally buying in with sympathy for others when I know I should be doing one of the above three things. I am consciously aware of it; I guess no one is perfect. We can at least bring awareness to it.

Small Steps & Major Leaps

A really important lesson I learned in my journey, in relation to life and how the Energy Source guides us with signals, is this: you don't have to make it all fit.

What does this mean? You don't have to know exactly what, exactly how, where it will lead, what will happen next, why certain things are happening to you, why you are getting a particular signal, or what you should or shouldn't do about it. The mystery of life can seem frustrating, but in fact, that mystery is the beauty and challenge of life all wrapped into one.

When signals come to you, you simply need to trust and take small steps. Take a step forward without knowing the reason or the result. For anyone who likes to have a back up plan, you can always step back if you want to, need to or have to.

Here is a wonderful message from the daily email quote service, *Notes from the Universe* by Mike Dooley, and it perfectly illustrates this point. "The thing about making it big, and doing it fast, is that invariably the first steps will be small and slow, which oddly, for many, is the same reason they don't take them..."[20]

Small steps add up to major leaps. If I receive a tiny signal and I'm super busy, there are times when I almost pass them by. Then I stop and realise that if I had done that with the long series of very small signals I received in this 18-month period, I would never have made the big leaps I have. Never underestimate the power of the small things in life.

Small insights open up your thinking, which in turn opens up your understanding, and piece by piece the jigsaw builds, until eventually the full picture is revealed.

> *Just because you can't see all the pieces now doesn't mean the masterpiece isn't there awaiting you.*

Creating & Supporting the Future

What is the future? There is nothing mystical about the future; it is not a scary beast out there, waiting to trick you; fate, waiting to throw hideous challenges at you; or lady luck, trying to find you. It is simply a space in which you can create whatever it is you want. That space is there for you to cultivate. It is a resource that is there for the taking.

In relation to creating your future, think about how you would feel right now if I told you that tomorrow you will lose all your money and your home, and you will be diagnosed with an illness. That hasn't happened yet, but how does that thought make you feel? Miserable, right? However, in this present moment, everything is as it has been. Nothing has changed. You are simply now living into a different future, and so your thoughts and feelings have changed. Remember, your thoughts and feelings create your reality.

Now, think about how you would feel right now if I told you that tomorrow you are going to spend the rest of your life surrounded by people you love, doing only things that you love, in places you love, and you will live a long, happy, healthy life with not a worry in the world. Now how do you feel? Better, right? You are now living into a different future. Again, your thoughts and feelings create your reality.

If you create a future that makes your heart sing, and you believe it, think about it and feel it, then while the tangible aspects of it may not be here in the present moment, somehow your current reality has changed as a result of the future you are living into. You feel lighter, more hopeful and your energy resonates in a different way.

This doesn't mean you live in denial of your present circumstances, but just the opposite. Accept your present circumstances, as everything is always just as it should be. It is no mistake that you are where you are now. You have learned life lessons on the path that got you here today. It is all part of your journey to get you where you are going. Accepting the present situation doesn't mean you must embrace it as what you want. Accepting it simply means surrendering any resistance to it, being at peace with whatever is—be it relationships, finances, career, health, material belongings and so on.

As the old saying goes 'what you resist persists'. If you are obsessed with focusing on all the things that are wrong in your life, that's what you'll get more of, and you'll have no energy to focus on manifesting the actual future you want. Most importantly, obsessing about the faults in your present circumstances will block you from enjoying the present moment, which is all we ever have.

Opening the Safe Box

If you have ever gone through experiences where you have been told something is not possible, you have tried but not succeeded, or you have been laughed at or ridiculed, you may err on the side of caution going forward, keeping your dreams in a safe box. In a safe box, your dreams remain a secret. Goals and dreams in a safe box can't be picked apart by others. They are private. They are cosy all tucked up in that safe box. But just as they are safe, hidden away from being challenged by others, they are also suffocated and constrained by that same box. Although you can strategise and scheme about your dreams in the safety of your own mind, and there is nothing wrong with that, releasing them out into the world through verbal statements and actions will accelerate their manifestation.

> *What dreams do you have hidden in your secret safe box?*

I lived by the safe box philosophy for a long time. It didn't work. My game plan went like this: open the box and let the dream out to only a select few, as carefully worded whispers, to be kept on the 'down low'. Those dreams were so big and audacious that I never dared say them aloud like it was fact that I could do it. I was scared of being told it wasn't possible or of being embarrassed that if they never happened, it would be testament to my failure.

But then, it occurred to me: *If I really believe these dreams will happen, why am I so afraid of sharing them?* The question begs:

> ***How much do you believe in yourself
> and your dreams?
> Do you believe anything is possible?***

When we decided on a relative whim that we were moving to Waiheke, we started telling people, 'putting it out there'. Although at that time we had no clear plan in place to make it a reality, we began stating it as fact. One person laughed with the rhetorical statement, "Oh yeah, that's a dream is it?" Actually, no, it's reality. When we released it from the secret safe box where our dreams had been kept, it then became our reality. We were spurred on to achieve what we wanted in the face of comments like this, spurred on to show that whatever you desire is possible if you follow the signals.

What dreams do you have secreted away in a safe box? Sit quietly with your eyes closed and picture whatever you dream of. Ask yourself: *Is my dream worth standing up for?* If the prospect of living your dream or achieving your goal makes your heart sing, then who are 'they' to rain on your parade?

Dream Crashing

Just like it is no one else's place to do this to you, you also need to remember that if someone else chooses to share their goals, dreams and future vision with you, then it's critical that you support them in a positive way.

To be let in on someone's goals and dreams is a privilege, as you've been brought into the circle of people that are helping that individual to manifest their life. When you think about what they are achieving, when you provide encouragement, ideas and support, you are feeding your positive energy into that person's goals and helping them to manifest it into reality.

There is nothing wrong with robust debate and practical questions, stemming from a position of constructive support. However, there is a definite difference between that and dumping on someone's dreams. My friend Pia calls this 'dream crashing'.

Are you a dream crasher? Do you know any dream crashers? Is anyone trying to crash your dreams?

I used to find myself silently observing what someone else was doing and admiring the possibility they were creating, but sometimes underneath questioning the viability. This wasn't because I thought there was any actual issue with the goal, but just because my mind automatically went into auto pilot mode, looking for faults. That is just as bad; it's called unspoken dream crashing! It's easy to fall into.

The Energy Source responds, whether we speak aloud or not.

Circumstantial Influences

In the corner of a crowded café, I sat chatting to Ben, a new acquaintance. We spoke about signals and the pinch-me way of living. He started to recall dreams he had when he was a young man, before he married and had children. He talked about how his dreams had changed, morphed into family related dreams, ones he was equally passionate about. However, as Ben spoke, I could see his mind drifting back, I could see in his eyes that he longed for those personal dreams and goals he had set a long time ago. They had not become any less important with time, though to him it seemed they had become 'less possible' due to circumstantial influences.

In not so many words, it became clear to me that he perceived his ability to turn dreams into reality, to live a pinch-me life, as heavily impacted by his circumstances.

For example, a parent reading this may think that my intention to flit off here and there chasing my dreams is only possible because I don't have children or other circumstances influencing my decisions or outcomes. Given I am not a parent, I can see that parents reading this may not relate to my situation and may find it challenging to see how 'anything is possible' when seemingly yourself and your dreams come a natural and rightful second place to caring for the most important person or people in your life: your children.

My parents did this for me; they sacrificed an awful lot to give us a wonderful upbringing. I know this is reality for many people, and this is the practical side of life.

I am told that when children enter the picture, your own goals and priorities change and things that seemed important before may not seem so important anymore. Do dreams and goals seem less important, or do they simply change shape to fit the new reality? Perhaps it depends on the individual.

If you are a parent, do you feel you have willingly and gladly lost opportunities for yourself due to taking on the important role of becoming a parent? Are you interested in reigniting lost opportunities or sidelined dreams, or creating new and more meaningful dreams to manifest all you truly desire in your life for yourself and your children?

Reflecting on my conversation with Ben, although I can most definitely understand his perspective, I don't believe for one second that our circumstances influence our outcomes. It is *we* who influence our outcomes.

We have all heard stories, read books and seen movies of people who have beaten the odds, come out of challenging circumstances, and at times overcome horrendous situations to go on and achieve what look to be impossible dreams. These are inspiring stories, uplifting examples of the human spirit.

You have your own equally significant versions of circumstances and/or choices in life that may make your goals and dreams look like impossible mountains to climb, that you could *perceive* as roadblocks. It may look like lack of money or a lack of confidence. It may look like health issues or a disability. It may look like lack of time, too many commitments or any number of responsibilities that seemingly must come before all else.

We all, as individuals, will face circumstances that make it seem like our goals and dreams are too big, too far away, too hard to get to or too difficult to achieve. We will always have such circumstances and challenges. These will not go away. This is life.

Your relationship to your circumstances, and your perception of your ability to live the life you dream of *despite* your circumstances, is what makes the difference. In a world where the signals will show you *how*, you can surrender up the worry that what you desire looks impossible due to your circumstances. If you live in alignment with the Law of Attraction, defining your end goal (however vague or specific that may be), living day to day with your tap turned on, recognising and following signals, then you *will* be led in the highest and best way to the attainment of your goals. Be honest and ask yourself:

> *Am I using circumstantial influences as an excuse not to move towards my dream life?*

Chapter 16

Goals Go International

After achieving all my goals, what would the next phase of my life hold?

I felt strongly compelled to spend more time exploring healing, coaching, writing and spirituality. I wanted more and more to put myself in situations where my own trust and beliefs could be tested and extended, where I could set new challenges and goals for myself, and where I could take an evidence-based approach to proving 'following the signals' as a very real way of creating a life you love.

This was where my heart was singing the loudest, and I knew I had to follow that natural instinct. The joy had started welling up, and I did not, for one second, want to move away from it.

However, I had a full time job, a long-standing career, and most importantly a stable income. How could I balance all of that with what I felt compelled to do? I needed income; we all do! Was I to give away my job? Was I to somehow create an income from these new things that seem to be creating my joy?

Aaron and I had always been clear on one thing: we wanted freedom. Both individually before we met and together as a couple, we had held no doubt that we wanted to enjoy freedom in our lives, to have time to experience life and the world around us.

However, the standard 'work to live' way of life that we had already experienced did not seem to allow for the type of freedom and life we desired. We wanted a life that had more flexibility, choices and time. We wanted to create and contribute at the times and in the environments where we felt the most creative, most ourselves, most passionate, most at peace. We wanted to do this in a way that naturally felt right.

Although having full time jobs as employees and working to necessary rules and structures certainly had its benefits, it also had its restrictions when considering our dream. We knew this because we had tried it. We tried it for many years, turned it inside out, in different forms, and looked at how to have what we wanted in life by living this way. It had only worked to a certain extent. We were grateful for what we had and practised that gratitude every day. However, we simply knew that there was more freedom, more time, more choice and more flexibility available to us, if we defined it and asked for it. All we had to do moving forward was to confirm the *what,* and look for signals to show us the *how.*

Settled in our new life on Waiheke Island, we had created a greater level of contentment. We could have been happy with that and continued with our full time corporate careers. That was the way we knew how to earn money, and it was reliable. We could have continued with our careers for another 20 years and perhaps our desire for true freedom would have faded.

Perhaps we would no longer want or need that level of freedom.

However, we both knew that was a lie. We couldn't hide from our desire for that type of freedom. We decided that we needed to embrace it.

A Compelling Pull

After considering all of this, we agreed the time was right to set in motion a big goal, a huge goal, a goal we had *no idea* how to make happen. This was going to be a goal that would seriously inspire us.

We listened to our hearts. Something was beckoning us; we had known it for some time. It had previously seemed too outrageous to consider possible, until now. With the pinch-me way of life embedded in our minds, and the signals flowing to us daily, we released this dream from the safe box.

Leaving the New Zealand winter behind, we dreamed of embarking on a journey to explore a land rich in history, culture and spirituality. Here we would learn and grow. A desire rose up in both of us, one that had lain dormant, perhaps waiting for us to see that truly anything was possible. Sitting in the sunshine, we had jokingly articulated the dream. However, within minutes, the goal took on a life of its own—a living and breathing reality asking us to join it. This land was calling us to come forth and live in the freedom that was available to us.

Which land? Thailand.

Unbeknownst to us at the time, Thailand stands for 'Land of Freedom'.

Living three months of the year in Thailand over the New Zealand winter and the rest of the year on Waiheke Island was mouth watering. It did not seem even remotely possible in any shape or form, considering time, money, careers and commitments. It was inspiring to consider that something like this could actually be possible, that we could feasibly do something like this, something this big! If we were drenched in money, with all the time in the world, then of course this would be normal, if we lived *Lifestyles of the Rich & Famous*.

We questioned whether or not we could do this. Considering our circumstances, this would test my 'follow the signals' philosophy to its limits.

What I affectionately and officiously termed Project Thailand, not only represented exploration and adventure, but also a means for me to immerse myself in all that I desired. In the midst of eastern culture, I saw myself writing, coaching, energy healing, doing yoga, meditating, learning new customs and beliefs, and discovering new things about myself. In the Land of Freedom, I would be living in a culture so strongly founded on mind, body and spirit connectedness. This was what I wanted and needed to move myself forward.

The beauty of this dream was that it would allow us to return to Waiheke in time for spring. Spring and summer were months to be spent between the beach and our garden, planting and harvesting in the sunshine; zesting, marinating, pickling and preserving our produce; and watching the insects and butterflies flit amongst the sunflowers and marigolds.

Thailand was a place reserved in our hearts. We were married there some years ago: a tropical garden, a white dress, my handsome new husband and I. It was my heaven on earth. What is there not to love about Thailand?! I was captivated by the unassuming, open-hearted people, the colourful and symbolic culture, the engaging environments, the lush and natural landscapes, and don't forget the food!

How could we make this happen? We had absolutely no idea! There were plenty of reasons not to do this, and there were no clear ways *how* to do this. However, we couldn't ignore this dream, even if we tried to. It had escaped from the box and there was no putting a lid on it. The little feeling of anticipation in my gut grew each day.

With winter less than five months away, there were conceivably a million things to do and questions to answer for Project Thailand to become a reality—commitments, jobs, bills, mortgages, income, accommodation, flights, house sitter, dog sitter...

The most wrenching decision was what to do with our beloved Cash. He was blissfully unaware as his Puppy Mummy explained that border control regulations prohibited his attendance in the Land of Freedom. We would need to leave him behind with someone that we trusted. I pushed this to the back of mind. I didn't want to focus on leaving him; it was not a pleasant thought, as any loving dog owner will understand.

We set about manifesting Project Thailand, waiting and watching for signals. Our job was to recognise those signals and to follow them. And so, as the many questions arose in our minds, we reminded ourselves that anyone who is striving for big goals, doing what they love, following their passion, knows that hurdles will present themselves—hurdles of different types and sizes. That's how life is. Nothing is an easy ride. Where would the fun be if everything were handed to us on a silver platter? We'd have no sense of achievement and no sense of comparison between what we want and don't want, and between what we have known before and what we have now achieved.

> **Isn't it as much about the journey as it is the destination?**

When our questioning minds attempted to take over, we just calmly acknowledged the uncertainty and remembered that the answers were not yet clear, but they would be... all in good time.

Unveiling the How

On my way home from a business trip, I was loitering around the airport, waiting to board the plane. I thought I'd grab a magazine for my flight. As I marched down the first aisle in the bookstore, something caught my eye. Abruptly, I stopped and reversed. There at eye level, the only book displayed with its front cover facing out was *The 4-Hour Workweek* by Timothy Ferriss. I was sold on the synopsis, and after devouring a few chapters I called Aaron. He didn't get a word in as I proceeded to rapid-fire share my thoughts before boarding.

One of the main concepts in the book is taking mini retirements throughout your life, allowing you to travel and experience life, rather than saving it all up for retirement. Ferriss shares how to structure your life to break out of the traditional work mould, how to work remotely, how to automate your work, how to deliver on commitments while doing so flexibly. Words leapt out at me: TIME, LIBERATION, MOBILITY.

I couldn't believe it. This was just what we had been thinking about, creatively considering how to tend to our commitments, to deliver on what we needed and wanted to do, but doing so in a way that would give us freedom. My eyes were opened to new possibilities from a logistical perspective. I had been caught up in a confusing story in my head. *How can I fund my life in Thailand for three months, given we have two mortgages, bills and commitments just like everyone else? How can I walk away from my commitment to my job?* Ferriss' book showed me a different way of thinking, and as a result, it reminded me that thoughts and feelings create reality. Change your thinking and your reality changes.

I realised I could potentially structure my work and time in ways that might make it feasible to bring in an income in order to pay our living costs. It made me think outside the box and seek input from others, generating ideas of how we could logistically achieve this dream on a budget. House swap? Short-term tenant? House-sitting dog sitter?

I considered ways that I could create income remotely. In my new role at work, I had discovered I was pretty darn good at performance coaching. It was feasible to consider I could do coaching from overseas, thanks to the wonders of technology. I also pondered whether this sojourn in Thailand would end up with me discovering more about 'in service of the common good'.

Project Thailand quickly became more than a desire. It morphed from a goal I felt drawn to achieve into a necessity. New concepts and ideas drew me in like magnets. I could see myself voluntarily sharing English language skills with local Thai people that I would meet day to day, a way to help them in their own lives, a service to others. Perhaps they would share the Thai language with me. This connection with local people might help me gain insights into eastern culture, healing traditions and spiritual beliefs.

Maybe I could take a long holiday from my job, paid or unpaid, a leave of absence. We momentarily investigated buying a business in Thailand and the rules around it. Although this looked interesting, it didn't feel right, and there were no signals pointing us in that direction.

We frequently meditated on and visualised our Thailand dream. We made it as specific as possible: living nine months of the year on Waiheke and three months living in Thailand. We said we would go on 1 June 2011 and return on 1 September 2011. We felt this level of specificity would drive a result—a deadline to aim for. We were leaving nothing to chance, the Energy Source would be clear that this wasn't 'pie in the sky' thinking. Most importantly, we agreed to keep our minds completely open to the myriad of ways we could end up achieving this goal: no parameters, no restrictions, no determining the *how*.

It was at this point that I created a simple incantation, one that I use to this day. I repeated this over and over in my mind on the way to and from work in the city each day: "I am ready and willing to receive the signals. I am ready and willing to receive the signals. I am ready and willing to receive the signals..."

What happened next was comical. Deep in the flow of life, with taps gushing forth, we recognised signals instantly. They kept coming and coming. Life had become so free and easy. I knew that whatever I manifested would show up in my life sooner or later. It became a deep knowing within me that if I followed the signals, there was bound to be plenty of pinching.

Thai-Style Signals

A photo hung in our bedroom. Printed on a small rectangular canvas, it was hung on sturdy double threaded wire over plastic hooks. Days after I started incantations, the canvas fell off the wall. The wire broke. It wasn't frayed or worn, but it looked like it was cut right through—a clean break. The hooks were fine. The canvas was on the floor, so I affixed new wire and rehung it.

Each morning when we awoke, the canvas was crooked. I'm talking about a serious angle here, not a little off centre. Hung in a spot where no one walked past it, it couldn't have been nudged. Even a breeze through the opposite window couldn't have knocked it so far off centre. The picture had hung happily on that wall, straight, since we had moved to Waiheke.

Each morning, I straightened it, but then I realised, "Ah-ha! This is a signal!"

I knew this because it was our wedding photo, of us standing on a beach in Thailand. I said to Aaron, "If this keeps moving, then it's definitely a signal we are on right track, that everything is conspiring to help us for Project Thailand, and that we should continue just as we are."

The next morning, the canvas was crooked again, and we agreed it was a signal. I straightened the canvas. It never moved again after that moment.

Days later, on his usual bus route to work, Aaron saw a newly erected billboard covering the entire side of a building; it was a tourism poster for Thailand.

Travelling home from the airport one evening, I glanced out the taxi window. One word was perfectly framed by the window and my obstructed view through a myriad of roadside advertising; it read, "Bangkok". Sometimes, if you let your eyes take you where you need to look, you'll see random things like this—words on a sign, a license plate on a car, a picture on a bus going by. Pay attention, especially in your usual day-to-day routes during your usual day-to-day routines.

Twice in a week, Thailand came up in business meetings. One with a manufacturing client who had moved operations offshore, and the client proceeded to share with me all about their Thai operations. The second was a meeting with a client who had previously been consulting overseas.

"Where did you work?" I asked.

She answered, "South East Asia, mainly Thailand."

On his bus ride to work, Aaron texted me, "Do you think we should have made it our plan to go to some other place for three months of the year. Are we sure it's Thailand?"

I texted back, "No, it's Thailand. We are being drawn there for a reason. I feel it."

A moment later he called me, sounding like he'd won the lottery. "I was walking from the bus stop to the office, and for some reason, I just looked over to the side of the footpath and down, like my eyes were moving of their own accord. There was a card on the ground. It looked like a credit card. I picked it up and flipped it over. It was an airline frequent flyer card."

"So what?"

"It was for Thai Airways."

We meandered to the beach one weekend and ordered a treat from the creperie. The gentleman asked us if we had ever had crepes before.

"Yes," we replied.

"Where was it?" he asked.

"Oh, that's right. It was in Thailand on honeymoon."

We laughed at another Thai reference, and I threw my arms around Aaron's neck for a hug. Over his shoulder, I saw a group of Asian tourists emerging from the sand dunes. They were huddled under umbrellas, taking shade from the midday sun.

I prodded Aaron, "I guarantee you this is a signal. Go and ask them where they're from."

He approached and politely asked, "Excuse me, whereabouts are you from?"

"Oh, we from Thailand."

With family coming to stay for Christmas, we needed to stock up on glassware. Racing through a Department Store after work one day, I grabbed several boxes and lugged them home on the ferry. As Aaron later gulped back his drink, he kept staring into the glass. Laughing, he handed it to me and said, "Look!"

I looked in. Everything looked very small and distant like the reverse mode on binoculars. *Oh, dear,* I thought, *he's lost the plot.*

"Ah, that's very interesting..." I said with a raised eyebrow.

"No," he said, "look at the bottom of the glass."

The word Thailand was imprinted into the base of the glass.

We believed the signals were coming to us for two reasons. Firstly, it was as confirmation that Thailand was definitely a positive move. Signals only guide you in the direction that will serve you best. Secondly, the signals were there to spur us on, reminding us of our goal.

Eye of the Beholder

The beauty of following the signals, when you truly believe in the power of this way of living, is that you effortlessly let go of the concern about *how* to achieve your goal, and you simply focus on the joy of what it is you want. When you know for a fact that the signals will arrive to point you in the right direction, and that all you need to do is follow them, then life will feel free and easy.

In that feeling, you will start to resonate so positively that you will attract back to yourself more of the same. This is a never-ending, self-perpetuating cycle of Law of Attraction. You either spiral up and up, or down and down. Trusting and knowing, combined with positive feelings, acts like fertiliser on your dreams.

You may still be feeling stuck on how to recognise the signals. My advice to you is this: question things, be curious, investigate, explore and most importantly...

PAY ATTENTION to the smallest details of your everyday life.

Signals do not generally come by way of a big slap in the face. Signals are often small; they are things you would ordinarily think nothing of and signals are most definitely in the eye of the beholder.

Let's say that you lived in my house, and you didn't notice the canvas was crooked. Or, maybe you did, but you thought nothing of it. Let's say you walked the same route Aaron walked to work. You didn't notice the card on the ground, or you did but didn't think anything of it. That's natural. They were not signals for you. They were signals for us. We saw them and recognised them. Equally, I will not recognise your signals. They are yours; only you will recognise them. Authenticity is in the eye of the beholder.

Oh, that canvas is crooked.

Oh, that canvas is crooked again, frustrating.

_Oh,_ that canvas is crooked again!

Crooked canvas = signal.

Oh, there's a card on the ground.

Oh, there's an airline frequent flyer card on the ground.

Oh, there's a Thai Airways Frequent Flyer card on the ground.

_Oh,_ what are the chances that on that street, on that side of the road, on that pavement, someone walked along, someone who had a Thai Airways Frequent Flyer card, someone who accidentally dropped that particular card, and dropped it on that very street, on that side of the road, on that pavement where Aaron walked by, and Aaron was the person who saw it and Aaron was the person who decided to pick it up.

Card on ground = signal.

Interpreting signals is brilliant fun, particularly for an inquisitive mind. I often debate and dissect signals with friends and family, wondering if specific things that are happening in each of our lives are signals. It's a game, and it's intriguing. Life becomes full of child-like wonder and mystery.

Synchronistic Meetings

Sometimes, new people come into your path, or people already known to you will show up in your life at a particular time, because they are part of the signal machinery. People form part of the intricate web that has been woven in reaction to your beliefs, thoughts and feelings.

I refer to the coming event as 'Night of the Twilight Zone'.

Arriving at a dinner party hosted by my friend Rachel, Aaron disappeared off with beer in hand to chat with a group of people in the living room. He sidled up next to Susannah. Visiting from Australia, she was staying with her son on Waiheke. She certainly got Aaron's attention when she said she wanted to move to Waiheke for three months and was hoping to find somewhere to housesit. She thought her willingness to pet-sit would make her a particularly attractive option.

Inter-Country Living Club

I was introduced to Penny, a woman with a riotous sense of humour and a passion for life, exactly the kind of person I love to be around. The conversation became intriguing when she told me that a few years ago she had decided to travel and live overseas with her husband. They split their time between Europe and Waiheke for several years. Before I could share with her our plan to live between Thailand and Waiheke, she went straight on to tell me about her friends on the Island who spent part of the year in Borneo and part of the year on Waiheke.

I enthusiastically told Penny that this was amazing to me, and I shared our Thailand goal with her. My mind was reeling, because earlier that week, Aaron had sat chatting to a stranger on the ferry who had voluntarily told him all about her life. She said she lived half the year in Bali and the other half on Waiheke.

Like Minds

As it turned out, Penny was new to currency trading. Having started six months ago, her passion was fresh and contagious. I felt Aaron gravitate towards us. With a big smile on my face, I was delighted to introduce him to Penny and to fill him in on our discussions. And so ensued a passionate conversation about trading and the freedom it gives you by providing an income that can be generated while living anywhere, doing anything, being whatever you want to be.

Penny's presence at the gathering was, I am sure, planned. Rachel did of course know that Aaron was currency trading, and I presume she thought it would be nice for him to meet other like-minded people on the Island. Rachel did not, however, know about Project Thailand.

Penny's comments and observations were mirroring our own beliefs and approach to life. She talked about the 10,000 hour rule, a concept outlined in Malcolm Gladwell's book, *Outliers*.[21] Extraordinary people are created out of extraordinary commitment to their endeavour, and this, mixed with determination and hours of effort, will create extraordinary results. Extraordinary talents and outcomes can be developed by ordinary people. The tipping point is once 10,000 hours of learning and practice have been reached. She knew of other traders who had done their 10,000 hours and were now reaping the benefits. We all agreed on one thing: it wasn't about the money. It was about the freedom.

Sitting close by was a brilliant man, a professor. He had developed a complicated algorithm for currency trading, beyond my ability to understand or even attempt to enquire about—let alone explain! Being around extraordinary and like-minded people is important for Aaron, for myself, for anyone. I call them Shiny People. Shiny People are those who are passionate, willing to chase and live their dreams, who live in a world of possibility, and stand up proudly to say so.

The Train

Enter Debbie. Penny was on one side of me, and Debbie flanked the other. I didn't know these people, but it seemed they were compelled to tell me things, out of the blue—unprompted, helpful things. I received some seriously intense advice.

All of a sudden, Penny looked at me, and it was one of those moments when someone looks you directly in the eye and you're locked in their gaze. Needless to say, I listened.

She said, "The train is going to come through. Be ready when it comes. You have two choices. Get ready, grab that train, and jump on it. Or, you can watch it go by. If you watch it go by, you will always wonder what could have been, what would have happened, and you'll have regrets. What's the worst thing that can happen if you jump on the train?"

The evening was anything but normal; it was downright bizarre and absolutely delightfully so. Running through the night rain to reach our car, we leapt inside and slammed the doors shut.

Aaron exclaimed, "That was like the freaking Twilight Zone! Can you believe all the signals we just got? It couldn't have been more obvious."

We were wound up like someone had plugged us in to a high-volt battery. We knew that things would continue to come to us freely, easily and quickly. Our taps were in perfect working order at that time; in fact, they were performing better than ever.

Out fishing that weekend, peacefully waiting for the fish to bite, Aaron and his friend Toby mused about our accommodation dilemma.

"What about a home swap? Surely, there would be plenty of people open to something like that," Toby suggested.

As it turned out, he was right. Online I found numerous people with properties in Thailand, who were willing to house swap for particular destinations at particular times of the year. We started to take tangible actions towards making Thailand a reality.

Chapter 17

Ah-Ha! Moments

As we trundled off to work one New Year morning, we both felt morose. After an amazing summer break, we were again facing the 9-5 life, commuting into the city, battling to find time to commit to our passions. Thailand seemed a world away and impatience crept in.

This impatience was coupled with absolute mystery about how our Thailand plan would play out. We were consumed by the fact that we had no solution to our major commitments, including the very serious consideration of our jobs. On the commute that morning, Aaron pulled a deck of cards from his bag— not just any deck. They were *Medicine Cards,* based on animal totems, by Jamie Sams and David Carson.

I pulled the Ant card. Ant = Patience. It read, "Oh tiny Ant... your patience grows, like the sands of time. Can I learn to be like you?"[22] Aside from the fact I was waging war against ants on our property, liberally spraying ant killer everywhere, I couldn't believe the coincidence that the novel I was reading at the time was entitled *Sands of Time* by Sidney Sheldon. The medicine card told me, "If Ant meandered into your spread today, it is time to show a little trust and patience in some life situation."[23]

I reminded myself how very lucky I was to have such a great job and that my desire to do more healing, coaching and writing would be fulfilled all in good time. My commitments, including my full time job, were helping me achieve many things in my life. Everything else would manifest in the best way—ways I couldn't yet decipher. *Patience B.*

Aaron drew the Snake card. Snake = Transmutation. Snake medicine represents the power of creation, embodying alchemy amongst other things. Aaron has long had an affinity for all things alchemy. It is a word and concept that seems to pop up in his life frequently. It read, "Look at the idea that you may fear changing your present state of affairs because this may entail a short passage into discomfort... In order to glide beyond that place which has become safe but non productive, become Snake. Release the outer skin of your present identity."[24]

We both had a gut instinct that it was time for Aaron to leave his job for good. This would free him up to spend more time on his currency trading business. Aside from the fact that we knew it was the right thing to do, it would also show the Energy Source that we were very serious about what we were creating in our lives. He needed to glide beyond his safe but non-productive situation. All things considered (our current circumstances), dropping an income would quite possibly involve a passage into discomfort!

Days later, Aaron received a phone call. The business he had declined to invest in wanted to engage him on a contract basis. He negotiated terms that allowed him to work remotely. He quit his job. In doing so, we had taken the first tangible step towards creating the flexibility we needed to live in Thailand.

Working through his notice period, he pondered his changes. Leaning back in his seat at work, he stretched and looked up. He noticed the sticker on the ceiling that had been there ever since he started his job. Although he had never paid particular attention to it before, this day was different. He almost fell off his chair. The sticker had a symbol on it. The symbol was the logo of the company he had just signed a contract with.

Understanding Washes Over Me

I was furiously writing, pulling together the book manuscript from my catalogue of hand written notes. Charlotte raised an idea with me, "Why don't you enter a writing competition?" She alerted me to a competition for unpublished manuscripts in this genre.

I reviewed the entry criteria and application form, and then, I read the list of past winners. The names of the authors and the titles of the books all sounded to me to be very spiritual, very serious, very academic and very refined. I felt my book was too blunt, too rough and perhaps too crude in parts. My writing seemed to me too light hearted to fit in a competition for serious, spiritual authors, writing serious, spiritual books.

"Thanks Charlotte, but I'm not like them."

She asked me, "B, who are you writing this book for? That is what matters."

I said, "People like me who are searching for answers."

Our conversation continued down this track, her asking me to speak aloud why I was called to write this book. She said to me, for what seemed like the hundredth time...

"Have you read that book *Synchronicity* yet?"

She was referring to *Synchronicity, The Inner Path of Leadership* by Joseph Jaworski. I had read it some years ago, but I struggled with it. I wasn't ready for it then. I resisted reading it again, and I told her, "No, it's about leadership, and I'm not interested in leadership!"

Note my further resistance, despite everything I had learned to date. I was still consumed with frustration. *Why won't everyone just quit about this leadership stuff? I am already doing a leadership role at work. Surely that's enough. Why won't this leave me alone?*

"I appreciate your advice Charlotte, but it's all about the corporate leadership centre he developed, and I want to get away from all that corporate stuff." I did not want to spend my personal time reading a book that related to business. I wanted to absorb myself in the area of mind, body and spirit. I told her this.

She challenged me right then to look at why I was resisting it so much, to look at how I really felt about it. What was blocking me and rearing its ugly head in this situation? Charlotte had never demanded anything of me, or anyone else for that matter, but she said, "I insist you read it."

She knew I had missed the book's underlying message, and knowing it was valuable for where I was at in my life, she prodded me in the right direction. That night, I reluctantly picked it up off the bookshelf and read the back cover review by Phil Carroll, "*Synchronicity* illustrates that leadership is about the release of human possibilities, about enabling others to break free of limits..."[25]

A torrent of understanding washed over me. I saw flashbacks to all previous conversations about leadership, Augustus, Stephen, my life number, my desire to immerse myself in coaching, healing and writing—all things designed to help other people to reach their true potential and to break free of the box they may find themselves in.

Ah-ha! Finally, it clicked! All the misunderstanding, fuzziness, uncertainty and confusion were clarified in an instant. I had been drawn to share with others what is 'out there' for them to access, to show them what is possible in life. I was clearly passionate about what Carroll described. When I read his quote, all I saw was...

RELEASE possibilities. Break FREE.

What the book described as leadership made my heart sing without a shadow of a doubt. I thought: *This is leadership? YES, this is leadership! This is what I am here to do. This has nothing to do with my corporate career and has everything to do with this pinch-me way of living!*

Peter Senge wrote the introduction to Jaworski's book and on second reading I saw a reference to something I had not seen before. Senge referenced Robert K. Greenleaf's book, *Servant Leadership*.[26] Glorious alarm bells went off in my head. Leadership was definitely a service to others. It was *my* service to others.

The following words by Senge further cemented my new understanding, "[Leadership is] not about positional power; it's not about accomplishments; it's ultimately not even about what we do. Leadership is about creating a domain in which human beings continually deepen their understanding of reality... Ultimately, leadership is about creating new realities."[27]

I became crystal clear that my version of leadership was to share the 'follow the signals' message, so others could also break outside the bounds of a life lived purely in the physical dimension and turn their own dreams into reality.

Although I completely appreciate the above statements are just words on a page to you, this moment of realisation was profound for me. It was a moment of connecting what had before been separate and indecipherable signals into one cohesive message—a message that resonated strongly within me.

It had taken a long time to get to this. It had taken steps, conversations, thoughts, feelings, introspection, discussion, debate, boundary pushing, risk taking and fear facing for me to reach this point. I can't describe how extraordinary the feeling was in that moment when it all clicked into place. I honestly felt like the stars and moons aligned and the sun shone down through the clouds onto me. It was like the Energy Source was saying, "Finally, she got it!"

Standing for My Beliefs

After sharing one of my unusual experiences with someone in conversation, they subsequently challenged me on the validity of that experience. I felt attacked. I knew this would happen eventually, being challenged.

It was clearly part of my journey and a lesson for me to learn: to stand in the face of that debate and criticism, and to stand for my beliefs and find my voice. It was a test for me to have solid faith, so that my message could be heard, for the good of both myself and others. My message had to find its place in the world for those whose path it is to seek it.

> *Being questioned, challenged or criticised*
> *is not negative;*
> *it is only negative if you perceive it to be.*

Debate is healthy, and it is through debate and questioning that we move forward in our understanding. I believe what I believe, and I respect that the opinions of others may differ. Some people will read this book and take something from it. Others may read it and discard the information. It may be a book that makes no sense to them, perhaps it will challenge or confront them, or maybe it will add nothing to them as they hold different beliefs—ones that will not be swayed by what I have to say. Is there any point worrying about something I cannot change? Again, in the words of my wise father, "Why worry when it's wasted energy?"

The following prayer is renowned for its pearl of wisdom, "God grant me the serenity to accept the things I cannot change, courage to change the things I can, and wisdom to know the difference."[28]

I actually had this realisation after something else happened to me—something that helped me reach this realisation. It was another type of attack.

The Attack

Out running past the beach one morning, two seagulls attacked me. I ran fast, but they followed. So I ran faster. As they swooped at my head and squawked, I ran up a side street away from the beach and lost them.

Considering signals, Aaron asked me, "What do you think it means? Think about what actually happened here and tell me." Without a thought, I just opened my mouth and said aloud, "I was attacked, and I ran away."

During a passionate discussion with my friend Laura about interpreting life's hidden meaning, we laughed about the time she was caught in the rat race of life, exhausted from stress and over-working. Her body started to fail, breaking down with ailments and illness. She got in the car one morning and her battery was flat.

You might hear, "Her *car* battery was flat."

She heard, "*My* battery is flat."

Can you see the difference? Do you see her interpretation of this seemingly normal every day event. This is precisely the type of signal we get all the time, but we pay no attention to.

As I reflected on how I was challenged about the validity of my unusual experiences, and my subsequent seagull encounter, I knew I wouldn't run away if attacked again (by people, not birds!)

I didn't *need* others to agree with me, to believe me, or even to like me. These are things that we want as humans. Of course, I want that too. However, I realised I didn't *need* it. My message reaching people felt more important than my desire for acceptance.

Are there times when you hide your true self for fear of ridicule?
What's the worst that can happen if you stand proudly in your space?

Stepping into Peardom

Throughout this journey, I had grown and changed a lot. I was still the same person, with the same values, personality and sense of humour, but my beliefs, thoughts and ways of being had changed. The way I had chosen to live my life had significantly changed.

Let's say that before all this change I was an apple, and after all this change, I was a pear. When I was an apple, there was nothing wrong with me. Apples are great. I should know, because I used to be one! But I had become a pear. In my own view, I made a much better pear than I ever did an apple.

However, some people in my life loved apples, and perhaps they even preferred apples. At this stage of my journey, I didn't know if they liked pears. Here's the bottom line: they thought I was still an apple. I'd kept it a secret that I was really a pear.

Reflecting on the attack and my resulting decision to stand proudly in my space, I wasn't sure that it really mattered to me if they didn't like pears. It had just been easier for me to keep up my façade of 'apple-ness' while I figured out for myself what was happening. I didn't know where my life was taking me; I didn't know I would end up a pear. And, I didn't want to provoke questions from people when I myself didn't know the answers.

If we drop the fruit salad for a moment, the straightforward summary is this: I changed, but I didn't tell everyone about it. I felt different, but some people were still relating to me as the old B. One day, I woke up feeling like the new B. There was a two-way disconnect going on. The new B didn't know how to relate to some of the people she knew, not in the way the old B did. Some of the people who knew the old B perhaps wouldn't know how to relate to the new B. Jeepers, what a predicament!

I'd been living the last year in a state of transition, still outwardly doing the same things for much of that time, but I'd been 'being' a different me inside because of changes that were unrecognisable to the passer-by. This in between state was like a tunnel between two places; it was an unusual place to be. I was looking back at what was, and looking ahead and wondering what next. I was about to exit the tunnel and pop out the other side. With Thailand looming, I was ready to start telling people I was a pear.

Clinging on to Person B

I felt myself, my soul, literally lifting to a whole new level. I felt light—light hearted, light in body, light in spirit. I was experiencing the feelings I had read about so often—feelings of complete connectedness to everything around me, particularly in the beauty of the natural environment, the world in its original state. In these peaceful, uncomplicated moments, I literally felt like I'd melted into one-ness with nature.

I had always longed to feel that way before. However, in the past I had only experienced it in fleeting moments, like when seeing a sunrise or watching the gleeful smile of a baby.

All of sudden, I started to have those moments often. Everywhere I looked there were things that made me feel that way. It seemed that these moments were not caused by the external things that I was looking at or experiences I was having, which therefore required those things to be around me or for those experiences to occur in order to feel like that. Rather, it was caused by my feeling of connectedness.

If you hold that feeling inside, you have it all the time, whenever you want it, wherever you go. Everything holds that magical potential to wow you, if you feel connected to it. I don't think this is something that you can intellectually create. I never really 'got it' when I tried to logically understand it. I only got it when I *felt* it.

It was pouring rain as we walked through the Regional Park one day. The native bush was thick and the towering trees and palms created a ceiling of foliage that the rain couldn't penetrate. It created a misty and intensely green scene under the canopy. I rounded a corner with Cash running ahead of me on the track, and I was faced with a sloping bank, blanketed in ferns, tall trees looming upward. They were vivid in colour, mist settling all around them. The trees had been there for decades, if not hundreds of years, growing quietly. They were strong but moving with the breeze. They were forever peaceful, with the turbulent world carrying on around them. I had to stop. I actually raised my arms up on both sides of me, smiled and breathed it all in. I must have looked a bit odd! Fear not; I was not getting my arms in ready position for some tree hugging, although I'm sure Aaron (a few steps behind me) thought perhaps I was about to transform to true-blue hippie status and do the final deed. I could sense him willing me on, "Hug them, B. I know you want to!"

It happened again when I found a bright yellow and black striped caterpillar hanging from a leaf in the garden, preparing itself for cocoon stage, to become the butterfly. I actually sat there next to it, staring, and I felt like crying. How ludicrous! But I couldn't help it. I'd turned into one of 'those people' that sees beauty in everything. I was determined not to convert: *I must retain my Person B-ness!*

Butterflies on a Mission

It started in the morning. I awoke to a crisp, clear day and stepped out onto the deck. A butterfly flew straight past my face, flying at speed in a straight line. *We're on the move,* I thought.

As I sat down to write in the courtyard, I looked up and a butterfly flew straight past me. I rhetorically asked aloud, "They're reminders, aren't they? Signals." My head lurched to the left unexpectedly—a yes. Guidance is gold, overwhelming, and yes, it brought tears to my eyes. What is worse than a hippie? A weeping hippie. *Crikey, I'm in trouble now!*

Before writing, I meditated. I asked, "This book is really going to be published, isn't it? This is definitely happening, isn't it?" My head snapped left again.

I just couldn't help myself, "I'm not making this stuff up, am I?" My head clicked right.

After an inspired writing session, I walked inside and a butterfly flicked right in front of my nose. It was so close that I felt the air as it moved past. When your tap is turned on, the signals come at you with as much clarity and force as they can muster. Sometimes, they fly straight into your face.

Show Your Intent

What more can you do to support the manifestation of your goals?

Start living the dream before it has arrived. Do things—any things, little things, fun things—that simply show your intent. This is not necessarily about action in response to signals. What I'm talking about here are intent-filled behaviours that show you are 'in the game'. This is just as much about putting yourself in the moment, feeling your dream come to life, as it is about outwardly showing your intent to the Energy Source.

On one particular day, to signal my intention about Thailand, I used jasmine aromatherapy oil in the house. Jasmine oil smells like a day spa. There are a lot of day spas in Thailand. I intended to visit them. With no immediate ability to book flights, I also printed off prices and flight schedules to Thailand, and pulled out our passports so that I could see them every day. When dinnertime rolled around, we bought Thai takeaways.

In relation to your dreams...
what can you do today to show the Universe
your intent?

How Are You Being?

Doubt crept in leading up to 1 June. There were moments where I wondered: *Am I still in the flow? Where the heck are these signals to show me how?!*

I asked myself: *Am I meditating enough? Am I visualising enough? Am I consciously creating my life enough?*

None of these were founded concerns. These were all just symptoms of my incessant need to do things perfectly.

There is no such thing as 'doing enough' in this realm or way of living. There is simply consistent believing, thinking, feeling and acting.

Although I wanted to try to control my staying in the steady flow of life, I should have known that the way I was 'being' was enough. Being is just a result of how you view the world and how you view life.

> ***Right now, how are you 'being'?***

Whether we are in or out of the flow is just a natural consequence of the way we are being. I soon knew I was still in the flow...

Seeking feedback on my writing, Charlotte suggested that perhaps I could find a local on Waiheke with writing and editing expertise. Sometime ago, Jessie had told me about her friend Lisa who also happened to live on Waiheke. Lisa was a Communications Consultant. It all seemed very convenient, so I put two and two together and followed the signal. I intended to meet with her and blurt out my whole book writing situation, hoping she would advise me on editors or, better yet, be willing to give me editing tips for my manuscript.

Covering the usual pleasantries, I asked about her work, and she mentioned she was only contracting on a job until April.

"Why?" I asked.

"Oh, I'm heading overseas."

"Exciting! Whereabouts are you going?"

"I'm going to live in Thailand."

Laughing, I shared with Lisa about the changes in my life, and she showed great enthusiasm for my book and healing work. She asked many questions. I felt a trust and connection to her, and that she could be the person to help me refine my manuscript.

Within minutes of me picking her brains about editing, she offered to review my work and to provide me feedback regarding how to polish it. She said that no fee was required, and that she'd do it as a favour to help me out.

Chapter 18

Clicking into Place

Guardian Sister

Charlotte is one of my five amazing siblings. Every one of them is unique and exceptional, and each one plays a big part in my life in different ways. Charlotte features in this story because she featured prominently in this period of my life, beyond the usual sisterly support you might anticipate. She went beyond the call of duty, beyond the endless phone calls, emails and Skype chats, as I hollered out for help, guidance, support and advice. Many times, she kept me level headed, moving me up the spiral of life, instead of spinning down and out of control. She assured me that I was not losing the plot.

I pondered: *Perhaps Charlotte is one of my spirit guides.* Augustus had told me that sometimes guides are present in the physical realm with us, playing a role in our life. When I thought this possibility about Charlotte, I had a flashback to a time long ago.

My partner had just left me. 'Left' is probably not the right word; it was more like he asked me to leave the house we shared together. Feeling abandoned, I was devastated. I had lost myself in a relationship and had no real idea who I was. I was blinded by what I thought was good for me. This sounds comically tragic, like the typical young love gone wrong scenario. It was anything but comical to me.

Charlotte took me in. I lived in her spare bedroom. She never once asked me how long I would be there or when I would stop crying. I was there for months. And I was there being miserable for months. She never once asked anything of me. She didn't ask me to clean, to cook, or even to pay rent.

She found me one day, soon after my sadness descended on her normally happy abode, in the bathroom. I was sitting on the toilet—pants up, toilet seat down, crying... again. I was staring blankly into space with red eyes and tear stained cheeks. She crouched down in front of me and held my hands. The silence was broken with, "I can't go on. I don't know how. What's the point?"

As soon as I said this aloud, the gravity of how truly alone and lost I felt hit me. Life seemed to have no direction. She looked at me with eyes that mirrored my sadness yet beamed with love. Gripping my hands tightly, she moved closely to my face. Quietly, with conviction, she said, "You will go on. This will pass, and until then, you have me. I'm not going anywhere."

She propped me up high enough so that I could see that no good could come from allowing myself to sink deeper and deeper into this self-pitying sadness. I had to pick myself up, and I was the only one who could do it—and, I was not alone.

It occurred to me that this metaphorical rescuing has been happening all my life. When I was three, we were visiting the neighbour's house. I remember it like yesterday. On hearing an airplane fly overhead, we raced around a corner path to see it. We ran past the in-ground swimming pool, hidden under a dark cover. I stepped too far, disappearing under it. I don't remember much, other than quiet, watery darkness and then a hand reaching down and pulling me out— Charlotte's hand.

Somehow, at the moment I disappeared under the cover, she turned to see me gone, knew I was in the pool, and reached under the cover to grab me. And somehow, at six years old, she managed to drag a fully clothed and waterlogged three year old from the water.

If she is not a guide for me, she is certainly a guardian sister.

My Calling

I'm not sure how it dawned on me, but sitting there alone at the dining table, staring out the window, dawn on me it did. It was like my stillness had allowed my mind to make sense of a jumble of things that had been swimming around inside my head.

I had long been questioning how to create a future and income for myself out of my passions and love for this way of living. I was unsure what I could offer. I couldn't see the forest for the trees. Then three things occurred to me all at once. More pieces of the jigsaw moved and fell into place.

My corporate life was performance coaching. I helped people to develop into their full potential, advising how to overcome hurdles, how to achieve goals, diagnosing issues and finding ways through them. This had started to go beyond my workplace, with friends and acquaintances asking for advice and coaching. The odd questions here and there were first in passing, and then, they became more in-depth conversations.

In my evening and weekend healing sessions, I found people were facing challenges, a broad range of obstacles in life, and they often had questions in relation to what was happening to them in their lives. These questions and answers often formed a part of the healing that was facilitated.

People had begun to ask me about finding their tap and following signals. They wanted advice about how to manifest change for themselves—change unique to their own circumstances.

In an instant, I saw these things come together. Further clarity on my service to others — pinch-me coaching and healing, blending all I could offer to help others transform on any level.

Perhaps, step-by-step, this new reality would gravitate to me over time, building steadily, until one day I would wake up, look around me, and realise this is what I now do with my time. Perhaps the day would come when this would be my full focus.

When Your Future Surprises You

If I had been asked 18 months ago to sit down and logically think of what 'to do' with my life to find my joy, I'm convinced I would never have found it. The physical realm and logical thinking did not hold the answers.

When I was five years old, I wanted to be a Mr. Whippy. In New Zealand, that's what we call the ice cream truck that drives around in summer playing the happy music as the neighbourhood children flock to it. Happy music and ice cream, to the five year old B these seemed to be the makings of joy.

Then at eight years old, I wanted to be a florist. Flowers are pretty, and they smell good. How can you be anything but happy when surrounded by flowers all day?

With Mr. Whippy and flowers no more than childhood memories, I knew that I would be 'living' as an author, coach and healer. It was happening, it was growing and snowballing. Never in a million years would I have thought that this was what I would love, be inspired by and actually do.

When I say living, I specifically choose this word instead of working. When you turn on your tap and jump in the river, finding your calling, then work ceases to be work and becomes living when you do what you love.

I decided to do one small thing to show my intent for my new calling. With my handbag slung on one arm, laptop in the other, racing out the door on my way to work in the city, I grabbed a piece of paper and cut out a small rectangular corner. On it, I scrawled:

Bernadette Logue
Author, Coach, Healer
Ph +1234567890 – Waiheke Island
Ph +2345678901 – Thailand

It was a mock up of my new business card, to show my intention. The signals had come to the party so far and played in my favour by showing me the way; the least I could do in return was to signal back that I was listening, watching and waiting for more...

Living on the Edge

I followed plenty of other signals that are not detailed in this story—signals that led me down unusual paths, taking unusual actions. Signals do not always end up in the result you anticipate. Sometimes they take you on a detour to teach you something, to show you something you need to know. If you follow a signal and don't get the result you expected, just remember one golden rule: dreams come about in the most unexpected of ways. You can't see it, but the Energy Source can. Trust and follow the signals anyway. I have done this many times at the risk of looking silly, which by my own advice, does not mean I am silly.

Maybe some of the signals I received were just there to test my resolve and my faith, to see if I was willing to really put myself on the line. Nowadays, I do all sorts of things I consider crazy and outlandish; there's no harm. It's fun to live a little on the edge.

Blood, Sweat, Tears and...

Considering everything I have shared so far, let's consider how one reaches a point where one stays continuously in this flow of life.

The answer, as I painfully discovered, is that you don't. I mean you don't stay *continuously* in the flow, unless you're super human. We have already established that I am not super human, and I learned the hard way that you will definitely realise when you're out of the flow. Then, you need to get yourself back in it quick smart.

How do you know if you've hit a bend in the river and been accidentally washed ashore on the muddy, grassy riverbank? How do you know if your tap has rusted up and is malfunctioning or, worse, not functioning at all?

The answer is that things turn to shit. Things become hard. You start trying to make life happen, emphasis on the *trying* as opposed to letting it be. You begin struggling, wondering why, wondering how, frowning, feeling lost and unsure, sometimes crying, definitely feeling sorry for yourself, and verbalising lots of 'why me?', 'why now?' and 'woe is me'.

Let me give you a fairly absurd example of how I got washed up on the riverbank, face first in the proverbial mud, and how I realised what was happening.

Although signals for Project Thailand had been frequent, all pointing to our going there, nothing was showing us *how* this would logistically happen. We lacked clarity on key things like where we would live, what we would do with our empty house, who would look after Cash, and how we would go given we had full time jobs. Let us not forget the other critical unknown... how on earth would we finance this entire experience! There was no rainy day 'savings to splurge on living in Thailand' bank account.

I was having little panic episodes, worrywart moments that enticed me to try to figure out how to make things happen quicker. I tried to take control. Time was counting down to 1 June. My positive, trusting thoughts and feelings changed.

With tense and anxious feelings emanating from me, I began forcing things to happen. This involved me strategising, calculating and planning all the scenarios of how things might play out. I didn't realise I was putting parameters and boundaries on what we wanted to create. I was suggesting 'how' instead of sticking to my job: 'the what'.

My usually calm husband was very close to telling me to get a hold of myself. This is my politically correct way of saying what he really did say, which was, "Seriously, will you give it a break? You're doing my bloody head in!" And he would be right.

If you add any negative emotion alongside whatever worries you, then you're pretty much guaranteed to get that which you don't want. Negative emotion acts like steroids for manifestation; they are as strong as, if not stronger than, positive emotions.

Naturally, within a few short days of my anxious forcing behaviour, things started breaking down. I felt tired and couldn't fit enough into my days. Work was busy. I had to get the book written. I had to work out finances. I had to fix things!

After a night of very little sleep (due to, not surprisingly, bad dreams) and tension in the household the night before as Aaron attempted to tolerate my mood, I awoke to the next day—a day I shall now refer to as 'The day the shit hit the fan', or perhaps we should say 'The day the shit hit the carpet'.

Yes, this is gross, but I'm going to tell you anyway, because it will show you just how obviously the Energy Source can provide you a signal when you are out of the flow. It does this by making you sit up and take notice, forcing you to breakdown in order to breakthrough. This happens when your tap has been turned off.

In this situation, who turned my tap off? I did. I allowed this to happen to myself. This is being human. This is why we all need to learn how to recognise when this happens to us and have the tools ready to fix the tap!

It was my work from home day. I decided to cram in a chore just before starting work: clipping Cash's claws. The final claw, as I raced to be ready to start work at 7:30am, got clipped too short. If you've ever seen this happen to a dog claw, you'll know the claw bleeds like there is no tomorrow. There was blood everywhere. I was sure he was close to needing a blood transfusion; well, maybe that's a slight exaggeration. But there was a lot of blood nonetheless. He yelped and whimpered.

So I did my best to tend to him, after harming my own beloved puppy. Then I raced to start work and ploughed through the morning. I was completely in my own head. I was not aware at all of the day, of how I felt or of my surroundings. I was consumed by my worry, by how busy I was, and by the full list of things to be done.

I spent the afternoon weeding the garden, planting and mowing the lawn—all to make things look nice for our guests that were coming to visit. This was entirely about looking good, rather than doing what really needed to be done.

Doing, trying, busy, hot, sweaty and tired—I came inside, and Aaron arrived home from working in the city. He went into our office to start trading, lucky for him, as things were about to take a turn for the worse.

Cash had been a little confused. Normal he 'toileted' way down in the bush area in front of the house. More recently, he had taken to using the olive grove as his toilet. The olive grove is a steep sloping bank covered in rock shingle.

Here is what happened...

He 'went', slipped and stood in his dog poo. (This is not what I refer to it as normally, but I don't want to completely offend anyone with sensitivities. Normally, I just call it dog shit.) What did he do then? He ran into the house and all through the lounge. Dog poo on paws, paws on carpet, vis-a-vis dog poo on carpet.

The hilarious thing, I suppose (in retrospect!), is that we had a 'no shoes' policy inside our house, as we believed that all the toxins on the bottom of your shoes weren't good to traipse onto the carpet. Oh, yeah, but don't worry about the dog shit!

I was beside myself. "Why did you do that, Cash? Why is this happening? You're so naughty. I am so sick of this. Why me? Why now?"

But I managed to maintain some composure, and although I was borderline hysterical, I cleaned it up. I used carpet cleaning chemicals to kill any potential remnant of the poo, while trying not to gag in the process.

Then Aaron decided to take Cash walking. He returned, and Cash knocked his claw. It was bleeding profusely again, but of course, I didn't realise it until Cash had—that's right—walked all over the carpet. Wonderful! Blood and poo!

Down on my hands and knees scrubbing the carpet, I started crying. This was a full blown 'woe is me' moment. *I am so tired. This is disgusting.* Blah, blah, blah, self-defeating rubbish...

I took care of what needed to be done and called Charlotte. I was crying, and she said that I sounded maniacal. She asked, "What happened?" She did not recognise the person on the other end of the phone. It surely didn't sound like I was in the flow. The calm, happy, 'life is a joy' B was momentarily far away.

Sobbing, I told her that I couldn't understand what had happened.

She told me to, "Go and ask."

So, I did a meditation seeking guidance on what had happened and why. The answer came clearly: "Shit happens."

Oh, that's funny? So you have a sense of humour up there! I'm asking to be shown clearly why this has happened!

The next morning, I awoke to a realisation that I couldn't see the day before: I was simply out of the flow, washed up on the riverbank.

How did that happen? I swam out of the flow and beached myself. I chose to try to make things happen, to force my progress, and I added negative emotion to all I was doing.

I had unconsciously turned my tap off and then suffered the consequences as the Energy Source reacted to my sharp change of course. Perhaps it reacted so suddenly with the intention of snapping me out of it. I realised that's all it was.

Try Hard, or Let it be Easy

Have you ever noticed how the word 'trying' sounds a little hard and abrasive, and how the words 'let it be' sound peaceful and easy? It's no surprise, then, that when you 'try' things can sometimes feel hard, and when you 'let it be' things generally feel easy.

But, for some reason, for most of my life it has felt like I'm hard wired as a human to naturally try, and it feels very foreign to just 'let it be'.

> *What would life be like if you mastered*
> *how to let it be?*
> *When trying hard steps aside, is there a*
> *vacuum created where your actions*
> *become more powerful?*

The Letter

After this ghastly and smelly incident, Aaron suggested that I write a letter to myself, that I could give to him so that he could give it back to me if I ever got beached again.

He proposed that if he ever saw rust forming on my tap, he would find the letter and have it ready, poised to shove it into my hand.

The letter is my own words, reminding me of why these things happen, snapping me out of my funk and getting me back into the flow.

The letter reads like this:

Dear B,

It's B here. Aaron has given you this letter because you are most likely behaving erratically, and you are possibly hysterical, potentially crying, and it is very likely you have beached yourself.

You agreed to read this letter when you exhibited signs of behaving like a mad woman. These signs are indications to your husband that he needs to stage an intervention, using this letter to drag your face out of the mud and get you swimming in the flow again.

Take a look. Is your tap rusty? Don't tell me you can't even see your tap! This is more serious than I thought. This is one of those moments when you need to sort your shit out.

Speaking of shit, do you want it to hit the fan again, like that day Cash trod poo and blood into the carpet? Now you're smiling. It's funnier in retrospect, isn't it?!

Answer one question: Are you creating the life you want by manifesting the end result, trusting that the signals will show you the way? Or are you trying to make it happen, worrying and working at it?

Life is not a chore. Stop making it one.

Love, B

Consider writing your own letter to yourself—one that you can read when things seem impossible and you don't know why life has become so hard. Let your letter be the access to your own wisdom—wisdom that is seemingly lost when the shit hits the carpet.

Accommodation

It was time to see if this house-swapping lark was one answer to our financial dilemma. We decided to see if it would work freely and easily. If it did, then it would be the right choice.

Researching online I found a home swap website that looked suitable, despite having homes that were, in the majority, quite luxurious. I didn't consider our home to be luxury by any stretch. There were only seven houses in Thailand available for a swap. It would cost $220 to register—a reasonable sum to throw at something with no guarantee of a result.

I figured I'd just throw it out there and see what happened, submitting swap requests to all seven members. Within 48 hours, "Swap request accepted." It was the only positive response we received. The owner's email commenced by saying that due to a newborn baby arriving in their family, and the fact they actually live in the Northern Hemisphere, travelling to the other side of the world to stay on Waiheke Island for a house swap was not on the agenda.

Then, things got interesting. They explained that their property, in Koh Samui, was located in a complex under development. Opposite their house, several other villas were being built, and as a result, their house had not and would not be rented out over the June – August 2011 period. If we were happy to put up with a bit of construction noise and some dust around the pool (yes, a pool!), then we were welcome to stay in the property.

I rubbed my eyes to ensure I had read it correctly. We could stay there? They were not suggesting we could rent it? They were giving us their home to stay in for three months? Our only cost would be the management company fees for maintenance and utilities. Come on down, and pinch me now! I must be dreaming!

A brand new, luxury, three bedroom, three bathroom, fully furnished villa with a swimming pool! Was this really happening? Yes. Do things like this really happen? Yes. Holy cow, this was really happening!

Who were these outrageously trusting and generous people? I was tempted to look for the catch, to wait for the 'but', but the 'but' never came.

Puppy Love

Amongst the unresolved logistics for Thailand was a loving home for Cash, and it weighed on my mind. It was not long after we first got Cash that I came to understand first-hand why childless dog owners act like crazy obsessed people. He is my dog child. There, I said it. Scoff if you will, but he is.

Aaron and I discussed the possibility of house sitters that like dogs. We thought back to the dinner party conversation with Susannah. There was one reason we didn't follow that signal: not yet one year old, Cash stood solid at 35 kgs and was growing by the day. He was quite a commitment to take on. Any house sitter would need to be up for some seriously energetic daily walks to keep up with him!

We thought about sending him down to Wellington to live with one of my sisters who was happy to look after him for a few months. Then, I thought about what I really wanted: *If I am truly living life like anything is possible, then undoubtedly I should manifest the ideal scenario.*

That scenario would be a dog lover on Waiheke who would go beyond walking and feeding him. I wanted someone who would love him.

I knew that someone. Her name was Kelly, and she had really fallen in love with Cash when she met him many months before at puppy training classes. Kelly worked at the vet's office. I recalled how she took pictures of Cash on her phone. She always asked after Cash whenever we bumped into her. I told Aaron that someone like Kelly would be a dream.

But I couldn't ask her to take care of him; it was too much to ask of someone. I didn't even really know her. However, reminding myself that anything is possible and sometimes you have to take a risk, I got over myself and called the vet's office. Kelly was not there. I asked the owner about dog sitting. They said they could actually have him to stay onsite at the clinic if we wanted and they drew up a quote. She said,

"Kelly is actually the person who looks after the dogs for walking and grooming." Great! This could definitely work.

I thought on this more: cost, length of time, Cash being onsite at the clinic versus in someone's home... You can see my emotional dilemma. Later that day, I drove past Kelly as she crossed the road. She yelled out, "Bring Cash in some time! I'd love to see him!"

We wandered to the beach that weekend and talked about solutions to this situation. I said to Aaron, "I really hope we bump into Kelly again." Ten seconds later, she walked around the corner with her partner Brent. Out of nowhere she said, "I'm happy to have Cash come and live at our house if you organise it through my boss. There's only one catch..." *Nuts, a catch.* "... so long as he doesn't mind my cats."

AWESOME-ER!

Kelly was excited. Brent was excited. Cash was excited. We were excited! The cats...*not* excited.

Chapter 19

I Can't Hear You!

Nauseous Reminder

I continued to wonder how my full-time job was going to be compatible with three months in Thailand. Awaiting signals, I was afraid that I would potentially have to move out of my current company and job in order to make this dream a reality. I wondered if circumstances were going to push me in that direction, in order to pursue my new passions. I sensed I was somehow meant to make a living from these things.

Although leaving my job seemed like the obvious option, as there did not appear to be any other clear way to make this viable, it was completely outside of my sphere as to how to step away from a place I had been for many years with people I actually loved being around. Moreso, how could I generate an income equivalent to my current job and do that in a matter of mere months?!

Alternatively, I needed to organise my current employment in a way that would give me flexibility so that I could retain an income while in Thailand. This seemed like a very nice yet impossible idea.

As I calculated figures, analysed our mortgages, bills, commitments, budgeted for Thailand costs, and tried to intellectually work out how to make a square peg fit in a round hole, I did not immediately recognise the signal.

I started to regularly experience full-blown nausea. I usually felt fine at home, but it kicked in on the way to work each morning. *Could I accidentally have fallen pregnant, or did I eat some bad chicken?* I wasn't overtired and had been sleeping really well. I considered maybe the ferry was making me feel sick on the commute, but the sea was calm and the nausea continued when I hit dry land. People at work passed comments like, "You look really tired. Are you okay?"

Travelling to Wellington for work, I was milling around the departure lounge at Auckland Airport when I bumped into my former colleague Jean. "Oh, you're looking wonderful!" she said to me. We chatted, and just before boarding my plane, she stopped talking, touched my shoulder and looked me in the eye. "You look tired. Are you okay?" Then, the nausea kicked in.

Why on earth did she say I look wonderful, and then minutes later say I look unwell? Odd. Then, it hit me. I had bumped into her for a reason. She made those comments for a reason. It was no coincidence that another person had said to me that I looked unwell when I wasn't even feeling unwell!

I felt nauseous all the way to Wellington. During the flight, I asked for guidance, but I felt so sick I couldn't focus. Staying at Charlotte's that night, I asked again for guidance, "Why do I feel nauseous? Please tell me."

The summary version of the answer was, "You will feel nauseated as long as you remain doing what you don't love and ignoring that which you do."

This was at once confirming and confusing. I knew there were things I needed to be doing with my time and particularly for my future (writing, healing, coaching), and I wanted to follow my heart. At the same time, my confusion arose because I was enjoying aspects of my corporate coaching and was surrounded by what had become my work family. That being said, if I was to be truly honest with myself, my job was not where my heart was leading me. I knew my calling, and that wasn't it.

And so it seemed, I had to be reminded of this. God help me if I became too complacent and comfortable that I might forget that fact.

I passionately shared this latest insight with Charlotte as we drove along, and it did not escape my attention that these lyrics blared from the radio: "...It's my life. It's now or never. I ain't gonna live forever. I just wanna live while I'm alive. It's my life!"[29] This Bon Jovi song had been my anthem since this journey began; it inspired me to reach for the stars. My body shivered as the words came to remind me.

Silent Screaming

Day by day, logistical arrangements progressed. It seemed we were really on our way. The time to stop living a double life was nigh; it was time to announce my pear-ness. I had to tell everyone, and I mean everyone!

My workplace felt like an area of my life where I was a double agent—a pear dressed up as an apple. I had hidden from them what had been happening to me, the fullness of my transformation and my goals, and I had most certainly hidden Project Thailand. And yet they could conceivably have been considered the most affected party. I felt guilt.

It was this day that I realised that my life could not manifest into its full glory, its entirety, if I was hiding any aspect of it. If you are hiding it, it signals to the Energy Source any number of things: you are quite possibly not trusting yourself, not trusting the signals, ashamed of your goal, afraid of your goal, or afraid of other people's reaction to it. Or perhaps, quite simply, you are not really committed to your goal.

The feeling of guilt was not doing me any good. It was a negative feeling amidst my endeavour for positive outcomes.

This company had done an immense amount for me. I felt indebted. It was an internal struggle to feel like I might not work there anymore, or that working there in future would look very different. It wasn't because I didn't want that for myself, but it was because I felt guilty for wanting that.

The nagging feeling inside was becoming louder and more insistent by the day. It wouldn't abate. *This isn't it. This isn't your joy. Life is ticking by. What are you waiting for?*

Pinch Me

Every time it niggled, the guilt goblin visited. I felt terrible that I knew I wouldn't do this job forever (which is strange when you consider the fact that no one really commits to a job forever these days!), but nevertheless, that was the reality I had created.

I had made myself guilty for wanting to pursue other endeavours. I was ashamed at myself for not having the guts to stand up and say it. I had avoided doing so for fear my job would be pulled from under me before I was ready to go. I battled myself every day, swinging between my head-based commitment and my heart-based calling.

Life doesn't have to be one thing or another; it can be what you make it: a mixture of both. I had once before been caught in that moronic loop, back in 'my old life', thinking I had to give it all away to chase my dreams. I had previously chased my dreams all the way to Waiheke without needing to jump to the polar extreme. *Why can't that work again?*

I knew at some point I would have to tell my work I was going to Thailand. I would have to because it would involve me leaving (certainly for three months, if not for good), which was something they were sure to notice! "Hey, has anyone seen B lately?"

I foolishly decided to wait for the sun, moon and stars to align... again.

Once we have booked the flights, I will tell them.

Once we have more certainty on the duration of Aaron's new contract, I will tell them.

Once we hit our next trading goal, I will tell them.

Once we have more income saved up for the trip, I will tell them.

And on and on and on.

It was time to listen to my own advice. All of these things could be sorted in their own time, and none of these things were interdependent. My work was the only commitment that required foresight to morph and change to suit my new life. I was in no doubt that this was my new life and that I was going to do this. I had to; I could not ignore the signals.

Work was either going to come with me on this next leg of my journey, or it wasn't. I had to be at peace with that and trust that the signals would guide me in the best direction. If it didn't, and that was logical to expect, I would then be presented with serious questions over how to immediately create an income for myself. This was big-time scary, and maybe this was why I had been delaying telling them. I was scared to hear the answer. Putting myself out there by telling them made this 100% real and truly the point of no return.

The current status could continue no longer. 1 June would wait for no man (or woman). I had made my work life at odds with who I had become; it was at odds with my peardom and with Project Thailand.

How do I make it 'at one with' and not 'at odds with'?

It was the day of the owners' planning meeting. Face to face, one on one time would potentially be available. As the ferry glided on silky still water towards the city, I meditated to the hum of the engines. I asked for an opportunity to present itself to me that day where I could share what was really happening to me. They would just miraculously say, "Hey, B, something is really different about you. Tell us what is going on." This would force me to speak the truth.

Amidst my request for signals, I was interrupted by loud and clear music blaring in my mind. Annoyed at the distraction, nervously working out how I was going to manage the day ahead, I suddenly realised the signal had arrived that fast.

"You scream in silence, but I can hear you..."[30] These words blasted through my mind, just as the song is sung by The Feelers, with powerful desperation, calling out. I furiously scrawled the lyrics in my notebook. With the ferry lumbering over wake as we docked at the wharf, I stared at the page. Was the message reflecting that I had been screaming out silently inside my head, screaming about what I wanted the next phase of my life to be, and the Energy Source was saying that it could definitely hear me? I already knew the Energy Source was not restricted by the confines of my mind; it senses everything.

Although the Energy Source could hear my silent screams, I knew a few critical people could not. Sure, I could look Stephen in the eye that day and scream my intentions inside my head, and hope to heck that he would hear the silent wailing, perhaps by using extrasensory perception?! However, I was fairly sure that unless I actually told him directly, I probably wasn't going to get very far. I cursed that I didn't have more time to get my head around this before going to the office. But time would make no difference. I just needed to man up.

Before disembarking I asked, "What does this mean?"

"Tell them."

Foolishly I asked, "Tell who?"

I was told again, "Tell them."

I asked, "Tell them what?"

The answer: "Everything."

Despite being extremely nervous, I somehow felt more peaceful, like there was no other way forward. *If they do not understand or accept me, so be it. If I encounter difficulties or roadblocks, I will at least have clarity.*

And so I told them everything. I told them everything about my journey, the book, my newfound spirituality, my energy healing, and about my want and need to live overseas. I told them of my fear and of the fact I was a pear and I didn't want to pretend to be an apple anymore (not quite in those terms). Then, I asked a question: "Do I have to leave my job, or somehow can I continue to do some coaching remotely while I'm gone?"

Stephen simply said, "Yes." His comments went something like... "That's great! That is exciting. That's certainly possible. That is admirable. That will work. We are onboard, and we think all of this is great for you."

Pinch me. I simply did not know what to say. Normal people don't go off and make glorious lives like this happen, do they? Apparently, they do.

Apparently, we do. Apparently, I do. My self-imposed selfishness syndrome dropped away.

When Stephen embraced who I had become, I could not even speak to say thank you. A tear escaped. I (almost) never cry at work, but sometimes, there are no words when something hits a nerve inside you. To quote from the heartfelt novel *The Shack* by William P. Young, "Don't ever discount the wonder of your tears. Sometimes they are the best words the heart can speak."[31]

In this situation, a tear simply said thank you.

Pinch Yourself

Pia has been a good friend for many years. I had not seen her in six months. Over a glass of wine, we caught up on all the latest news. She asked how life on Waiheke was going, but she knew the answer coming was "great" when she saw me beam from ear to ear.

She asked what big adventures we had lined up next. I smiled wider, and she laughed. "Of course, you have your next project underway. You guys are on the go!"

I told her everything, and she replied, "Don't you just want to pinch yourself?"

"Yes, I do. Often."

I could see her mind ticking over, thinking: *What if this is how life works? What if this is available to me as well?*

Anne's Retreat

Our house was going to be empty when we left. There had to be a way to make sensible use of this resource to fund our plans. I had mentioned to my friend Emily, who lived on Waiheke, that I intended to get a rental agent around to assess the property for short-term lease. In my meticulous plan, this money would go towards paying for Cash to be looked after.

It was then that a series of catastrophic earthquakes hit Christchurch, New Zealand. In the days after the quakes struck, as aftershocks rocked the city, I wondered how we could help the people affected. The news bombarded us with stories of houses ruined. I thought: *We have spare bedrooms. We should be helping these people somehow. People are homeless.*

Emily texted, "Are you still looking to rent your house? My friend's mother needs somewhere to rent on the Island over winter."

Anne was affected by the earthquake. Her Christchurch house was damaged, and she was devastated by what had happened. Eager to get out of the city to seek solace, she was coming to Waiheke to be near her daughter and needed somewhere to live.

The rental assessment was double Anne's budget. However, Anne's budget was exactly the cost of the dog sitting. I texted Emily back immediately, "Yes!" Anne had been drawn to me. I was certain our home was the place for Anne to retreat.

I warmed to her as soon as we met. Kind and open hearted, I knew within minutes that she would be living in our house. Anne went on to tell me about her work, providing therapy to people who experience trauma, a woman who gives to others. It felt like I had known her for a long time. I even told her I was an author, having officially taken on the title!

As we walked outside to her car, she told me she was overwhelmed and full of joy to have found somewhere like this to stay—a sanctuary to recover from the events back home. As she opened the car door, she turned to me and said, "I just want to pinch myself."

I couldn't help laughing. "Funny you should say that. *Pinch Me* is the title of my book!"

I emailed the owner of the Thailand property and told him that because of his generosity to us, someone affected by Christchurch's earthquake was now benefiting as a flow on effect. He was helping Aaron and I realise our dream, and indirectly, he was helping this lovely lady to be in a place she felt safe.

Although this was for certain, there were *still* things that were unresolved for Thailand—financial things. Aaron's contract work had begun looking shaky and potentially unreliable, and while I could do some coaching remotely, my hours would be reduced, resulting in a pay cut. We had two mortgages to service. The feverish and conservative money worry was rising like bile.

BUT... I said no to the bile. I refused to listen to my fear. I refused to buy into the things that could go wrong or could make this impossible. This had gone beyond being about just Aaron and I. This was now also about Anne. This was now also about Kelly. This was now also about Stephen. This was about all the people who were excited for us and had helped us get this far. This was also about the flow on effect of other people seeing what is possible when you follow the signals.

I yanked out my notebook and flicked to a blank page. I wrote a message to the Energy Source...

I DON'T KNOW HOW TO MAKE OUR FINANCES WORK TO HAVE THIS HAPPEN. I WILL FOLLOW THE SIGNALS. PLEASE SHOW ME.

Chapter 20

Berries & Bastions

Thorn Berry?

There is something I must share with you now, something that happened some months ago. At the time, I preferred to ignore it, wishing I didn't have to share it, and moreover, wishing I didn't have to follow it.

I lay in the dark, curled up in bed. It was some unearthly hour. Stirred by something, I tossed and turned. I don't know how long it took me to realise what was happening; time seems to have no meaning when you're crossing in and out of deep sleep. My mind dragged itself from the haze, and almost immediately, I knew. It had happened again.

Another word in the middle of the night, over and over again, the same word came to me. Just like the time Asara came to me at the start of this journey. I wanted to ignore this latest word. But knowing that this is how life works now, I couldn't ask for help and not listen.

"Thonburi."

This word rattled around in my mind as night turned to morning. I didn't really know what it was, but there was no doubting it had something to do with Thailand. It most definitely sounded like a place.

My friend Trina giggled when I told her. "What's the word? Thorn Berry? What the heck is a Thorn Berry?"

"No, Thonburi," I repeated.

I googled it to find out more and discovered Thonburi is an area outlying Bangkok city, a vast area covering the west bank of the Chao Phraya River.

Okay, here we go! Please don't tell me I have to go to Thonburi. Listen Energy Source, get with the programme! I have a wonderful place lined up to live, amidst the glorious golden beaches and azure blue waters of Southern Thailand. Don't make me give up Koh Samui for this. Please!

But I could not deny this signal. Damn this new philosophy and way of living! So I asked, "Do I need to go to this place?"

"Yes."

So I asked the obvious question (one I am sure you will also be asking right now),"Why would someone leave idyllic Waiheke Island for a sabbatical in a seemingly random outlying district of Bangkok?"

With some exasperation, I had asked this very question and was told, "You'll see."

When signals make no sense, and you have no idea why you are being guided in a particular direction, this is when your faith is tested the most. This is when your faith must be greatest. These are the moments when you have to trust without knowing why. This was especially the case for me in this instance, when the path ahead seemed most unusual and, quite honestly, highly undesirable.

As I sat there and saw my dreams of a sabbatical spent entirely on a beach in Southern Thailand slowly re-orienting to a very different picture, I simply reminded myself that there was something beneficial to be had here and while I didn't know the answers to my questions yet, the signals had served me well so far.

This was a true turning point. We all have options in life. No one was forcing me to do anything. I had the option of returning to a life led by my mind, where I ignored this guidance and intellectually chose to spend the whole three months in a tropical paradise— a place we had also clearly been led to by a series of signals. That option sounded nothing short of divine. Or, I had the option to have faith, to continue living a life led by this 'other dimension', and to go to Thonburi. This option was a mystery to me.

Let it be known that for most of my life Bangkok had been on my list of places *never* to go—mainly because I was small-minded, narrow-minded, and also petrified of the city from childhood memories of watching the movie *Bangkok Hilton*. (If you haven't seen this, it's horrifying!)

When we were married in Thailand, we had to go to Bangkok to sign marriage paperwork at the Embassy. I discovered that it was, in fact, a colourful, fast paced, vibrant city, where your senses are overloaded on a minute-by-minute basis. It's a place where the world is at your doorstep, whatever you wish to do. Nevertheless, after three days there, I was more than ready to move on.

So, again I asked, "Do I really need to go there?"

I didn't need to hear an answer though. I had been told once. I knew that if I wanted to find out the answers to all my questions, if I wanted to experience whatever I was meant to discover there, then clearly I had to go. Otherwise, I would never know. My curiosity would be my undoing.

I decided to follow both sets of signals. We would go to both places—six weeks in the villa in Koh Samui and seven weeks in Thonburi, Bangkok.

Another task was added to the list: accommodation in Thonburi. I searched online for short-term, furnished rentals and found apartments that looked new, modern and perfectly set up. It seemed too easy. Selecting the 'ideal' location within Thonburi was a bit of a challenge. I had no idea why I was going or what I was trying to get myself 'near' to (the usual way I would book accommodation). Thonburi is an extremely large area, covering many districts. B's planned, prepared, researched and controlled approach could not find a way through this situation. There was nothing more to do than to randomly pick an apartment and hope for the best.

It was some days later when it clicked—something else that invited the bile to rise. Aaron had long ago booked a trip to the United Kingdom for the end of July, to be best man at a wedding. We had known this for almost a year. Back then, he had conveniently booked his flights via Bangkok, so he simply needed to change the dates. However, the point I am truly making here is not that he was going to the United Kingdom, but that he was going away for ten days during our newly planned stay in Thonburi.

Thus, leaving me ALONE in Bangkok.

For some people, this would be nothing. This would be exciting. This would be someone's version of great. For me, this was a version of very scary. I am being polite here, as I really want to say I was shit scared to stay in that crazy city alone. One day, maybe two days, possibly even three days... but TEN DAYS?! I was anxious and afraid of being there for that long, in a place I didn't know, moreover a chaotic, immense city where I didn't speak the language.

Clearly, I had a fear to face. This fear went straight to the top of my list of things to conquer during this three-month sabbatical. The list covered all sorts of things that my heart desired, that I had been drawn to do in Thailand, and the things I was not so drawn to do but still needed to. My list looked like this:

- ✓ Overcome anxiety of being alone in a foreign place where there is no one I know, no one expecting me and no one to look after me, by spending ten days in the city of most dread since childhood.
- ✓ Overcome fear of the ocean, and of sharks, and all other creatures therein that could get me, and my very lacking ability to swim in water that is anything deeper than one metre and my strong preference, nee... absolute requirement,

to avoid water on my face, in my eyes and up my nose at all times, by learning to scuba dive.
- ✓ Write, write and write some more.
- ✓ Heal, heal and heal some more—myself and anyone who is willing, wanting and needing.
- ✓ Learn language. Share language.
- ✓ Learn about local traditions, healing practices, beliefs and spirituality.
- ✓ Do daily yoga. Healthy body, healthy life.
- ✓ Grow as a person. This falls purposely short of saying 'find myself'.

The Last Bastion

Life was about to go global. What better time for more things to turn to shit—well, more like mini-versions of shit. I'm not talking about the type of clear warnings that something is bad, that catastrophe lies ahead, not the 'turn back now before it's too late' type of shit. I mean more like the testing, trying type of mini hurdles that bother you when you're outside your comfort zone.

Over a period of two weeks, I was repeatedly faced with a variety of money-related challenges. Again, the financial side of things was not entirely nailed down. It was no wonder I was feeling outside my comfort zone, as money had always tended to put me on edge.

A work bonus, which I thought I was getting, which was pre-allocated in my finely balanced Thailand budget to pay for my flights, had really been a figment of my imagination. I was not going to get any bonus; I never was because I had totally miscalculated the figures. Me, a person who is anally retentive about all things numeric (in fact just all things!), had managed to miscalculate something that was so critical to me. I never get figures wrong. I got this wrong.

I called Charlotte in a flurry. She reminded me, as did Aaron, that, "When you ask the Energy Source to provide for you, when you manifest the money you need for Project Thailand, you don't get to dictate where it comes from. It will come, just not necessarily from where you think it will."

Next my accountant announced, "As you know, the rules for property investing are changing." No, I didn't know! Our Wellington home was now a rental investment. I learned that the rule changes would possibly impact my tax payable, thus impacting savings that I had previously set aside to pay for such tax, thus impacting the overall budget (currently calculated to the cent) for Project Thailand.

Then, the company Aaron was contracting for advised that their circumstances had changed. They now needed someone working onsite for the next phase of work; his work flexibility was gone, along with the income from it.

These issues arose to test me, to push my buttons. The reason I knew this was because I was the only one in our happy little household reacting like an insane, headless chicken whenever money situations arose. The money gremlin would frolic around me and sing an ugly little song that went something like this: "Oh, no, money, money, money! What if we don't have enough, money, money, money? How will this work, problems, problems, problems? La, la, la, la, laaaaa." Fear not. I did not actually see a gremlin, but something inside of me acted like one.

Aaron patiently sighed and waited while I did my money gremlin worshipping ritual, where I listened to and embraced my concern. As soon as I stopped to draw a breath, Aaron reminded me that I'd had a constant, negative belief about money for as long as he'd known me. In all honesty, I had been that way about money for as long as I could remember, well before meeting him.

Aaron suggested that perhaps this money fear was simply showing up time and time again in my life in the hope of giving me the opportunity to heal myself of it. He interrupted my chaos at just the right time, with just the right comment, before I let all of it suffocate me.

On my lunch break the next day, I wandered to the rose garden near my office. I parked myself in the sun-filled courtyard surrounded by rose covered trellising. I used to go there often, watching the birds play in the water fountain. I called Charlotte and relayed Aaron's observation. She pointed out the same thing to me. "Yes," she told me, "haven't you realised it yet? It's been with you a long time."

Mmm....

Aaron could it.

Charlotte could see it.

B could not see it.

But I felt it, like a tightening in my gut. A foreboding 'oh, my god, I might lose everything' feeling. I felt like I had to protect my interests, protect my money in case I lost it all. They say if you close your fist tightly to hold onto something, then your hand isn't open to receiving at the same time. On that basis, I thought: *How can I receive the money I need for Thailand if my fist is tightly gripped around what I currently have, panicking at any sign that it might slip away?*

Any changes to money had always made me very uneasy. There was no logical thinking going on; it was just a feeling that always inhabited me, like I had to be very careful. Amusingly, I'd always had enough money to sustain myself, and I'd never had true reason to worry about money. This hadn't stopped me; I had always found a way.

Sitting there in the sun I had crystal clarity on money for the first time in my life. I realised it made me act like a crazy person. *Not all people act like this, to this extent. Not all people feel this way. Why do I?*

This had to be blocking my way forward, holding me back. This sort of negative energy and crazy reaction was surely attracting back to me more of the same. That was not what I wanted. Were my imaginary bonus, my accountant's news and Aaron's contract changes all 'happenings' designed to call me to face and resolve my fear?

So I asked for guidance. Within one minute, I had it. It flooded my mind as a mixture of words, feelings and flashes of information—much like a movie reel.

It was a past life. I asked questions and received answers.

I had lost everything. I was desolate. I was in despair. It was caused by my own poor decisions.

Then, I was told, "Listen to what Augustus told you. This is the last bastion."

Addressing this unnecessary money drama would allow me to move forward and live in freedom. Augustus had told me something very important—one key thing. How did I not truly hear what he had told me? It had taken me over a year to 'get' this. It was quite possibly one of the most important lessons for me to learn and overcome in my life, and he had handed it to me on a silver platter in that session. Still, I had missed it.

As soon as I got home, I pulled out the CD recording of my session with him. I navigated my way to the part I needed to hear. He described my need to control everything. He explained this was my way of protecting myself, my money and my security. He said I was living in a box, all safe and protected. I had made a choice to live this way.

My controlled, planned and protective way of living, and my meticulous money management were my strong suit. These traits had been the foundations of my success. It was affronting to hear they were, in fact, also my downfall.

And then the gold: "This is definitely a past life attitude for you. You are living like you have got to stay in control, like something bad might happen, like you might lose everything. In a past life, you had no control. You had no say over what happened. Because of that situation, you lost out. You lost money and/or your life. In this life, your soul decided you have got to be in control; you are organised and focused. You are not going to allow yourself to be drawn into mess. You must cross every t and dot every i. You have to ensure all the foundations are strong. You have created an incredible intensity around this, but it has only created anxiety and fear."

Listening to these words, my ears instantly started burning. They burned red hot, and then, they started itching. Sitting alone in the room, I blurted out, "Yes, I got it. I know this is what you wanted me to hear!" The burning sensation stopped immediately.

That was the last bastion, the last thing to cling to, my security blanket, my habitual way of being. Don't get me wrong; it was not the last thing ever, just the last thing for now. It was the last thing to overcome in order for me to achieve my Thailand dream.

A healing for limiting beliefs was on the cards. Done and dusted, I tumbled that wall in front of me with one big kick. (Think Miss Piggy from *The Muppets* when she does her karate chop move, and says, "Hi-yaaaah!")

This personal progression seemingly signalled to the Energy Source that I was truly ready to be shown the 'how' for funding the rest of this sabbatical. Within days, our accountant sent our final year-end accounts for sign off, with confirmation of two very helpful things. Aaron was receiving an unexpected tax refund, and my tax bill was less than anticipated, immediately releasing savings. I then discovered I had more paid holiday leave owed to me than anticipated, which could be spread over my time away, allowing me to maintain a workable income level. And to put the icing on the cake, our Wellington tenant emailed me asking, "My friend needs somewhere to live for two months. Could they please move in temporarily? They will, of course, pay additional rent."

Project Thailand just grew wings.

Chapter 21

Lost in the Jungle

Our departure was set. Everything was in place. I marvelled at the fact we had created this from nothing, against seemingly impossible circumstantial influences.

In the lead up to going, life became extraordinarily busy. I was on edge, tired and feeling unwell. The beauty of Aaron is his directness. "Why are you so anxious and overwhelmed? Aren't you some guru who knows everything? So just stop it, or fix it."

I'm no guru, that's the whole point I've been trying to make. I'm just an average person who wasn't born with any special gift. I battle each day to control my undiagnosed OCD, desperately wanting things to be easy and often falling back into habits perfected over a lifetime. I reach out for advice when needed, and at times I advise myself to stop trying and start trusting.

Still more signals flowed. It seemed I had opened a can of worms when resolving my relationship to money. Other challenging personality traits came to the forefront, and under the microscope they were much more significant than I had ever realised.

Fix-it Lady

One such trait I was shown was my inability to be with other people's problems. This had been a theme throughout my life. I usually jumped in to try to fix such problems; driven by an incessant need to. I suddenly realised it had little to do with other people or problems, and everything to do with my own need to fix things. I couldn't 'be with' other people's problems simply because it distressed me.

At times, this had been a little joke within my close circle of family and friends. If something happened, they would tease, "Don't tell B, or she'll try to fix it." It happened when Ryan was diagnosed and an endless number of other times. Asked for or not, at times not even wanted, I still dove straight into fix-it mode. I could now see it wasn't healthy, and it was leaving no room for other people to help themselves.

In time, this lesson would come to meet me face to face; I would soon be confronted with the perfect opportunity to practice 'no fixing'.

Getting What You Ask For

My time became consumed with more and more healing work. Word of mouth had expanded beyond family and friends; people I didn't know were coming to me. I was using literally every waking moment outside of my job to either facilitate energy healings or to write. Most days involved 5am – 10pm doing. I got a little lost in all the frenetic activity.

I strived to get a balance between focusing on *doing*, which achieves an outcome, and focusing on how I was *being*. It's in the 'being' where action combined with awareness can also achieve an outcome, but it can be achieved in a much more powerful (and far less stressful) way. Less doing, more being. The guidance I received at this busy time, as my new life took off, was, "This is what you asked for."

In response, I thought: *Dammit, you're right! You're always right. This is what I asked for. I manifested all aspects of this life and wanted it and still want it, but now that I have it all I simply don't know how to juggle it. I am hitting a wall physically, mentally and emotionally, and it is all of my very own making.*

I was anticipating that much more of it was yet to come, because I was manifesting a big life—a life full of all the things I wanted in both Thailand and at home afterwards. I knew I had to quickly learn how to manage all of these things while remaining happy and healthy.

You know something is not quite right when you are having a crisis just before going on a sabbatical trip of a lifetime. Songs were flowing through my mind every morning when I awoke. The Eurhythmics serenaded me, "Another day, another night has taken you again my dear. And you know that I'm gonna be the one who'll be there when you need someone to depend upon, when tomorrow comes..."[32]

While chasing my dreams, I felt like I had bitten off more than I could chew and had lost my 'presence' in the process. However, I never felt alone; the Energy

Source and the signals gave me comfort that whatever I needed would come to me.

Beyond Coping

"Wow, only a week to go until we leave!" he said.

"I know, and I have a million things to do before then."

Aaron was quick to ask me to list those 1,000,000 things, which I naturally failed to do. My response showed how precariously close to the riverbank I remained. Putting things into perspective, there were about 15 things on the list. If I didn't do them immediately, the world would not stop, and no one would die.

Charlotte laughed when I told her that Aaron had called me out. She suggested, "Perhaps this is just one version of 'being busy' and learning how not to sweat the small stuff. Drop the unimportant things and reprioritise the important things. Most importantly, find time for yourself. This may be your practice run for how to go beyond coping and into living life enjoyably before you step fully into your future as you have designed it—life as an author, coach and healer. You will surely need to learn these skills to live that life fully."

Still, I am a little ashamed to admit to you, I had a further meltdown. Charlotte lovingly laughed, and it was so ludicrous I had to laugh too. "You are so far out of the river now. I think you're well past the riverbank this time! Maybe next time you won't get so lost in the jungle?"

I reassured myself that the signals had not gone away, but I was just too caught up to recognise them. My guides were apparently right there too, watching me spiral down, spinning and waiting for me to stop. As a coach and healer, I knew it would do me well to remember that moment at the bottom of the spiral, to remember:

- What it feels like to be lost in the jungle;
- What it feels like when you're in a rut; and
- What it feels like when someone tells you that all you have to do is jump in the river and you instinctively reply, "But I'm stuck!"

And so in the midst of that meltdown, I closed my eyes and took a mind, body and spirit snapshot. I etched that moment into my memory and promised myself: *I will remember this day when I come across other people who are living their own version of this moment. I will remember what it's like to be swimming, then beached and then lost in the jungle, simultaneously wondering how on earth you ended up there. I will remember what it is like to then ask the Energy Source to recalibrate the compass that got you there in the first place—the compass that just responds according to the thoughts and feelings you create. I will remember all of this so that I can help other people find their way back.*

Searching for a solution to situations like this externally is not the answer, the answer is simply to be quiet and still. The answer will come from within.

Simultaneous Signal

Aaron patiently watched and waited as I dragged my sorry arse out of the jungle, remaining nearby, quietly supportive. The next morning I awoke, humming a tune to myself "...I just need you now."[33]

Brewing the coffee, I heard the same tune playing down the hallway. I followed the sound and found Aaron. He looked at my bewildered face and said, "What?"

I couldn't believe it. "Why are you listening to that song?"

His response, "I woke up to this song going over and over in my head, so I figured it was a signal. I think it is about you. I think it's telling me that I need to support you more."

What I call 'coincidentalism' at its best! Did I tune into his signal or he to mine, or was it a newfound form of signal—a simultaneous one? Who knows?!

Shrinking Away

With only days to go, people were constantly asking why we were going. Why Thonburi? I was uncomfortable responding to questions about how I came to that point. They wanted answers about the guidance I received, and about energy healing and how it worked. The more people asked, the more I realised that I didn't know all the answers and the more uneasy I felt. I could hear myself attempting to explain. I saw a few screwed up faces amongst the predominantly shining sea of smiles and support.

I could hear myself belittling my experiences in order to sound less unusual to people, in the hope of blending in. I could hear myself answering questions and thinking I sounded a bit like Person A. *Do they understand what I'm on about? How much of a crackpot do they think I am?*

Shrinking away from being who I really was served no one—not myself and not others. I was reminded of something my mother gave me to read when I was younger. As Marianne Williamson wrote, famously quoted by Nelson Mandela, "...your playing small does not serve the world. There's nothing enlightened about shrinking so that other people won't feel insecure around you. We are all meant to shine..."[34]

I was pretty sure people weren't feeling insecure at all. They probably just felt confused by my lack of ability to explain myself. So I shed light on my fear and my desire to shrink away, and I addressed it.

It continuously amazes me how much negative belief baggage one person can carry around. *How much more baggage does B have to uncover? I'm not sure, but referring to yourself in the third person is never a good sign!*

Coming Home

The day had come to depart.

How is it possible that diving into the unknown, embarking on an adventure where risks are taken and outcomes are unknown, can at once seem uncertain and at the same time seem like coming home? By this,

I mean coming home to myself. Ah yes, the 'finding myself' bit! This leap of faith felt like I was opening the door for me to discover my true self, even though I felt totally exposed and out of my comfort zone while doing so.

Opening an email from Trina, I saw before me the famous 'quest' passage from Elizabeth Gilbert's *Eat Pray Love*. Trina thought it was timely for me to read it. I was filled with a sense of calm. It was a signal to me, showing that if you are willing to step away from all that you know, in search of meaning, with an open mind "...then the truth will not be withheld from you."[35]

I was very excited to discover the truth.

Chapter 22

Days & Nights Samui-Style

We did it! We arrived!

Koh Samui—stunningly beautiful, steaming hot, peaceful, carefree—it was heaven. There was a familiarity about the place, not just because we had been there once before, but because it felt strangely like a homely place to be. As you know, we were living in someone's home, and what a home it was!

To see it first-hand, we were more than overwhelmed by the generosity of the owner who had let us live there. There were far too many rooms for just the two of us, and I felt that it was necessary to dance around the house to make use of all the space! The rooms all opened out onto the veranda overlooking the in-ground bliss, also known as the swimming pool—a watery retreat from 35 degree heat and 90% humidity.

And... there was no construction to be seen. The building project opposite the villa was indefinitely on hold. There was no noise and no dust.

Aside from being called the Land of Freedom, Thailand is also known as the Land of Smiles, for a very good reason. Thai people are beyond friendly. To add to this joy, Thai food is delicious and cheap.

Sights, smells and sounds abound wherever you turn. And the not so joyful... sweat constantly trickling and sticking skin to clothing.

We visited the local temples, and I had taken a moment to consider what they mean to the local people. The colourful and elaborate decorations held meaning and symbolism that I couldn't decipher.

We had no great desire to shop or sightsee. We were there to marinate in the quiet and solace of no day-to-day errands and interruptions, as I focused on what I came to do—to quiet my mind, to give attention to my body, to connect to my spirit and to write.

Mind

To quiet my mind, I used meditation, just like at home. My mind was quite naughty and regularly interrupted meditation to go over lists of things that could be done—checking in at home to see if Cash was alright, checking in with Anne at our house, calling family to say hi. I resorted to regularly shushing my mind and refocusing.

Body

To give attention to my body, I fortunately, and also regrettably, chose to do Hot Yoga. Like it wasn't hot enough already! Humorously, the most economical option was actually the month unlimited membership—unlimited hot pain.

I had never done yoga on a regular basis. In my first class in Thailand, I thought I would die and could not last the 90 minutes in 38 degree heat without lying down to skip a few of the rather aerobically challenging postures. I gritted my teeth (not the point of a meditative yoga practice at all!) and made it through, while mumbling, "I am over this body-loving stuff. I don't need to do this."

After showering, I met Aaron out front to alight onto our trusty scooter to head home amongst the Samui night traffic carnage.

He said, "You know it's hot when you have to blow on your water bottle to cool it down!" We cackled with laughter as we flew along the poorly lit, pothole ridden back roads leading to the villa.

But, in all seriousness, doing hot yoga every day was not only a gift to my health, but it really tested my commitment, determination and resilience. It took some physical and mental endurance to sustain hot yoga, and it was the perfect way to get present. It also showed me how much of 'giving up' was in my mind and how much was actually my body. My body was fine; it was my mind that was waning.

How often is it true that our minds give up before any other aspect of us is ready to quit?

Spirit

To connect to my spirit, I wrote. This may sound odd, but I guess that was my version of getting in touch with myself—where hours could go by unnoticed, when nothing else mattered, when I got lost in what I was doing.

For everyone, it is different...

> *What things in life give you this feeling?*
> *What do you love getting lost in?*

I started writing as soon as we arrived, and I can't explain how blissfully happy I was sitting in my writing room, tapping away on my laptop. As I remembered what my 'old life' used to be like, joy suddenly welled up when I looked out the window. Beyond the gloriously aqua blue pool, I saw coconut trees waving in the breeze, hills rising majestically in the background, covered with thick tropical jungle. Dragonflies flitted about. What was before a dream, was now very much a reality. My musing was interrupted when I heard Aaron yell out, "Do you want some chicken on a stick?!" Ah... music to my ears!

Samui Antics

One of the most amusing moments of our first week involved lying by the pool as we watched two workmen nearby felling a four-storey high tree, using nothing more than a chainsaw and a rope. Thailand is a very efficient place when it comes to matters that appear much more complex in other countries.

Someone had tied the rope to the top of the tree, one man held the rope to guide the direction of the fall, while the other wielded the chainsaw. We heard a loud crack, and then, we saw them run. That was that. Whether the tree not hitting all the surrounding buildings was luck or experience, I am yet to decide.

Another amusing moment, as I stood in the verge of the road paying for my noodle soup, was feeling something brush against my leg. I looked down to find a face peering up at me. All of three years old, this little Thai boy stroked my leg and grinned. I think perhaps he had never seen anything so white. (Note to self: get a tan!)

In addition to learning basic Thai words so that I could converse politely with hello, please and thank you, I also learned several very important lessons regarding how to ensure one is understood for matters of a more detailed nature.

For example, when the motorbike man rented us a scooter that kept backfiring, I had to resort to imitating the event with loud 'bang bang' noises, combined with hand expressions, much to his amusement and Aaron's embarrassment.

I also learned that the appropriate response to the one worded question, "Spicy?" is a one worded answer, "No." My initial use of "no spicy" was a fatal mistake that resulted in long jaunts doubled over on the toilet. Seemingly, they do not hear the 'no' and only hear the 'spicy'.

We soon mutually agreed on three essential daily must-haves: plastic rain poncho, iced Thai coffee and deep-fried bananas. With the exception of the poncho, I was sure I would never leave this heaven!

I failed my audition for Zen Idol, when, after carelessly leaving my credit card in the money machine, I ran back like a crazed woman to discover the machine had eaten it. I was not calm, not peaceful.

However, all was made well again, when I made a new dog friend to fill the Cash void. I nicknamed him Chad. Chad slept on the dusty roadside every day and night near our villa. As we zoomed by on our scooter, I called out, "Sawasdee ka, Chad."

The owners stared, and I suspected that they thought I was a little odd. They indeed may have been wondering what "Chad" meant in English, and why that crazy farang (westerner) kept shouting it at their dog.

Kop Kun Ka

Before leaving home, I was given an origami set for beginners as a sabbatical gift with the suggestion that I make origami butterflies for people who helped me during my time in Thailand, as a way to say 'kop kun ka' (thank you). [36]

Let me tell you that origami for beginners should actually be called 'don't try origami unless you're super smart and very patient'. My first butterfly was a demented one-winged monster. They improved little by little, and I enjoyed giving them to bemused (or more apt, confused) locals who helped me. Kamnan, the Security Guard, let me practice my Thai greetings with him. He tied his butterfly to a ribbon, and hung it from the security desk at the front gate. It swayed in the breeze each time we whizzed by.

Chapter 23

Lessons in Unexpected Places

Local Healing

Arriving in Samui, I waited for signals in relation to several things I wanted to learn—one of those being local healing traditions. How do Thai people view healing? Do they use energy healing? Is it aligned with their spiritual beliefs? In fact, what are their beliefs?

I asked around at the local hawker market where we ate lunch each day. I began to get to know all the stall owners. The lady who made iced coffee had reasonably good English skills, so I asked her, "Where do Thai people go if they feel sick and don't want to go to the doctor?"

I wasn't sure that my message was understood, because after conversing with her neighbouring stallholder, she turned to me and said, "Massage. Go massage."

Okay. Surely they don't head down to the cheap massage place on the beaches and get the usual Thai massage. I've had those, and I can't see how that pummelling would fix anything other than tight muscles and stiff joints.

A Thai massage is amazing, but quite vigorous to say the least! Was there some other type of massage that had healing properties? This remained a mystery for some days.

Then during yoga, I hurt my hip. Something pinched; it felt like a nerve. Over the coming days, my lower back seized up and the hip just wouldn't come right. I facilitated healing after healing. It would momentarily get better, but then, the pain would come back. How odd! Why wouldn't it go away? One day after class, one of the locals asked me what was wrong, as she noticed I was gingerly favouring that hip. I explained.

"Okay, I am going to give you a name. She works at a little place, a massage healing centre. It looks like nothing from the outside; you'd never notice it. I will draw you a map. Her name is Charunee. Ask for her when you arrive. Tell her you have a sore hip. I go to her no matter what is wrong with me. She does the same healing treatment every time, never a deviation, no matter what my problem. It works every time."

Ask and you shall be shown. There was one reason I hurt my hip and the pain didn't go away. It was an opportunity to find what I was seeking. This situation had arisen to allow me to get me in touch with the right person to find out about local healing practices.

The next day, armed with map and name, I headed off to find this inconspicuous place. After driving up and down the road several times, I finally found it. The staff spoke next to no English. I asked to see Charunee. Either my pronunciation was off or I wasn't inflecting it with enough of the unique Thai sound, because they didn't know what I was saying. I gave them the piece of paper with Charunee's name on it. It took about five minutes to establish who that person was, after the lady who seemed to be in charge disappeared out the back of the building and returned with Charunee in tow. This was the woman I was here to see.

I pointed at my hip and grimaced. She led me into a room, and it began: an hour of the most unusual healing massage I have ever experienced. If you're thinking about relaxation, you're sadly mistaken. It goes something like this 'no pain, no gain'.

She pinpointed and pinched at every internal organ, applied serious pressure under my ribs, in my abdomen and pelvis. She put her fingers into joints and her elbows into odd places. I spent most of the hour wishing I wasn't in my body as the pain was intense. I left feeling like I was having an out of body experience.

That night, I was sick. Aaron thought he was going to have to take me to hospital; I had a fever and was burning up. It lasted most of the night. Despite the air conditioning tempering the room to a pleasant 18 degrees for sleeping, I was sizzling like a hotplate.

I awoke the next morning to find myself lying on the wooden floorboards. In my delirium I had vacated the sweat ridden bed sheets and decided that the floor was the coolest place to be. Empty water bottles were strewn around the room, and wet flannels surrounded me, but... no hip pain. Apparently my body had purged everything it needed to purge. It seemed that this was the local healing way, working with the whole body, igniting the body systems to let the body heal itself from the inside out.

Aquatic Adventure

I was healed just in time to turn my attention to my fear of water, specifically my fear of deep water and the ocean. I had been diligently reviewing my dive course manual, becoming familiar with the theory, absorbing the number one rule: don't forget to breathe. I was perturbed to read, under the 'Aquatic Life' section of my manual, what one should do if one comes across a dangerous or aggressive animal. I was thinking shark. I would rather actually die before facing a shark in the water. Like many people of my generation, I was ruined for life as child by watching the movie *Jaws*.

The manual reassuringly said, "Remain calm, and lie on the bottom." ARRRGGH! Remain calm? Okay, that in itself would be an issue. At least I knew how to lie on the bottom, surely that couldn't be too hard? Look like sand. Become the sand. I am the sand. Most importantly, I decided that perhaps I wouldn't wear a wetsuit. I figured that if I were to wear a black wetsuit, I would look like a seal with arms and legs. If I didn't wear a wetsuit, my white, white skin would ensure that any said sharks or other dangerous animals wouldn't mistake me for a seal.

So, my game plan was: Breathe. Look very white. Make like sand. Remain calm! I was told that if we were lucky enough to see a shark (I'm sorry did you say lucky?), it would probably just swim right past me. If that were to happen, I was sure to pee myself. *Are they attracted to other bodily fluid or just blood?*

Pinch Me

I was about to break 32 years of water trauma. I remember getting swimming lessons when I was six. The teacher instructed me to hold the edge of the pool and put my face in the water. It was seemingly not too much of a problem, despite the water going into my eyes and up my nostrils. Some basic instruction on blowing out one's nose could have been quite useful. The most interesting teaching technique (I question her training in retrospect) was when she held my head in the water and turned it left and right for me, controlling my breathing—an excellent way to instil fear of water in any child: not allowing them to breathe of their own accord.

Day One—survive the pool—also known as confined water dives. Even the word confined freaked me out. Day Two—survive the ocean, also known as open water dives, down to twelve metres. I do not 'do' water deeper than my waist, and I had never left the surface. I was super excited, despite my fear, and I was determined in every way not to let it beat me. I refused to leave the island without my certification. I had been visualising Aaron taking photos of me after the course with my dive card and thumbs up to prove I did it, and I created the feeling inside myself of what it would be like at that moment when it was done and the type of elation and personal triumph I would feel.

Aaron was anticipating the course with much glee.

Snorkelling Reminiscence

He knew how big this water thing was for me. He could still remember our mere snorkelling trip on our honeymoon.

Bikini? Check.

Mask and snorkel? Check.

Fins? Check.

Life jacket belted up around my waist and between my legs (that's right, between my legs!)? Check.

Snorkelling in waist deep water with much trepidation? Check.

Seeing a fish that looked a metre long with teeth poking out and me standing up, trying to move hurriedly away from it with my fins still on, wet hair draped chaotically over my mask, spitting out my snorkel, waving to Aaron onshore for help? Check.

Scuba B

It was just my instructor Tim and I in the pool. Because I was not a water baby, and in fact, my reflexes were built to resist water in any place at any moment, there were many times during the day where the strangeness of it all overrode my common sense. I snorted instead of breathing, sucked in instead of blowing out and thought my nose was my mouth. As a result, there was much coughing, spluttering and spitting—very attractive. I was hoping Tim had seen it all before; surely, I wasn't the first water-phobe to try this.

I was delighted to discover my 450 minutes worth of hot yoga every week was paying dividends. Although I ordinarily breathe at a hyperventilating rate in water, yoga promotes calm, slow and deep breathing, an essential skill for diving, and I was now well practised at this.

Tim then nonchalantly announced that we were going to flood our masks under water, and my fear got the better of me. Stepping back, I shoved my mask off my face and looked away. My eyes welled up from instinctive panic. I reminded myself that nothing could beat me and that this was what I came here to do: face my fears. If I could do this, then I could do anything.

Tim said it was all the more triumphant that I passed the 'losing the mask, recovery, replacement' test, given I did the whole thing one handed with my eyes closed. My other hand was busy holding my nose.

What normally takes 90 minutes, took three hours. Tim earned his money that day. The only tears, post mask flooding, were ones of triumph.

Next would be the open water, ocean water, deep water, call it what you will. It was water that was vast and had lots of things living in it.

The boat full of accomplished divers (and me), sped away from the island, out into the wild blue yonder. I marvelled at the fact it was me on the boat, me about to go into the ocean, me about to scuba dive. Then, my pondering was interrupted. A large fin rose from the water, and the boat slowed. Dolphin? No. Shark? No. Pilot whales! They were majestically rising and falling around the boat. They were breathtaking. I was mesmerised. Still, as we moved away, I quietly hoped they would stay well away from the dive site.

We entered the water off the beach, following the sea floor down. I couldn't see any sharks, good. I couldn't see any large fish with sharp teeth, good. I couldn't see any pilot whales, good. Some level of scuba instinct kicked in, and I marvelled at the underwater world. It was like another planet, and despite my nerves I was lulled into a sense of underwater freedom, floating along as the loud sound of my breathing apparatus rhythmically calmed me.

At the second dive site, Tim announced that we would be jumping straight into the sea off the back of the boat. Really? Jumping into the dark abyss with all this gear on like real dive people? (I am still today most proud of this moment.) Fully geared up, mask on, regulator in, BCD inflated, fins on, tank on (most importantly!), I stood at the back of that speedboat, and holding my regulator in place, I jumped into the one place I had most feared all my life. Did you know you can holler a little scream right through your regulator?

My diving experience was nothing short of extraordinary. I actually did it. I cannot to this day fathom that I swam around under the ocean like that. It goes against everything I thought I could or would ever do.

> **What fear-striking things do you think you could or would never do?**
> **What do you think it would feel like to overcome it?**

It made me realise something about human willpower and about my own willpower. Diving gave me something that I was not intentionally seeking and a realisation I didn't know was there to be had. Aside from it breaking my fear of water and the ocean, it came with a cherry on top. The cherry is this: if you feel fear, if panic rises within you, you can let your thoughts run out of control in ways that do not help you. This can happen in relation to anything in your life, in any situation, for any reason. It is different for each of us.

However, when your life actually depends on it, as is the case with diving, a will power emerges that perhaps you didn't know you had. In diving, you cannot let your fear win. You must breathe calmly. You must move calmly. You must rise slowly. You cannot pop to the surface in a flurry of panic unless you want to burst a lung. Somewhere from deep inside of me came a calm that overrode my fear. It seemed to me that perhaps there is a hidden reserve of willpower inside of everyone that most don't even realise is there.

I thought: *If I can be calm in the face of a fear this strong, because my life depends on it, why can't I muster this willpower in the face of lesser fears,*

others situations and challenges that arise in my life.
The answer, of course, is... I can.

Surprisingly more enlightened than I was before,
you can now call me Scuba B.

Jao

Thai was not a language I had ever been
interested in learning. It's not a language that is easy
to speak, and it certainly doesn't hold the romanticism
of other languages. But then, learning Thai wasn't
really about the language at all. It was about the
interaction with people. It was about taking away with
me some piece of Thailand, and it was about leaving
some piece of me there. It was about helping someone
who might benefit from what language I could offer
them, who hopefully in return would help me. This
was what I had been manifesting back home and since
my arrival in Thailand.

Aside from it being fun, if nothing else, I knew it
would be a challenge to figure out how to convey
information and meaning when the one means of
communication I normally relied on, that I took for
granted, was gone—common understanding, common
language.

We flew through villages one night on our way
home from yoga, and I noticed an art studio on the
roadside, just like every other art studio you could see
on the island. But for some reason, it caught my eye,
and I felt an instinctive need to stop. We had gone
well past it by the time I managed to tell Aaron this—
me shouting from the scooter back seat and him

trying to watch the road and hear me as the wind whistled in our ears.

I yelled, "I think we need to go back. I need to see that place. Maybe there is a painting in there we should buy. I don't know, but let's go back!"

It was some distance from the villa, and Aaron assured me there would be similar paintings in every other art studio closer. But I had a feeling this place was somehow different.

The next day, we returned. This is when we met Jao.

Jao could speak some English. We chatted about his work and the meaning of his paintings, particularly the symbols in several. I explained the type of painting we wanted, and he confirmed he could paint it for us.

He wrote down the details of our request, and he spelled out the word "B U D D H A" letter by letter, saying each letter out loud to himself, slowly and meticulously as he wrote. Then he went to write the next word, "H..." He then looked at me, unsure of himself. Thrusting the pen into my hand, he said, "You do..."

I vocalised the sounds for the word 'head' and helped him with each letter as he spelled the rest of the word.

Then, we shared a few sayings in English and Thai. Just like that, just as I had imagined it would happen: he told me he needed to speak English to customers, and he needed to learn more. He said, "me English no good, little." As we alighted our scooter, he grinned and said, "Lap fan dee." He explained it meant, "Good sleep, good dream." He invited us to come back again and said, "You come, you welcome."

The next day, Jao invited us into the back of his studio (his house). He introduced us to his wife, Sarai, and they shared Thai coffee with us. As we perched on stools, surrounded by palettes, paint pots and canvases, it turned out that Jao was a very good teacher. He loved to chat and shared the meanings of many Thai words, pronunciation and quirks of the language with us.

He patiently, yet firmly, reiterated the words over and over with the correct inflection. I said that one of his paintings was very beautiful, and he insisted I say it in Thai, "Suay maak maak." But I got the inflection wrong; apparently I had spoken too low. Shaking his head, he explained it needed to be higher. He then said it the correct way for me to copy him. I got high-pitched, perhaps even shrill; I didn't care. I just didn't want to get it wrong! Then, he explained to me why this was so important, by way of a short skit. Aaron and I doubled over laughing as we watched Jao's studio turn into a stage.

Looked at the painting, Jao pretended to saunter on by while saying in a high-pitched and happy tone, with upwards inflection, "Suay maak maak!" Got it. Then he walked along and pretended to trip over, stumbling forward. He shook his head with a scowling face and said, with low tone and downwards inflection, "Suay maak maak." The latter apparently means something like bad luck, or at the very least, something not at all good!

When Jao spoke in short sentences or one-word answers, I could understand him. When he started to explain in detail, I would catch glimpses of information, but often, I would get lost in a series of sounds and intonations that were unfamiliar to me. In turn, I realised that it was the same for him. To him, I probably sounded like a gabbling goose.

A loose fitting singlet slung over a lean, wiry frame was perfectly matched with Thai pants; Jao's daily uniform for painting and working in the cloying heat. He was clearly hard working, and I wondered how many fumes he had breathed over the years, as I watched him spray a finishing coat over a large canvas. He was not sun-ravaged like many people on Samui. His skin belied his age; he was youthful looking for 63 years old and had spent many years under the awning of his studio painting in the shade. His wavy hair was the only give away, with its salt and pepper tones. With a small goatee and a cigarette perpetually hanging from his lips, it occurred to me that in some ways he reminded me of my dad.

My dad does not have a goatee, and he does not smoke, but what reminded me of him was Jao's warmth of personality and a generosity that made me feel very much at home, just like my dad.

Over the coming weeks, I discovered that Jao was very a knowledgeable man. He spent many years in Bangkok studying art, before moving to live in Samui where he had been for over two decades. He was responsible for caring for his wife, his grown children and his parents. He explained to me how family responsibilities in Thailand work. It was an interesting glimpse into their culture.

In his dusty roadside studio, he had a shiny laptop. It was at odds with the environment. He said he had never left Thailand, but that he loved to travel the world on the internet. He said, "It dee maak maak" (very good).

A Meeting of Minds

On our next visit, out of nowhere, Jao announced, "People say no speak same same." He meant that people often say there is no common language between cultures and that we all speak different tongues. However, Jao stated that everyone speaks in two common ways. We laughed as he explained that when a baby is born, its cry is its language before it learns to talk. The sound of "wah wah wah" is a common language in all countries—babies communicating the same way across cultural divides. The other common language is laughter. No matter what country you are from, no matter what language you speak, Jao said that we all laugh "ha ha ha ha ha." He imitated this as he leaned back on his chair, laughing, cigarette smoke swirling and his eyes grinning.

On our next visit, I gave Jao and Sarai a butterfly each to thank them for their friendship. Jao looked at me, and with a frown and a raised eyebrow, he exclaimed, "What it?"

Really? I thought my creations had developed from one-winged monsters into real butterflies.

Apparently, I was mistaken. I explained that it was something I had made—one for him and one for Sarai—to say thank you. He yelled to Sarai, who was out back, something in Thai with the word butterfly somewhere in the sentence. I laughed to myself and made a mental note: more practice required for origami.

Over afternoon tea of fresh fruit and juice one day, I realised Sarai was not there. Jao told us that her mother was sick. Sarai had gone back to her village to look after her. From what I could gather, this was somewhere on the mainland, further south. He didn't know when she would be back. This led me on to ask Jao about local healing practices. I asked him, "If sick, you go doctor or hospital?" (I had taken to speaking pigeon English in order to get my message across). It took several attempts to explain what I meant, with a variety of hand gestures and one word prompts. Jao then explained to me, in great detail (from which I grasped bits here and there) all about heart power.

He explained that the body is powerful. "You eat, drink, sleep and have quiet mind. Then, you good power in heart, body well. If body sick, must first close eye and listen to body, and ask, 'why body sick?'"

He went on to explain, "You then sleep more, eat more, drink more water, have more quiet and empty mind of problem. Then, more heart power and body no sick." However, he did momentarily marvel at the "bone scanner" at the hospital as he rubbed his arm. He told us the bone scanner was very useful if you snap your arm (deciphered via the use of charades).

"Yet," he said, "before hospital, heart power come first."

I explained to Jao, as best I could, about energy healing. I asked if he understood. He looked up above himself and then signalled as if he was pulling down the energy into his heart. Then, he touched his heart before he outstretched his arms towards me. He understood. Jao said, "I think also."

As it turned out, Jao had much more to teach me than merely how to speak Thai. He went on to tell me that to have strong heart power, I needed to empty my mind. "Very important."

"No problem. No carry problem in mind. No tell everyone problem. No think about problem. No wake in night with problem." Instead, he suggested, "Have problem. Quiet mind. Fix problem. Empty mind. Have good heart power."

He changed the subject abruptly. "You speak happy, other people speak happy you, only good things. You speak problem, bad things, other people speak bad and more problem."

It was clear that we shared the same beliefs—that you attract back to yourself whatever you put out. Positive thinking, feeling and action create more of the same and vice versa.

He said sometimes that he had problems and that he thought those problems might have come from his past. He looked at me and said, "You understand, past time?" He pointed over his shoulder as if referring to some time ago. He was referring to past lives. I nodded, yes. I asked, "Karma?" He said, "Yes, I think too. Buddha says." He pointed to a painting of Buddha next to us.

Jao's world was a smiling and calm one. All the questions about life and all the seeming confusion in the world appeared to be so simply explained by him. He went on to say, "You see everything, concentrating all time, you walking see things, you driving see things, you painting, you working, you see people, you hear talking good things and bad things... it all nothing. It empty. No problem. No carry around things in mind. Just empty." I sort of understood, but I was a little lost as to where this was all leading.

He could see my confusion and started to use hand signals to explain himself, but I couldn't make out what he was trying to convey. He moved his hands coming down from above, through his body and then pushed his hands down to the ground. He masterfully adjusted the cigarette hanging from his lips, swiped his hair from his eyes, pulled out his laptop and typed in Thai, punching the keyboard with one finger—the beauty of Google Translation.

We were sitting huddled together on the bench in front of his studio. I watched as the website translated to English...

"Everything returns to dust."

I looked at him, and he nodded at me. "Yes? You understand?"

Something hit a nerve in me. He stared me right in the eye, like it was important for me to know and understand this. He said, "No problem, B. All empty. You come, you smile, you happy, you go."

There was freedom in that knowledge. Strangely, I felt tears inside me. I kept them hidden. Maybe they were tears of relief.

Days later, I read an article in a magazine stating that Buddhism teaches that we come from nothing and return to nothing.

As we were getting ready to leave that day, Jao asked us to come back for dinner the following week, pointing to his truck. "You come. We go truck, fish market." He wanted to cook for us. As we left, I wondered when Sarai would be back, and if Jao would be okay without her. Waving goodbye, I resisted my urge to worry about others, and I saw clearly that there was no problem there for me to fix.

Makruk Showdown

When we returned, Sarai was back, and her mother was well again. That day, Jao was busy finishing paintings for other people, and we didn't want to hold him up. However, he insisted that we stay and sit with him while he had a cigarette. He shepherded me towards the bench seat. "We talk, we talk," he said.

This brief chat ended up spanning hours, once Aaron and Jao discovered that they both play chess. Jao pulled out his chess pieces, and they played on the roadside table. Jao indicated that he played "little" and "no good". Aaron is a chess fiend. This, I anticipated, was going to be interesting. I felt sorry for Jao, expecting Aaron to run rings around him. However, within two moves, Jao attempted to explain that Aaron's rules were not rules in Thailand. I laughed and wondered to myself if these Thailand rules were in fact just Jao's rules!

However, as the saying goes, "When in Rome..." The playing field had just been evened. Aaron had to play by new rules. I later discovered that the rules that Jao referred to were, in fact, for Makruk (Thai Chess).

I saw Aaron's brow furrow as the game commenced, and Jao cunningly watched his expression. It was with much joy that I sat side by side with my new friend and watched him explain to Aaron which pieces could move which ways, and which pieces could 'eat' other pieces.

Aaron started to reply in turn, "So this one can eat this one?"

This was the most amusing game of chess I had ever seen. There were horses eating pawns and castles eating bishops.

Jao turned into a different person when playing chess. He shocked me each time with his very definitive action, as he slammed down each chess piece he moved. The peaceful, Zen version of Jao had turned into the Demon of Makruk.

The two of them ended up with just their Kings and one Horse each left. They called it a draw, and I winked at Jao. "Jao, you tell us you no good! No...you dee maak maak!"

Feasting with Friends

The week before we were due to leave, we had dinner with Jao and Sarai. We wondered why Jao had told us to be there at 4pm when the fish market was not too far away, but we soon discovered why. It was because Jao took a *long* time to decide what to buy! We went around and around and around the fish market assessing all the options, haggling over prices. Finally, we left with a whole fish, squid, prawns, fish pieces, crabs, and beef fillet, along with fifteen different types of vegetables.

We stopped to buy drinks at the 7-11. Due to all the hot yoga, I hadn't had any alcohol since well before we left New Zealand. That seemed very wrong, considering we were lulling on a tropical island! I quietly wondered how many drinks it would take before I would be asleep or passed out. Aaron helped Jao start the barbeque, and Jao explained that this would be, "Very good party." He said that we should "eat slow" and "stay long time." He explained that he would have to paint during the evening because a customer would be coming the next day to get a painting.

As it turned out, there was no painting, not while we were there at least. Jao told us that he and Sarai, "No party often—no drink and relax. This dee maak maak." He drank many beers and told us often that he loved the fun time with us.

Sarai cooked a meal that exceeded the flavour and quality of any restaurant we had been to in Thailand. It got late, and many drinks were consumed. We were all sitting shoulder to shoulder around the little table, swaying to the music and laughing. A friend of Jao and Sarai walked past the studio. She smiled and waved. Jao waited a moment until she had passed, and then looked at Aaron with a sly grin and said, "Man too!"

Jao started crooning to the music "...love you more than I can say..."[37] He was sitting between Sarai and Aaron, with his arms around their shoulders. He looked at them and pointed at me. He said to me, "Dee maak maak, more than I can say."

He was very happy, and his happiness was contagious.

I left that night with an experience not to be forgotten, with people that would never be forgotten.

The Painting

My new painting was glorious. It was a painting, yes, but specifically, a painting by Jao. It was a treasure. I knew that I would miss Jao dearly when it was time for us to leave, but I would leave with the knowledge that an empty mind and strong heart power would do me well in life.

> *With an open mind and heart, you can learn things in the most unexpected places, from the most unexpected people.*

I left Samui the most clear-headed, calm and happy version of myself I have *ever* known. It was all preparing me for...

Chapter 24

One Night in Bangkok

Well, actually it was 50 nights in Thonburi, but now you're humming that catchy tune "One Night in Bangkok", we're all in the mood to switch from Samui easy days and nights to city chaos.

Think non-existent road rules, overpasses, underpasses, skyscrapers, low rises, people riding four astride one motorbike, cars overtaking in the face of oncoming buses, shopping malls and apartment blocks as high and far as the eye can see, every conceivable form of entertainment, fumes, heat, smog, monks, temples, tourists, locals, yoga, tai chi, parks, rivers, hawker markets, mansions, shacks and... me. Dorothy was a very long way from Kansas now.

We hit Bangkok, known as the City of Angels, during rush hour with our taxi snaking its way slowly across the city. Up and down one-way streets, around road works and finally (two hours later) we arrived at our abode. I had sensory overload. Hot, bothered and feeling unsure, I dumped my bags and tried not to react badly to fact that Samui was now a memory—a memory that didn't much comfort me when I looked out the window at the unfamiliar territory outside.

Setting Me Free

Before I left New Zealand, I had an experience that acted like a signpost as to why I was going to Thonburi. At the time, I was perplexed and uneasy about this experience. It was easier to let it pass and see what happened when I actually got there. However, it seems I must now share this with you. It will require a somewhat detailed flashback.

In the lead up to our departure, Aaron pointed out to me that I was being my obsessive self, ensuring all the 'i's were dotted and 't's were crossed. As usual, I set rules around everything. Not only did I think it was necessary to follow all my own self-imposed rules, but I also had to follow everyone else's rules to the letter—be it my parents, my employer, at school, at University or the law. With regards to rules, you name it, and I followed it. I made sure I was the model citizen to the point of being paranoid and ridiculous. Never park one minute over your paid parking time. Never litter (very good rule). Never break a commitment. Never miss a deadline. Never turn up late for work. Never break the law. This is how I have lived my life and not in a relaxed way, but in a 'toe the line, you better be careful to obey authority' sort of way.

I thought this was what everyone did: obeying with intensity. Until I realised that I had irrational fear of breaking rules and an irrational fear of authority. During the ThetaHealing™ course, Janine had asked for a volunteer for a belief healing. *Great,* I thought, *I'm sure I have a truckload of negative beliefs and here is someone willing to resolve one for me.* I put my hand up.

As a starting point, Janine had suggested I look at something in life that made me uncomfortable. Out of nowhere came tumbling a list of things that had bugged me all my life. I honestly had not thought about this in any detail before, but the second she asked me, it was like my mind zoomed in. It all came pouring out. So I shared with her and, uncomfortably, with the observing course participants.

As far back as five years old, I didn't like being around groups of people I didn't know. I didn't like going places that I didn't know. I didn't like putting myself in situations that I couldn't control. I felt unsafe, and new people felt unpredictable. New places were unfamiliar. New situations were uncertain. None of this was good. Something bad could happen. Of course, this was completely illogical, and I'd always known that. However, it's not easy to rationalise a fear. This was a fear I couldn't explain. It had faded somewhat over time, but it still manifested in certain areas of my life.

When Janine asked me questions, I started to spill the beans on things I had not articulated to anyone before or myself really. I had just accepted it was part of who I was. Although my life had been full of happiness and great experiences growing up, these following perceptions framed much of how I felt inside.

I did not like going to school. I was afraid of messing up, being told off and being punished. I was afraid of other children. I avoided going to inter-school events. When I first started school, I remember being asked by my teacher to carry a message to the 'big kids' class and thinking I would rather die than do that.

I did not like high school. I often felt intimidated by my surroundings and other people. It all seemed unpredictable and unsafe. I did not like school camps. I avoided any situation that put me in the middle of people I didn't know and trust. If I went to parties, I thought about who would be there and I usually had a niggling nervousness about going.

I did not like University. I was afraid of being on my own in large groups of people that I didn't know. I didn't like it when my class schedule changed, meaning new lecture room locations, new lecturers and new people in the class.

I don't hate many things, but it is no understatement to say I hated the Halls of Residence at University. I was surrounded by unfamiliar people and the tiny shoebox bedroom felt claustrophobic and suffocating. I couldn't sleep. I didn't go to meals in the communal dining hall. At the risk of being the laughing stock of people who know me, I will admit that after weekends at home in the countryside when my parents drove me back to the city, I used to cry when I was dropped off—not because, at 18 years old, I was sad to say goodbye to my parents, but because I didn't want to be 'left there'. It got so bad I had to move out because I was losing weight and couldn't settle.

As a young adult, I didn't find new people and new environments so difficult. I suppose I gained confidence over time. However, I know I always engineered things so that I would be around people I knew and trusted, and I avoided parties or group situations where I didn't know the people or the place. I adjusted to the world around me, but I remained on guard, ready to protect myself.

Within minutes, Janine identified the cause. One belief had created all of this. She showed us how to remove the root of this recurring issue. When I questioned her as to why I was like this, she simply said to me, "There is a good reason you fear institutions." This was accompanied by a knowing look. Without a thought, these words came out of my mouth, "It's like I was taken away somewhere against my will or left somewhere by people I trusted. This is what happened, isn't it?"

This was a past life hangover—a very real fear created from some previous experience, carrying through at a deep level. She made it clear that it did not serve me to go into the details of this.

Everything made sense in an instant—my fear of these places, imposing places, institutions of a type. I actually didn't care to know the details of what Janine was referring to, though it explained a lot to me about why, since as young as I could remember, I had felt that way.

The Incident

When Aaron pointed out my incessant and ridiculous need to obey rules and my fear of any form of authority, I saw clearly that I had been adhering to things like my life depended on it. I wondered: *Perhaps in a past life my life actually did depend on it, perhaps in some institution where I was left or taken to.*

I'm not interested in delving into the past. I only care for the present and the future. But, you may be wondering how I put two and two together and ended up with five. You may be thinking how on earth this all added up. My answer: it resonated in me, in a way I cannot put into words.

Prior to coming to Thailand, I dug down and found as many negative beliefs as I could and moved them. In order for you to come with me on the rest of this journey, I have to tell you what the bottom belief was. The root cause of all this fuss and bother was a deeply held belief of being 'forgotten and unloved'. This did not resonate with me in the least on a conscious level, yet something triggered in me when the belief healing was done.

Not long after freeing myself from a lifetime of institution and authority fearing baggage, an incident occurred. I call it 'The Incident,' because it was not one of the fun, exciting signals that I revel in and love to share. It was a signal that scared the living daylights out of me.

I was in a taxi on the way to the airport to travel for work. It was not long after the abovementioned healing. I was talking on my cell phone when I heard:

"Open the magazine."

In response, I thought: *I'm busy here. I'm talking on the phone. I have a flight to catch. I don't have time for this. I don't have time to read magazines!*

I heard again: "Open the magazine."

Sitting in the seat pouch in front of me was a travel magazine. I knew this was going to be about Thailand; it had to be. I ended my call and flicked through the magazine. Sure enough, an article on Bangkok. I was literally minutes from the airport and furiously reading through the article trying to figure out what I needed to get from this. Was this *the* signal I had been waiting for?

The article was a traveller's account of a bicycle tour around Bangkok. *Ghastly*, I thought, *cycling with all the fumes and that crazy traffic, I'll be lucky to make it out alive!* Then, I saw what I was meant to see. They cycled across the Chao Phraya River to the west side... to Thonburi. And then... to an orphanage. Next to the article was a tiny photo of children sleeping on the floor, lined up perfectly in little rows. And, instinctively, I began to cry. I tried really, really hard not to, but I couldn't stop it. I leaned forward to hide my head so that the taxi driver couldn't see me.

I didn't think poor children. I didn't think anything. I just cried and felt very uneasy.

I can't really explain it. Sure, I logically and emotionally think it's extremely saddening that children are abandoned or left without parents, but this subject doesn't consciously upset me to the point of tears. Then, my old belief came to mind: forgotten and unloved. That didn't help the situation. It felt haunting.

Is this a signal of what I need to do in Thonburi? Or is this a signal of what happened to me in a past life? Was I left at or taken to a place like this?

I just wanted to know why the heck I had to go to Thonburi.

As we pulled into the terminal, I shoved the magazine in the seat pocket and gathered my bags. I was thinking to myself: *I can't go there. I can't even look at that article and not cry; I will be overwhelmed. It can't help me to go there. They don't need me. They have people looking after them, so it can't be about that. Like they really need some crazy westerner turning up and sobbing in the middle of their orphanage! Who's that going to help?!*

Could it have possibly been that going to Thonburi was about going to an orphanage to fully bring about my own healing, for something upsetting that I didn't even know was within me? Perhaps I needed to go to such an environment—an institution that I associated with 'forgotten and unloved'—to face that fear and learn to be with it, to rid myself of something underpinning a raft of irrational fears in this life. I thought: *But I've done that belief healing, so is this really necessary?!*

Waiting for my flight, I called trusty Charlotte. She could tell something was wrong. I relayed the story: taxi, hearing the signal, magazine, reading, right up to: "...and then they went to an orphanage..."

That was the last thing to escape my mouth before I couldn't say anymore. I couldn't because I was quietly crying, sitting in the middle of a café, in the middle of a busy airport, surrounded by normal people going about their happy Monday mornings. It was official: I had lost the plot! I didn't even know why I was crying for heaven's sake! This was not shedding one tear for the plight of the children; this was 'someone get me a box of tissues' sobbing business. I couldn't stop myself, and I couldn't speak.

I had to remind myself that I was a normal person, with normal relationships, with great communication skills, and a successful career. I was not this sobbing weirdo I seemed to have turned into.

Regaining my composure, I told Charlotte I thought it was a signal pointing me towards the reason I was going to Thonburi—a direction I very much did *not* want to go in.

Her wisdom was as priceless as always. "Let it go. It's not your reality, but it is reality for some people. Perhaps the challenge is this: can you be with it? Can you be around it? Can you be with their experience of it? Can you be with their suffering, their life circumstances, and do so knowing it is not your own and you do not need to fix it?"

Ah, more of this not needing to fix things. Dammit. I don't want to see the reality of forgotten children—not because it's an unsavoury flavour in my mouth or 'okay if I must go I will', but instead it is a deep down uncomfortable truth: I really don't want to go there.

I hate to admit I said this to Charlotte, but I did. I felt like a westerner going to an orphanage in a place like that was a bit cliché, and how could I possibly help children by turning up and then leaving again? They don't need more people leaving them.

Still, I could sense that my upset was not about the children; it was like a part of me was triggering some hurt related to their situation. Something hit a raw and hidden nerve. Perhaps people that visit orphanages go because they are drawn to. Perhaps they followed their own signals to go.

And so all my many questions continued and remained unanswered.

Will I go there to help in some way? Will I go there to do energy healing for children? Will I go to volunteer? Is this why Thonburi came to me in the middle of the night? Can I make a difference there? Will the difference be for myself or for them? Or both?

As I sat on the plane returning home later that day, I couldn't recreate that emotion; it didn't even upset me to think about it again. That upset was gone. It was like it came out of some hidden cave deep inside me and reared its head before crawling back to the dark recesses. I was left only with confusion and uneasiness. This was not helped when the man next to me started chatting and proceeded to pull out his camera and show me photos of his trip around Asia. A picture of young monks draped in saffron robes caught my eye. I tried not to look shocked when the man started telling me that orphaned children in these countries often end up becoming monks, taken in by the monasteries. My mind was going into signal interpreting overdrive.

Although I had no answers at the time, one thing I did know for sure, and always had, was that I had an inability to be around other people's suffering, just like I had an inability be around other people's problems. Even though I wanted to fix suffering when I saw it, sometimes you just can't fix it. Sometimes it is simply the other person's journey, not yours.

The signals became repetitive, following me all the way to Samui. At the end of my dive course, the owner of the dive centre invited me to a charity event that weekend.

I asked, "What is the charity you are raising money for?"

"An orphanage."

"Where?"

"Just outside Bangkok."

Crying Thomas

Following 'The Incident', all of a sudden I could see how 'forgotten and unloved' had played out all my life. I couldn't bear to see anyone feeling ostracised, alone or unloved.

I recalled a situation from last summer. I was standing on the beach early one morning, working up the courage to dip my toes in. I heard noise down the other end of the beach. There was no one else around, apart from a little boy looking out at the sea and crying. I ran down that beach to the crying child, in my togs no less. I live by the rule that no woman should run in togs unless they are Pamela Anderson off *Baywatch*. You see this proves how intensely I felt when I heard his cries; it was enough to break this rule! Yes, I can hear you asking now, "You broke a rule?"

As it turned out, Thomas's grandad had just rowed out to their boat, and his older brother had snuck back to their bach, leaving Thomas stranded on the beach.

I have fond memories of watching *The Littlest Hobo* as a child. It was a TV programme about a superhero dog that would always save the day. Only one episode sticks in my mind. A baby was left alone in a house, and the house was on fire. Of course the dog ran through the burning house and rescued the baby from its room. I don't remember the dog, but I do vividly remember wondering why on earth they left the baby alone!

Chapter 25

Fish out of Water

I was a bit disoriented for the first 24 hours in Thonburi, before full-blown culture shock took a hold of me. I had theoretically known what to expect, but I had mistaken how hard it would be to go from Samui to Bangkok, how hard it would be to transition to life in Bangkok, and to do so knowing that I would be there for nearly two months.

When you're faced with being somewhere you don't really want to be, for a considerable amount of time, with no certain answer as to why you are there, questions start eating away at you. The anticipation and excitement started to fade. Reality sunk in.

Of your own choosing, would you rather be in your version of heaven on earth, or would you choose to put yourself in a version of your own nightmare?

For a few moments, I considered turning around and going back to Samui—to my version of heaven. However, forfeiting the deposit and prepaid apartment rent, along with the fact I'd received a signal to go there, was enough to make me stay put. This in itself made me feel like I had no control. I was trapped, and worst of all, I had trapped myself.

I pushed all this down as we orientated ourselves. We quickly realised we were well beyond the reach of the underground and Sky Train systems. Working out how to cross ten lanes of never ending traffic, with no pedestrian lights and seemingly few road rules, added to the list of helpful distractions.

In the area we were living, for the most part no one spoke English, and nothing was written in English. Ordering food became a game. Aaron played 'pin the tail on the donkey', closing his eyes and putting his finger on a menu item. Whatever arrived on his plate, he ate.

This area was not frequented by tourists it seemed, so why would English be needed? Completely fair. The taxi driver informed us that's why locals like living in Thonburi: not many, if any, tourists. I had seen one other farang, and I was convinced there must have been one million people living in our district alone. I read online that it was more like 600,000 in the Thonburi area. Suffice to say, it's a lot of people in relation to the geographic size.

The apartment I booked was not quite what I was expecting. It was in the general sphere, just a stripped back, older and sanitised version of it. The most striking feature was the cube-like feeling, white walls and white shiny linoleum floor—much like a hospital room. Ah, the beauty of real estate photography: wide angled, soft lenses and properties dressed for photos. I particularly liked the window views inserted using Photoshop. Despite the fact our accommodation was missing all the basic essentials beyond bed, couch, table and TV, I knew that we could buy everything else we needed, and I was eternally grateful it was clean.

When we had first landed in Bangkok, and I gazed directly at the sun, thanks to the thick haze of smog protecting my eyes, I wondered if I'd be able to maintain my gift from Samui: my 'once in a lifetime' tan. Looking at the apartment balcony, protruding 60cm out, Aaron laughed, "Can't wait to see you sunbathing, B!" This evoked a small smile in week one and also cemented my lament.

After an evening wandering around in the humid chaos that was life outside our apartment building, we returned. I sat and catastrophised about the prospect of being there alone and felt selfish for doing so. For anyone else coming to Bangkok with the keys to our apartment and ten days of peace and quiet, I was sure they'd be excited and full of the adventure ahead. I felt trapped in the white box, in a city I didn't know, surrounded by people I didn't know, feeling unsafe and unsure. The anticipation of alone was looming, and this time, there was nothing I could do about it.

Aaron watched me spin about this. He said, "You can come to the United Kingdom with me if you really want to."

But I knew that there was no room in the budget to go, so I couldn't. I also had to know why I was there. If I left, I would never find out, and I knew that I couldn't live with that lingering question.

During meditation I asked, "Is this where I am meant to be?"

The answer was: "Yes."

I gave up pretending that I was okay, and Aaron watched while the worry inside of me boiled and soon spilled over. Hot tears were spitting out, tears that told a story that went something like this: *How can I live here for two months? But mostly, how can I be here alone? I am afraid and confused. Why did I listen to the damn signal? Please tell me why I am here!*

Seeing my red swollen eyes, Aaron exclaimed, "Do I need to stage an intervention? Where is that letter?!" He tried to reason with me that everything was fine, that we'd only just arrived, and that it would take some time to get used to. Then he resorted to suggesting alternatives, such as, "You can always go home," and, "How about you check into a hotel in the central city while I'm gone?"

All of a sudden I was full of answers. "I can't go home! I was guided here! We can't afford a hotel. We've already paid for this place." My normally sane self, full of positivity, possibility and options, was lost in the jungle. It was 3am at home, so I couldn't call Charlotte or Mum. The reality was that I knew what they would tell me: the same thing that my patient husband was telling me.

I could see it written on his face: he was frustrated that I wouldn't or couldn't see that this is not that big of a deal... to other people at least. I was in full breakdown mode, and his words sounded like something off in the distance, spoken by someone who didn't know what I was going through. It was pretty clear to me that I was in this alone. He was going to leave me, and no one was going to live this for me. No one was going to help me through this. I had to help myself.

My interpretation of being there without him was that I was being *left*. Logically, I knew that he was not leaving me anywhere. He was going somewhere, and I had chosen to stay. Still, that didn't stop the ridiculous, irrational fear rising within me. It seemed my emotions, fears and subconscious overrode all logic.

I don't mind being alone in New Zealand; in fact, I quite enjoy time alone. I'm certain I could have quite happily been alone in Samui too, but not in Thonburi. I definitely didn't want to be alone there.

This place has done this to me. It's this place's fault! This place has turned me into a psychotic crying farang!

The Cause

I believe we all have areas for development. My reaction to having my buttons pushed is to get upset in this way. For others, they might withdraw within themselves, or they might get angry or aggressive. They might bury it and carry on like nothing is wrong, or they might turn to humour to belittle the fact that anything is actually wrong.

What things in life push you beyond logic?
What types of situations or people
push your buttons?
What are your coping techniques?

No matter what the technique is for coping, the lesson to learn here is always the same. If you react and then carry on like nothing happened, you are ignoring the cause. The cause is not the external stimulus. The cause is within you. The cause will just wait for the next opportunity to come back and visit you, to come back to push your buttons again...and again and again.

I wondered: *What could my life be like if I face the cause?* I didn't want to spend my life avoiding, indeed at times running away from, circumstances that pushed my buttons. I didn't want this to beat me. I wanted to learn to be a different way, but I had no idea how.

All There is to Get

Unsure of how to drag myself out of this downward spiral, I attempted a calm meditation and asked my spirit guides to be with me to help me through. I asked for signals to show me the way.

Lying down to sleep, I silently whispered to whoever was up there listening, "Aaron is leaving. I'm afraid. No one here knows me. I will navigate my way around, and no one will know any different as to where I am or if I'm okay. I don't want to do this. I don't feel safe. Please help me."

The next morning, still unsettled, I emailed Charlotte in the hope that she would give me the much needed directions from Junglemania back to RiverCentral.

Pinch Me

*****

Hi Charlotte,

I am feeling very unsure and teary, in fact near on petrified about Aaron going away and leaving me. It is a mix of the reality of life in Thonburi and being in an area where I stand out like a sore thumb. Despite my desire to physically blend in, my tan is simply not that good. People stare at us constantly. I do not feel comfortable being out and about on my own, certainly not at night.

I don't know why I'm here, and most of me wishes that I wasn't. I couldn't stop crying last night, and I tried to do it quietly so Aaron wouldn't think I was a total baby!

Please can you tell me something positive, as I'm only just keeping tears at bay. I know I was guided to come here, but when I look out the window at this vast city stretched before me, I wonder how on earth will I find what I came here to find?

I miss you.

B

*****

Charlotte reminded me of what I already knew, logically, during a time when logic had escaped me. There was nothing for me to try to find. Just being there was enough. The signals would find me. They always did.

She pointed out something that was comically obvious to her; something that I could not see at all for the tears had blurred my vision.

*****

B,

Have you considered that how you are feeling now is exactly WHY you were guided to be there? That being with this level of fear and facing it (which isn't the same as not having the feeling anymore) is the WHOLE reason? That there may not be any more than this? That you don't have to be skipping down the road to find your next signal? That you may have thought you had something to do like find an orphanage, but maybe you don't?

Maybe you are there to face the fact that you somehow feel abandoned, trapped—indeed, orphaned—when in situations completely foreign to you, when faced with being alone, and when it feels impossible to avoid the situation you find yourself in? Perhaps this is a lesson you must learn, one that is important for your future, a lesson the Energy Source couldn't get you to face in Wellington, or in Waiheke, or even in Koh Samui, but it can guide you as you face it in Thonburi, alone, finally.

Love, C

*****

Perhaps none of us are here to adventure out in the external world to find some big goal to achieve or some big external experience to have. Maybe we are all here to find and face the big things *inside* ourselves.

You may not understand what I was experiencing, just like I wouldn't necessarily know or understand whatever your version of this may be. Perhaps by identifying and overcoming these things within ourselves, we will end up being stronger, more peaceful and more capable versions of ourselves. Perhaps we will only face these 'things' if we put ourselves in a place where they can reveal themselves to us.

There will be times in my life, I am sure, when I am left alone. People will come and go. People will die. People will leave me. I may travel on my own. I may get lost (literally and metaphorically). This skill of learning to be capable by myself, and living without reliance on anyone for assistance, was something I needed to learn first-hand.

If I had been in a cosy, homely apartment in the midst of modern Bangkok central, I wouldn't have been experiencing this. Maybe I needed to be out in Thonburi, feeling more isolated, more uncomfortable, more farang, more unsure and more unsafe.

The Little Girl

I sat on the tiles of our balcony at dusk with my knees tucked up under my chin, staring out at the unfamiliar territory. With the white walled and linoleum floored cubicle behind me and the wrought iron bars of the balustrade before me, I realised quite ludicrously that everything about the experience (the environment, the city, the district, the apartment, the impending situation with me alone...) could not have been more cleverly and carefully engineered by the Energy Source. Cogs had clicked slowly into place to bring it about in my life, to create that very reaction in me. By following the signals, I had found what sat undiscovered deep down. All the success and confidence on the surface was just a mask for what was beneath. To put this in perspective, I would have rather gone diving again, down deeper, for longer, with bigger and scarier fish, than stay there alone.

One week had passed. I wondered what days 8 – 50 would bring. I sensed my confusion was leading me towards a breakthrough. I realised: *When pain has a purpose, it feels more acceptable.*

My earlier cries of, "Why am I in this damn place? God only knows why I'm here! I wish I'd never left Samui!" were just echoes that lingered in my ears, and I wondered who that defeatist with all the tears was. She was just a scared little girl with nowhere to hide, no one to turn to, and no one to help her face what lay ahead.

When she felt like running away, she knew in the back of her mind that leaving was not an option. Leaving would be shutting the door on a path paved ahead, where great things might lie. Leaving would only tell the Energy Source, "I heard your message about Thonburi, and I don't like it. I'm done with this way of living." She knew very well that running away would not help her grow and expand, as unsettling and fear-striking as it might be. Like it or not, she knew that Thonburi was her place to breakdown, presumably (she trusted) in order to breakthrough.

Looking beyond the iron balustrades on that dark night, rain clouds threatened during a season of hot days and monsoon evenings. The dark alley below me was littered with carts, shacks, and motorbikes. The overpass nearby sent noise and fume pollution into the air. Smoke and steam rose off the nearby Soi where various unknown food items seared on sticks over hot coals. I breathed it all in, and I said to the little girl, "Don't worry. Remember what Dad told us: worry is wasted energy. I'm sure we'll be just fine."

Perhaps Charlotte was right. Maybe there was no orphanage or orphans to meet, no connection to be made between my time in Thonburi and how I reacted to that magazine article. Perhaps that incident simply showed me some hurt that was hiding from me. Maybe the scared little girl inside was the only one that I was meant to meet. I had to be in Thonburi for her to come out, for me to see her and to see how upset she was. *Feeling* alone and abandoned does not mean you are actually alone or that you are actually abandoned. Reality comes down to your perception.

Adjusting

I knew that it was time to face reality. Everything was just as it should be. The way in which I had been led to Thonburi was no mistake.

For some calm, I headed to a Buddhist Centre holding meditation classes in English, confident that it would give me new tools to apply while Aaron was away. I wanted to spend that alone time in any other way except hiding in the white apartment box, awaiting his return.

Enter Yut the teacher. He said things that mirrored what Jao had already told me—things that struck a chord. "Meditation is a way to know your true self. All you need to know is within yourself, seeking it externally in the world will only take you so far. You need to look within."

With a breeze floating through the temple window and a fountain trickling water beyond, Yut also said, "We are all alone. We all face our own challenges alone." I was nodding along, and I could feel it welling inside me. He continued, "As we become more enlightened, as we know ourselves more, truly anything is possible. When you connect to your true self, then life is limitless and anything you can possibly imagine can be your reality."

I was mesmerised. The girl next to me was staring at Yut with a frown, and then she stared at me, then back at Yut—like we had lost the plot. She asked several very sensible questions seeking verification on the authenticity of his statements. He was a bit like Yoda from *Star Wars*: simple answers, serene smiles and knowing nods.

Rescue From Self-Pity

As you can see, I was not alone in rescuing myself from self-pity. I did not come to these conclusions about my situation unaided.

If you seemingly have no one, thinking you are completely alone, there is *always* someone. Even a stranger may be willing to be there for you.

When I finally saw sense and realised Aaron, Charlotte and Yut were right, I also knew it was only their words that would help me. Not a single one of them would be with me over the ten days. I thought to myself: *In a city this big, surely I am not all alone. Surely there is someone.*

The next thing I knew, I met a Thai man named Nayan. Working in our apartment building, I soon discovered that Nayan used to live New Zealand! I had randomly selected this apartment from hundreds, and I had picked just the right one. When he learned that Aaron was going away, he gave me his phone number in case I needed anything. He then proceeded to translate all my favourite food from English to Thai on paper, so that I could present this to nearby eateries rather than playing pin the tail on the menu.

In my continuing efforts to drag myself off the riverbank, I considered what I couldn't change and what I could. I couldn't (or more accurately wouldn't) change the fact I was in Thonburi, but I could change how I felt about it. I could do things that I knew would make me feel better.

And so I announced, "I cannot live in this white box for one minute longer without feeling like I'm in hospital."

I yanked Jao's painting out of the carry tube and laid it out on the floor. With my wallet and USB stick in hand, I marched out of the building in the hopes of finding what I needed. Prepared to blow my daily budget in order to retain my sanity, I returned with fresh flowers, a portable DVD player (I reasoned this was an investment), cellotape and A4 sized photos of Cash, our garden and home. I put the photos up all over the apartment and hung Jao's painting amateurishly using cellotape around the corners. I put flowers on my newly adopted writing table. My bright pink and blue sarongs, which served no purpose in the middle of the city, formed colourful additions as a couch throw and bed cover. The DVD player solved my TV foreign language dilemma.

Next came yoga. Yoga in Samui was in English. Yoga in Thonburi was not. I contorted my body as I peered out between my legs to observe and mimic what was happening in the rest of the class. This made not falling over, as I precariously stood on one leg, very difficult. What is funnier than a sweaty farang who can't understand what is being said? A sweaty farang, who then loses her balance and falls over in class, trying not to take out the row of yogis like a game of dominos.

At one point I thought I heard the yoga teacher say 'option', perhaps suggesting a beginner's choice of a yoga move versus a more advanced option. He put his leg in some odd position and said 'option' while smiling directly at me. He then put his leg in a slightly less contorted version of the same position and said 'option' again. I wish I had heard him say option during the next move: when he put his leg behind, up and over his arm and hoisted it onto his shoulder. I stifled my laughter as he looked at me and nodded with a smile, as if to say, "Your turn." I was ecstatic just to get my leg at nearly 90 degrees to the floor, but it appeared that wasn't quite enough. With gusto, he nimbly leapt off the raised platform to 'assist' me.

Arm pushed further under leg. Head under leg and past armpit. Leg resting over shoulder. Really? Try this at home, and you'll see what I mean! Some things, no matter how hard I push, are just not going over my shoulder. My leg is one of them. Well, I had approximately 42 more days to master that one.

Standing Out

I started to make up stories about why the locals were staring at me. Aside from the fact it must have been amusing to watch a farang attempting to get a taxi or tuk tuk to the one place they didn't want to go (Thonburi, with all its traffic congestion), people seemed to stare every minute of the time I was outside of the apartment. Old people, young people, men, women, children—they were staring and smiling, staring and not smiling, staring and laughing. I knew I was different, but after a few days of the non-stop staring, it started to wear thin. I first became a little paranoid, then frustrated, and then overly sensitive.

Do I have food on my face? Are my clothes inappropriate? Do I look unhappy? Do I look ungrateful? Do I look mean? Do I look too happy? How the heck can I blend in?

A group of women in the public toilets laughed and one pointed at me as I raced past. I later discovered why they were laughing. I assumed it was because they knew I was rushing towards a toilet cubicle, busting to go, and was going to discover a hole in the ground and no toilet paper. I cursed myself for forgetting to carry my own toilet paper—a mental note that I had made to myself before, but seemingly forgot. Desperate to pee, tired, hot and laughed at, I could have turned around and run out of the toilets, but there was a high potential that I might have peed my pants in pursuit of an actual upright toilet that had actual toilet paper! That would certainly have provided for more opportunity for staring. Alternatively, I could squat, 'go' and shake what my mama gave me. I went for the latter. Aaron wondered what could possibly have happened in the toilets to make me so morose. I exclaimed, "I do not want to talk about it."

After yet more staring, pointing and laughing incidents, I decided that I could either let it get to me, or I could put my chin up and get on with it. Of course, people would stare. I was different, and I was out of place. Sure, I had no idea what people were saying to me or about me. Perhaps they were laughing at my glorious ignorance. Perhaps it actually had nothing to do with me, and I was being paranoid. For whatever reason, I learned something I had never truly known before: being different is not easy. Being different attracts attention, and sometimes it's not very pleasant.

I had heavy, coke bottle glasses with thick metal frames when I was five. "Four eyes, four eyes," I was taunted. As I laid in yoga class one evening, trying to be Zen and forgetting about the two women who had just pointed and laughed at me outside the classroom,

I felt like an ostracised five year old with bad glasses. I realised that people who are born different or who choose a different life to the norm must find it quite hard at times. Standing out comes with its challenges.

New Things I Can't Fix

Although I was quickly assimilating to life in Thonburi, there were some things I hoped I would never get used to.

I hoped I would never get used to the sight of the family of ten who lived on the corner of our Soi under the veranda of an abandoned building: an old woman, a baby and an assembly of others.

I hoped I would never get used to the sight of the old man without any clothes who slept on the overbridge nearby. He was so dirty that it was hard to tell he was there; he blended with the filthy pavement.

I hoped I would never get used to the man who sat on the pile of rubbish bags outside our local market, eating whatever he could find in the bags, day in and day out.

What I previously might have considered to be 'problems' in my life could no longer find space in my mind to register. As I walked past these people I wanted to avert my gaze. But instead I looked. I looked to see the reality of what life is like for some people, and I looked to acknowledge that it exists.

Chapter 26

240 Hours Alone

It was time for Aaron to leave, but he had to say it before he left: "I don't know how many more signals about orphanages you want, but don't you think it's time you find out why? Why don't you just go to one and find out what this is all about?"

He received a furious response. "No, I don't want to! It's not like I've had a really clear signal to actually physically go to one, and I'm not going off on some wild goose chase." Emotions welled, and I pushed them down.

Staring out the window I remembered what Yut had said: "There is freedom and inner power in knowing your true self." There was one thing that remained unanswered about my true self: why did I react so strongly and strangely to references about orphanages?

I meditated and asked, "If you want me to go to one because it will help me or help someone else, please send me a signal of *where* to go. I am ready. I am willing. I am ready and willing to receive the signals."

Although I was certainly willing to be shown the way, quietly I was not convinced I was ready. But when would I be ready? What more could I do to be ready to understand why this situation created such upset?

I asked, "So *now* will you show me a signal?"

"When you are ready."

And I said, "I am ready."

But I heard again, "When you are ready."

It seemed there was no tricking the Energy Source. It knew what was going on within me. My words were just words, and it could see right through them to what truly lay beneath. I would be shown when the time was right.

So for the time being, I remained aware. I was alert for signals and for opportunities to 'ready' myself. Aaron left. Not surprisingly, I cried. And I waited...

My First Day and Night

I awoke to hear the lyrics, "We gotta get out of this place, if it's the last thing we ever do."[38] *How about you hit me with something a little more inspirational?*

As I got out of bed and thought of the days ahead, marking them out in my mind, I realised Aaron was actually going to be away for 11 days. How did I miss that? 240 hours alone now stretched out to 264 hours. Charlotte suggested that I would probably love my time alone so much, once I got used to it, that I'd be grateful for the extra 24 hours. I was eager to believe it.

Alone, I didn't quite know what to do with myself. Once you strip away all there is to *do* in your normal life, what is left? It seemed the answer was nothing. There was no one to talk to. There was nowhere to go. There was nothing to do—no friends to catch up with, no husband to laugh with, no dog to walk, not even the dishes to wash. We didn't even have a kitchen in the white box.

My planned side emerged as I wrote a list of things to do while Aaron was away. Of course, that included a sub-list of things to do if I felt lonely or upset. At the bottom of the sub-list I wrote, "Create noise and distraction." It seemed my best defence against loneliness was to be doing things to make me not feel alone. That is...rather than work through the alone feeling, I would just disguise it by overloading my senses.

I had become a jukebox for signals. I awoke on day two and was humming Fergie's song, *Big Girls Don't Cry*. The lyrics told the story of why I did not run home to safety and familiarity, of why Aaron had gone away and of why I was alone. "I need some shelter of my own protection... to be with myself and centre, clarity, peace, serenity... It's personal, myself and I... And I'm gonna miss you like a child misses their blanket... It's time to be a big girl now, and big girls don't cry... The path that I'm walkin', I must go alone..."[39]

I had some growing to do. I had some establishing of clarity, peace and serenity to do. If I could find those things in Thonburi, then I could find them anywhere. If they were within me, and I could become at peace with the crazy environment that surrounded me, I would never be without them.

On that note, I ventured out into Thonburi alone for the first time.

I do not know why or how it was different to before, but I had a most wonderful day, not just an okay day, but a *marvellous* day! It was a day better than any day Aaron and I had had in Thonburi together. How was this possible? Somehow being dumped in what I thought would be one of the worst situations I could find myself in, ended up resulting in one of the best experiences I could have. This was becoming a recurring theme.

I covered up my glaring farang skin as best I could, creating a walking sauna, and I headed off to yoga. Yoga was not on, and somehow, I found myself in the middle of a class called Gym Ball doing the last thing on earth I thought I'd be doing: jazzercise. And it was to my anthem: Bon Jovi's *It's My Life* no less! I took that as a sign.

As I sat eating boiled pork hock and rice for lunch, I realised a few more things. If I tried to fill my 11 days with things to occupy and distract myself, creating noise and sensory overload to avoid feeling alone, I would probably not *get* what I was meant to get.

At home, I planned everything. My hours, days and weeks were planned with military precision. Constantly on the go, I would rarely sit down and relax. I was always writing a new list or executing items on an existing list. As I paid the stall vendor for a delicious feast, I laughed to myself that I actually wrote a list of things to refer to when feeling lonely. It seemed there was no shortage of situations where I considered a list to be the perfect solution to any problem! The list, including the 'create noise and distraction' suggestion, was promptly filed in the bin.

I had an opportunity to find clarity, peace and serenity. I would not find any one of those three things if I spent my time in Thonburi living according to my normal habits. I surprised myself and resolved to be as still and quiet as I could for my 264 hours alone. This would require me to be everything that I was not. Everyone who knows me knows I am anything but still, and I am definitely anything but quiet.

Sipping iced tea with my facemask on, I skimmed the channels and found a documentary with subtitles. A western teacher living in Japan after the 2011 earthquake and tsunami disaster was describing the aftermath. I went to remove my facemask in the bathroom, and the apartment went silent. Startled, I poked my head around the corner to peer into the living room. The TV was now off. A chill went down my spine. I went back to turn it on, and as the screen came to life, the subtitles said, "You are not alone."

I could only assume this was another signal. With a face half caked in mask and water trickling from my forehead, I sat cross legged on the floor as the next scene unfolded. A room full of young children, and a subtitle that said, "Don't forget about us."

Miss B

The following days involved many more 'alone' signals. I awoke to an 80's classic, "I think we're alone now, doesn't seem to be anyone around."[40] I wasn't sure exactly what I was meant to take away from all the repeating alone signals. I was pretty clear on the fact I was very much alone! I was hoping for signals that would show me what to do next...

The day became quite eventful when I booked myself a Thai massage, but became so engrossed in writing and editing that I forgot the time. Grabbing my bag, I literally ran all the way to the massage clinic. No one runs in Thonburi. I hadn't even seen a Thai person walk at a brisk pace, let alone jog or run. Of course, it was during this unexpected running expedition that my shoe decided to break. Now I was late and shoeless. This was a serious problem, especially since I was about to break one of my lifetime rules: never be late for appointments. I considered running with one shoe on and one shoe off, but that felt weird. So, I chose to run barefoot. That day, I completely and utterly failed at blending in. What is stranger than a crazed farang running down the alleyways of Thonburi? The answer is: a crazed shoeless farang running down the alleyways.

I arrived sweaty and out of breath. Hoisting open the door, I fell into the cool air conditioning and the sweet smell of peppermint oil. I was taken aback when a boisterous greeting in English came from the reception desk. "Good afternoon, Miss B! Welcome." This was followed by more enthusiastic and friendly comments, "This way please, Miss B. Have a wonderful massage, Miss B." *Did I blink and go to my own special heaven?*

Wait, it got better. We walked straight past the curtained massage cubicles. We were going upstairs. We arrived. The room was marked 'VIP' on a plaque outside the door. I had no idea how or why I ended up being given such treatment, but I will tell you about one of the other rules I live by: never look a gift horse in the mouth. That rule is closely followed by another rule: never think you don't deserve everything good that comes to you.

Since deciding to change my perspective on my situation and deciding on what I really wanted that time to be like, things completely turned around. The Energy Source responded to my about face in attitude. I couldn't even recall one instance of being stared at by anyone. As I wandered home from my massage, chewing on some unknown type of meat on a stick, I reflected on my own nonsense. I realised that for someone to have been staring at me, I would, of course, had to have been staring at them to know.

Magnet For Help

It was time to venture further out of our little area, to explore the rest of Thonburi and the districts beyond. It was all well and good meandering around the one square mile where we lived, but it was another thing to explore beyond alone. I resolved to really push myself out of my comfort zone further and not take a map.

I went by foot, boat, tuk tuk and bus. With the intention of visiting a temple on the other side of the river, I walked to the pier. I sat down for a breather and to dig my wallet from my bag. As soon as my backside hit that park bench, I had a feeling. Something was telling me to get up and get on the boat ASAP. So I did. I jumped up and raced to the pier. The ticket lady shouted at me in Thai, presumably to hurry me along. I managed to jump on the departing ferry. I didn't pay, but that didn't seem to bother anyone. Apparently, it was more important that I made that particular ferry.

I leapt off the pier with both feet flying forward towards the open deck of the barge as it pulled away from the wharf. Then, it occurred to me I had no idea where it was going! So I asked whoever would listen, "Where is this boat going?" None of the 15 people aboard responded. Then a man pointed to the shore opposite to indicate that we were simply crossing over. I said, "Kop kun ka," and sat behind him. He turned around and smiled at me. I was delighted when he spoke English and asked where I was going. As I told him the names of some temples that I hoped to visit, he pointed down river and indicated I could walk along the river's edge to get to one of them. He explained that he was an artist, a sculptor, studying at the University nearby.

The ferry docked, and people leapt off and on. The man was ahead of me. He kept looking back, and then waved me on, as if to say come this way. I followed him and as the throngs of people dissipated, he said, "I show you way."

We talked as we walked along a tree-lined street. The old me would have followed rule number 98.2.d that reads: "Thou shalt not talk to strangers, particularly men, particularly in foreign countries." This rule falls under the chapter: "How a Female Should Safeguard Herself When Alone." Somehow, I didn't care about this rule or any other rule. I figured if he was an axe murderer, then I'd be absolutely fine because the satchel slung over his shoulder was far too small to conceal an axe.

He asked me if I was alone. I said, "Yes, because my husband is away."

"You like coffee?" he asked.

I indicated the affirmative.

"We sit and coffee."

At a riverside café, sitting under the trees, he insisted on paying for my iced mocha. His introduced himself as Mok. We rallied back and forth as he clarified if my name was P, D, C, T, V or B. I kept trying to think of things like "B as in Bee," but that didn't help! Then, I made a buzzing sound like a bee. *Oh, god, I am terrible at this!* Then, I tried "B as in Butterfly."

That clicked for him, and he smiled. Mok instantly made me feel at ease as he exuded a quiet and gentle friendliness that was very welcome after several days alone. He told me all about his sculptures, and then, he proudly announced that he was having a solo exhibition very soon. He stated, matter of factly, "You come to opening." Rattling around in his satchel, he yanked out his newly printed invitations for the grand opening night at a gallery in Bangkok central. The invite was of course written in Thai. So, on the back he wrote:

> *To B*
> *New friend in Thailand*
> *Come to exhibition opening night*
> *9 August, 6:oopm*
> *Lucky Mok*

Without asking, he handed over a myriad of other useful things. His email and cell phone number included.

As I sipped my mocha, I wondered if I was meant to meet Mok, if he was part of this great unfolding. I asked if he knew of any orphanages located in Thonburi. He did not know.

Mok walked me all the way to the temple, dashing over roads and down alleyways, all the while looking back to ensure I was in tow. He fended off oncoming scooters and tuk tuks to ensure I safely arrived at my destination. As we waved goodbye, he shouted back, "See you at opening! Call me if need!"

Feeling buoyed, I decided to proceed on further after visiting the temple. There was another temple, but it was much further away. I would have to venture south. I found a pier and pointed south hoping the ticket vendor wouldn't ask me to go into any more detail than that. The response, in a very loud and direct voice to be heard over boat engines and crowds, was, "Something something something 10 something something 8 something something something 3 baht." I paid 3 baht, and to this day, I still have no idea what the 10 and the 8 were.

There was only one boat at the pier, so on I got. Alighting further down river, I knew I had to go south, so I started walking, declining all offers by waiting taxis and tuk tuks. After several kilometres, I momentarily basked in the air con of a 7-11. Paying for my water, I asked, "Temple?" to the cashier while pointing south. She smiled and pointed to a large tuk tuk outside and said "5 baht." Several people waved me towards the three-wheeled transportation. The driver shook his head and pointed me towards the one in front. I had no idea how the system worked, but it appeared there was in fact a system.

I climbed aboard the group style tuk tuk—the type that no tourists use. These vehicles congregate in seemingly random places. Any number of people clamber aboard, and even with no conversation with the driver, somehow everyone involved in this system knows where they leave from, where they go to, how much it costs and how to get off—everyone except me.

Looking for the driver, I had no idea when we were leaving, when I should get off or how in fact I should alert him to my desire to get off. I promptly scooted closer to the lady next to me as four children, two teenagers and a man all squished in.

The lady next to me smiled, and in English, she said, "Where your friend?" Bizarre. I told her my friend was away, and I was alone. Her eyebrows rose.

She promptly grabbed the 5 baht from my hand and paid the driver. After asking where I was going, she said, "I take you."

At one point, I misread the 'system' and thought it was time to get off, but my new friend pulled me by the arm to get back on. Finally, the system worked, and we arrived at the temple. My new friend chaperoned me all the way to the entrance. A few steps away, she instructed, "Come. Sit. We talk." She searched frantically in her bag and pulled out a pen and paper. Introducing herself as Tida, she handed me her contact details and insisted I should call her if I needed anything before Aaron returned. Before parting, I asked, "Do you know of any orphanages in Thonburi?" She did not.

After what seemed like an age of sitting quietly staring up at the temple which towered against grey skies, hearing tiny bells sounding in the breeze, I headed off to conquer another marvel: the Thai bus system. In rush hour traffic and sweltering heat, I hung my head out the bus window. Feeling peaceful and at ease, I considered how help had shown up everywhere I looked that day. I drew it in like a magnet.

So, I'm Going...

Wiling away the hours, I surfed the internet that night and came across a documentary clip. As I watched the video, I soon discovered that it involved footage of a trip to Thailand—and a visit to an orphanage. The signals were hunting me down.

After yoga the next day, I went to the movies. The trailers included a documentary clip about animals—orphaned animals.

Orphans, orphans, orphans!

I resolved that it was time to go—not home but to an orphanage. This had gone beyond a joke, beyond coincidence, beyond my ability to ignore. I had hoped it would all melt away into nothingness, but alas, no.

The Energy Source had been continually prodding me in this direction, non-stop, since 'The Incident' back home. The signals had been frequent and unwavering. However, as the old adage goes, you can lead a horse to water, but you can't make it drink. I knew I had been a very stubborn horse.

Failing to follow my own advice to date, it was time to take action. I knew I could sit in Bangkok for longer, perhaps forever, and never get the answers to my questions. I emailed two orphanages, and one volunteer organisation—all were located within two hours of our apartment. I waited, but heard nothing in return.

I didn't want to admit it to myself, but one of the places stuck in my mind for the rest of the week. They cared for abandoned babies—not toddlers or older children, just babies. I thought of babies alone. Those two words should NEVER go together: babies and alone. Never ever.

I went exploring in the area where the nursery was located. I had intended to go into that district to explore anyway. I got to a major intersection. To the left was the way home to our apartment, and to the right was the way to the nursery. I turned right and started walking. Then, I promptly did a 180-degree manoeuvre and walked home.

Why? Let me count the ways... It's not okay to turn up unannounced. I should really get home because it looks like rain is coming. I might get lost if I don't go back the way I came. They probably don't speak English... and so on.

I tried to console myself all the way home as to why I had made the correct decision, but the funny feeling wouldn't leave me. So I telephoned the nursery. I called once. I called twice. I waited another day and called again. Nothing.

In the end, I got hold of someone at a volunteer organisation, and the gentleman said he didn't know of this nursery. However, he did say that I was welcome to visit one of the other orphanages with him. He explained the process and was very helpful. I said I would call him in a few days to arrange the date and time. But, still, the funny feeling remained.

With little more than 12 hours until Aaron was due home, I packed my bag and left the apartment. I navigated my way into Bangkok central to do a few errands (i.e. more time wasting). Traffic was thick and so was the monsoon rain. The day was getting on, so before I let my 'running away self' take control again, my 'get out of your comfort zone self' jumped in a tuk tuk. After debating with the driver about whether or not we would be stopping at his brother's tailor shop on the way, we began our trip to the nursery.

Rain gushed in the side of the tuk tuk as we wheeled and bounced our way through the city—over railway lines, under overpasses, through intersections.

Once the city limits were breached, we moved through suburban outlying Bangkok and arrived.

I stood looking at the building that lay beyond large iron gates. A smile greeted me from within. The woman said I was very welcome, but perhaps I could come tomorrow as the rain was very heavy and tomorrow we could play outside with the children. She assured me that there was nothing to do and nothing to bring. She wanted nothing more than for me to be with the children. "Smile and play," she said. My baby steps had first taken me into the district, and then as far as the iron gates, and soon I would meet the children.

I returned home to find an email from the woman at the nursery. The email had been sent to me while I was venturing on my way there. At the very time that I decided to reach out and go, they decided to reply. It's funny how life works that way.

Make Me Real

I awoke at 2:58am to a haunting Evanescence song, "...My spirit's sleeping somewhere cold, until you find it there and lead it back home... Save me from the nothing I've become... you can't just leave me... make me real... Without a voice, without a soul, don't let me die here. There must be something more. Bring me to life."[41]

I tried to listen to the song online multiple times, and each time the song cut out after 'make me real'.

Chapter 27

Beyond the Gates

Aaron arrived home! The peas in the pod reunited. I was so thrilled to see him, but at the same time, I was sad to bid farewell to my 264 hours of alone. It had been a wonderful rendezvous with myself, and I discovered that aside from Aaron being my best friend, I was in fact my own best friend.

Aaron dragged his jet lagged self towards a hot shower. After I had unleashed 11 days worth of stories on him, it was time for me to venture out again. I was going beyond the gates.

I first had to navigate myself to the gates. This was quite a momentous journey by foot, taxi and ferry and then by foot and taxi again. Eventually, almost two hours later, I stood at the gates. This two hour calamity was simply a fact of life in the perpetual Bangkok traffic jam.

The journey was very much worth it. Two hours there and hopefully not two hours to get home would turn out to be a small price to pay. I sat on the patio with the nursery social worker. I had questions about their work, about the circumstances that had brought the children there and what the future would hold for them.

Although this was a broken English conversation, I was sufficiently clear that this was a wonderful, loving place where the children were anything but forgotten and unloved. The children and their wonderful caregivers were like one big family.

Bizarrely, this particular nursery adopted their children primarily to two countries, including New Zealand. I was delighted to hear that there were, at any time, between 200-300 families awaiting a child via adoptive agencies. It seemed, based solely on this conversation, that there were many families wanting to remember and love these children.

I was told there were 14 babies inside. It was consoling to know that every child in there was already adopted, simply pending paperwork. It's a fact of life that such paperwork takes a very long time to process.

It would have taken an idiot not to see the love emanating from the caregivers. They treated the children like their own, minding them until their new parents could come to take them home. With passion, the social worker explained very definitively that a family wishing to choose the child they wanted would need to go to some other place for adoption. This was not how their process worked. Here, the nursery selected the family for the child. Things that had previously stung in my mind seemed to be untrue in this situation. The children's needs and futures were solely what was driving the process.

Buoyed by all of this, and surprising myself by not being in the least uncomfortable, I leapt up as soon as

I was asked to go inside the nursery to meet a little girl named Malee.

Two steps behind the supervisor, I looked at my feet as we walked through the nursery room door. When I looked up, my heart was in my throat. I reminded myself to suck it up.

14 cots were in three neat rows, each containing a baby. They all seemed to be awake. 14 pairs of eyes turned to look. It felt like 28 hands all reaching out towards us at once. The older ones became vocal, calling for attention.

All I could wonder was: *What happens when there aren't 14 caregivers to cuddle them all? Perhaps seven is enough, since everyone has two arms. There aren't seven of us here, but maybe other days there are.*

Malee was one year old. She looked at me with suspicion for all of five seconds, and then, she did her best to leap from the cot into my arms.

An incredibly sociable little girl, she appeared to have no fear. The caregivers confirmed that her nature was just that: fearless. She was inquisitive and open. I found it inspiring, that after all she had experienced in her start in life, what I assumed to be her true self was still shining through undiminished. This was not what I was expecting. How much fear baggage had I accumulated in 32 years, and I assumed many lives previously? And yet, little Malee, all 12 months of her, was completely fearless. I quickly saw that there was something for me to learn in this place.

My heart returned to its rightful chest cavity as the following hours became absorbed in playing with

Malee. The caregiver asked me to come back often, to help her learn to walk. She scooted around the patio pulling at my hands, with her body and head ploughing forward. Musical toys elicited a wonderful smile and broke her silence as she made clicking noises while the melodies played. I made a mental note to look for a musical toy to bring the next time. There would of course be a next time, once I'd discovered I didn't break down like a sobbing idiot.

A caregiver joined me outside with a little boy. I quickly understood that each child bonded with one person. The caregiver clearly lit up like a lantern when she had him in her arms. She had cared for him since he was a newborn. I peered over to see her flipping through photos of his new family who would be coming to take him home soon. She said to him, "Mummy," and he grabbed the book. Pulling the photo close to his face, he kissed it. She said to him, "Daddy," and he turned the page and kissed the photo.

I looked at her beaming face and said, "It will be sad to say goodbye." She looked down and silently nodded. I thought that she possessed possibly one of the greatest human traits to achieve: to be able to love with her whole heart and still be able to let go. I suspected that the caregivers, some of whom had worked there for 20 years, had loved and let go of countless children.

As I made my way back to the apartment, I thought back to 'The Incident' when I made the remark about westerners visiting orphanages being cliché. I was utterly disgraced at myself for having thought it, let alone voiced it.

Now, I firmly believe that there is nothing at all cliché about a human being showing compassion, whether it is compassion for an hour, a day, a week, a month, or indeed, compassion for a lifetime. Compassion is never a bad thing, and compassion will never be cliché.

> *How improved would our world be if we all went beyond fear, hesitation and judgment into compassion?*

Hard Truth

My subsequent visits were not as easy as the first. The handful of caregivers and other volunteers dissipated. There were six arms and 14 babies. You do the math. It wasn't great. There was love, no doubt—love to be shared generously and unconditionally, but babies need a lot of love. Sometimes, it seemed, there just wasn't enough to go around.

Malee was handed to me. The caregiver explained that the children could get upset if they saw someone they had bonded with playing with the other children. Even at this young age, they were very much observant and alert, looking for who would play with them, who would cuddle them, and wondering when it would be their turn to get out of their cot.

As far as walking went, where there's a will, there's a way—and Malee certainly had will. I was sure she would be hooning around on her own in no time. I gave her a musical toy, and she shook and squealed with delight. The afternoon was spent between walking attempts, jiggling to music and throwing herself into my lap every few minutes, nuzzling her head close for a cuddle.

On the previous visit I had left without saying goodbye to Malee. After all, she was only one, and I was a stranger. However, that day, I gave her a cuddle, put her down and said goodbye in Thai. Her lip quivered, and she burst into tears, grabbing at my legs. I balanced her quivering lip with my stiff upper lip to cover the upset. I told the caregiver I would be back.

It seemed these visits were the warm up, and next came the main event. I arrived and went inside. There was one caregiver. I heard noises out back; someone was busy doing washing, cleaning dishes, preparing food and folding nappies. It appeared that nearly all of the babies were awake, and a couple somehow masterfully slept through the din.

Malee was screeching from her cot when she saw me arrive, flinging her arms towards me and smiling widely. I walked over to pick her up.

Since some of the children were able to pull themselves up from the edge of their cots and move around quite deftly and quickly, for their own safety, one ankle was gently tied with a long piece of soft cotton stretch cloth. The other end of which was tied to the cot. This was a necessary reality to ensure the children remained safe and well cared for. One, two or even three people cannot watch 14 children every second; it is humanly impossible.

I untied her ankle and scooped her up out of the cot, holding her close. We went beyond the patio and touched the grass and the leaves. We watched some type of squirrel scratch around in a tree in the yard. Wiggling to get down, it was time to practice and it was this day that she walked. Was this her first time walking on her own? Two steps turned into three— then seven. She walked seven whole steps on her own! No one was there to see it—no one other than me. I felt lucky to be there, but I felt sad at the same time. There was no video camera to record the event for posterity and no mother or father to delight in her progress, no grandma or grandpa to revel in pride, no photos to put in the family album.

It felt only right that I should teach her at that moment how to do a High Five! This was something she would become proficient at in the coming weeks. I thought to myself that whoever her adoptive family were, wherever they were, they were going to have a wonderful life with their little girl. She was certainly full of personality.

Visiting hours drew to a close, and I took Malee inside. The two caregivers were preparing a tray of bowls and bottles ready to feed the children. I turned around to face the cots, and all the many faces stared back, most of them crying. Again, one doesn't have to be a rocket scientist to work out how challenging this situation was. I'd seen my nephews when they were hungry and it was time to be fed; delays were not pretty!

I fed Malee first as the two caregivers fed others. One little boy in particular was beyond crying; it was the distressed level of sobbing with intervals of silence as he gasped. In order to get him up to feed him; I had to put Malee down.

As I lowered her down into her cot, she gripped on to me and started screaming. Her hands clawed at my arms, and her head leaned into my chest. I looked down and saw the cloth tie lying there, and my heart dropped as I realised I would have to tie her in. I could feel it coming, the upset rising from the dark cave. My fingers fumbled with the cloth. She sobbed, pulling at me with pleading eyes.

There was no other way to do it. I swallowed the lump in my throat, and I gently tied her ankle. As I walked away, leaving her desperate crying to continue, my heart literally broke.

Near on breaking into tears, I turned my attention to the little boy who had been so upset. He stopped crying as soon as I leaned into his cot. Attempting to feed him admittedly stretched my child caring capabilities beyond their tested limits! Who could blame him for wanting to move—any way, anywhere, just to move to experience freedom beyond the cot. It took me five minutes to realise why all the squirming, reaching and twisting while I attempted to interest him in his food. He was trying to get to the screen door behind us, which led outside. He pressed his face up against the wire screen and stared out, and that was all he wanted.

This visit broke me. It broke open the unwanted feeling. It broke me with the reality that I couldn't fix the situation in any meaningful or lasting way. I couldn't make it better. I couldn't do anything. Everything I was faced with in that situation challenged how I would normally react: logistical planning, then fixing. That's always been my way of being, but that way of being was not going to work at the nursery.

Leaving that day was hard. In the back of a taxi, on the way to the pier, I was only vaguely aware of the journey. Caught back in that moment in the nursery, I was lost in the knowledge that I couldn't help. On the ferry, people jammed in shoulder to shoulder as we lurched down river over muddy orange water lashing at the side of the boat. I stood sweaty and motionless, gripping on to a metal pole, my head resting against it. Staring vacantly at the water from behind my sunglasses, I tried not to cry. I failed at trying.

This had pushed me beyond my limits, expanding my ability to feel, to cope and to 'let it be'. There was no other option available to me; I had to let it be.

Turning Dreams Into Reality

Attending Mok's exhibition, I asked him to explain the theme underpinning his work. He struggled to articulate it in English. He asked his mentor from the University to help. The professor announced, "Turning dreams into reality."

He went on to say that there were other messages woven into Mok's sculptures. The art told us,

"Meditation by breathing is a way to release negative thoughts that come from our subconscious and the past, instead recall the goodness and beauty of life."

I presented Mok with an advanced version of a one-winged monster, and with congratulations on his achievement and gratitude for his friendship, we left.

His art had inspired me to put more thought and feeling into the next stage of my own adventure: for what lay ahead when I returned home. There were more dreams to turn into reality. I wanted to create my life as an author, coach and healer, doing that from my home on Waiheke. The dream represented doing what fulfils me in a place where I feel most inspired. I visualised all that my life would be like: my book published to share my message with people and my clients benefiting positively from coaching and healing, turning their own dreams into reality. I ensured that this movie reel playing over in my mind included income flowing to me.

Within hours, healing requests started flowing in. The ball was rolling already. One person insisted on paying me. I also had several new 'experiences' during the healings—new ways of receiving information and messages during the sessions.

Then, I met Nim, a volunteer at the nursery. We stood chatting with babies in our arms as she explained that she also lived in Thonburi. She offered to give me a ride. Stuck in traffic, moving nowhere for 75 minutes, we had a long conversation. After years of nursing, she decided one day that she wanted to be a self-made business woman. There was one small problem: she knew nothing about business. And it wasn't just any business; Nim wanted to make wonderful handbags.

"I know nothing of *how*. So, I say 'show me how, show me each step to make it so', and then, I just go bit by bit to get where I am now." As she said this, she was looking upwards. She told me that she was spiritual and believed in guidance from above. She literally went from nothing (no idea, no capital, no product, no factory, no staff) to owning and operating a hugely successful business exporting high-end fashion bags to the most exclusive stores across Europe and Japan.

Pulling out her camera, she showed me photos of her products. Next came the photos of her on the front page of a leading Bangkok newspaper, and one of her shaking hands with a Thai government minister who visited her factory.

Nim took her dream and turned it into reality. She was another example of what is possible in life when you desire something and ask for guidance.

Noname

I decided to get more efficient about my passage to the nursery. The traffic was stealing valuable time from Malee. There was only one way to get around Bangkok in a hurry: motorbike taxi. This, I was told, was definitely NOT advisable. However, needs must. I lived far away from the nursery, and time was of the essence. I manifested that I would be safe, and for practical purposes, I ensured that I knew how to say SLOW in Thai.

Unbeknownst to me, I was about to learn a very good lesson in Thai motorbike transportation: older men driving motorbikes drive slow. Younger men drive fast and furious. On arrival at the pier, all the drivers were young men, and as I subsequently found out, they all drove likes bats out of hell.

I clambered on the back of what could have been called a motorbike, or should have been called the skeletal remains of a motorbike! In an attempt not to behave like a complete farang freak, I did not wrap my arms around the driver's waist. Thai women demurely ride side-saddle without even holding on. However, I did want to make it there in one piece, so I gripped the back of my seat. As we bounced over potholes and wove our way between buses, I tried not to focus on the fact that the lever on the handlebar looked like it was loose, and nothing on the tiny skeletal dashboard was working. Although it was mildly concerning that we actually became air borne as we flew over a raised intersection, I did make it there alive.

Pale in the face and eternally grateful for having all my limbs in tact, I bowled into the nursery only to find Malee asleep. The caregiver present said, "Ah, Khun B..." and signalled for me to follow her. She grinned and looked like she had discovered this was the perfect outcome. She bent over a cot and turned around to present me with a baby: a little boy. She said, "New."

While definitely no baby expert, I was pretty sure this child was not newborn. I assumed she meant that he was new to the nursery. I took him outside to the patio and spent several hours with him. Through my powers of deduction, including various solid experiments including 'sit up on own time' and 'lift head tummy time' and 'how many teeth do you have time', I narrowed his age to approximately six or seven months old.

A caregiver walked by and I asked, "What is his name?"

She shook her head. Mmm, I wondered what that meant. I snuggled him close to me. "Maybe you have no name? I will have to call you Noname until I figure it out."

The caregiver returned. I asked if the baby had just arrived. The response was a nod.

I asked how old he was, but she shook her head with a look of dismay. I took from this that they did not know conclusively. I said, "Maybe six months?"

She shook her head and shrugged at the same time.

I asked, "What is his name?"

"No name," she said.

"No name?"

"Ka, no name."

Many afternoons were then spent with Noname in one arm and Malee in the other. Malee spent the time between wobbly walking and clambering over the top of Noname to commandeer my attention. Noname held close and never made a peep. He was always full of silent smiles and wide-eyed stares.

I whispered in his ear, "You will have a wonderful mum and dad soon. They will come for you, and you're going to have a great life, I promise." I wondered: *Where are his actual parents? Who bought him to the nursery? Was hard for them to do? If he's here, then he's meant to be here. They've given him a chance at a better life than they could offer.*

On the journey home, as a railway crossing barrier arm came down and the bells and lights were going, I cursed that the driver was young. *Why aren't there any slow driving old men around here?!* Anyone from any country knows that a railway barrier arm down means a train is coming. I actually shrieked when he ran a red light across a six-lane intersection, sped towards the barrier arm and performed an 'S' bend manoeuvre to beat the train. It was that day that I lost one year off my life and vowed to learn how to say STOP in Thai!

That night, I told Aaron about Noname. I couldn't shake the knowledge that he wasn't really institutionalised yet. Technically, he was, but in his heart he wasn't. It was his first few days in the nursery. He had been raised by someone to date, and now, he was orphaned—abandoned. From the constant smiles on his face, he seemed blissfully unaware of his situation. He did not have that slightly bleary eyed, slightly alone look about him that the other children had—the ones whose eyes followed me every second I was in the room, waiting, hoping to be picked up, reaching out to touch me with their hands, making noises in the hopes of engagement. Noname was not alert to his predicament.

I wished very hard that one of the adoptive families on the wait list could have just come and taken him home right then. Despite the love and care in the nursery, I wished that he wouldn't have to wait there while paperwork was processed and that his formative months and quite possibly the next year wouldn't be spent in a cot, waiting.

Lingering

Before leaving Thailand, we made a fleeting trip to nearby Cambodia to experience the awe of the Angkor World Heritage Site. Walking amongst the temples, marvelling at the history and spiritual symbolism, I noticed a woman. She was alone.

Aaron and I meandered in our own directions, exploring the nooks and crannies of the ruins. I saw her again. In fact, she was standing right in the middle of what I wanted to be a perfect photo opportunity. As I waited for her to move away, I wondered where she was from and what she was doing on her travels alone.

After two nights, we left. Boarding the plane back to Bangkok, we bustled our way to our seats. Aaron usually gives me (a.k.a. I jostle for and win) the window seat. This day, there was none of that. I climbed into the middle seat and settled in. Within seconds, I could sense the person sitting next to me in the aisle seat was staring. After a few moments, I turned to make polite conversation. It was a young woman, and she was strikingly beautiful. She seemed very genuine and friendly as we chatted. I was tired after a long day and not entirely 'with it', so I was shocked when she said, "I saw you yesterday at the temple. Remember me?"

It was her. We spoke at length.

I asked, "What brought you to Cambodia?"

"I've been working at an orphanage."

With little more than a week to go until our return to New Zealand, preparing for closure and an end to Project Thailand, I wondered to myself if these continuing coincidences were going to follow me home.

I awoke the next day to words of a song that didn't answer my questions, but they left some lingering.

"...it's no coincidence I've come..."[42]

Unforgettable

In the days before leaving, Noname continuously came to mind. I awoke one morning and put another dime in the jukebox baby because the songs kept coming. Nat King Cole warmed me from the inside out, "Unforgettable, that's what you are. Unforgettable, though near or far... never before has someone been more unforgettable, in every way. And forevermore, that's how you'll stay..."[43]

Sitting in the dentist's reception, waiting for Aaron, I flicked through a magazine, looking at pictures surrounded by nothing but Thai words. I don't know why I was surprised when I happened upon a picture of children playing happily in a playground, with the only English word being the article heading; "Unforgettable."

Goodbye

It was time to say goodbye. My motorbike taxi friend at the pier smiled and called out when he saw me jumping off the ferry. "She go Soi 36!" he exclaimed with his arm flailing in the air, pointing in the direction of the nursery. He knew where I was going because he had taken me many times. We often had broken English/Thai conversations as we zipped along. At first, he had been perplexed about where I was going, in the middle of this outlying residential area. I had explained to him, "Chuay babies" as I rocked my arms back and forth.

I knew it would be hard to say goodbye to Malee and Noname for the final time. I didn't anticipate quite how hard. Malee had been crying every time I left. She just wanted to be held. Putting her back in her cot was something she equated with being very bad news. I decided it was best to get her asleep before leaving this last time, perhaps for my sake more than hers. I didn't want to walk away with her cries being the last thing I heard.

I sang her a little ditty, my version of a song called *Que Sera Sera*. I've always hummed this song to myself for years, I don't know why. When I was alone in Thonburi, I changed the lyrics. The real lyrics go...

"When I was just a little girl I asked my mother, what will I be? Will I be pretty? Will I be rich? Here's what she said to me: Que Sera, Sera, whatever will be, will be. The futures not ours you see. Que Sera, Sera..."[44]

Holding Malee, I sung my version to her...

"When I was just a little girl I asked my mother, what will I be? Will I be pretty, will I be rich? Here's what she said to me. Que Sera Sera, BE WHATEVER YOU WANT TO BE. THE FUTURE IS YOURS, YOU SEE. Que Sera Sera..."

I hoped Malee would come to know this truth for herself one day. When she fell asleep, I laid her down in her cot. The last thing I saw of Malee, she was quietly sleeping—legs sprawled, arms sprawled, hopefully dreaming of good things to come.

Looking down into Noname's cot, he beamed up at me. I picked him up for a cuddle, and he smiled. I put him down, and as I said goodbye, he smiled—Noname, who forever smiles.

I had hugged them goodbye knowing it would be the last time I ever saw them. As I looked at them one last time, I took a mental snapshot of their faces, hoping the picture in my mind would never fade.

I didn't want to get upset, especially not in front of the children. It was the one thing I promised myself I would not do, but as I left, I broke my promise. My tears said, "I am sad I will never see you again."

Conclusion

Today is the day. I miss home, and I'm ready. It's time to go. As much as I want to go, I will miss this place and these people. I actually ache when I think about leaving.

I will walk away from Thailand, this experience, leaving things behind.

I will leave behind wonderful people who have been very kind to me and who have taught me a lot. I will leave behind things I can't fix, things I have learned are not there for me to fix. I will leave behind parts of the old B, bits of fear and anxiety here and there, bits of B that don't serve her well for the future. These old bits have left necessary gaps for the new B to emerge. Thailand has allowed me to shed the old to make room for the new.

My metamorphosis, for this journey at least, is completing. I believe I have come out of my cocoon fully, and as I ponder the fact I will soon be going home, I feel like my butterfly wings are stretching out ready to take flight. I take flight not as the old B, not as Scuba B, not as Miss B, not as Khun B, but as Author, Coach and Healer B. The B I said I would be.

I also leave behind butterflies. Butterflies of various shapes, sizes and colours (and made with varying degrees of skill and quality!) now adorn many nooks and crannies, corners and walls, ceilings and doors in Thailand—a 'thank you for your smiles' butterfly swinging from a security guard's desk in Koh

Samui, a 'thank you and good luck' butterfly sitting in an art gallery at a solo exhibition, and a 'you're special and memorable' butterfly pinned on a nursery room wall for a group of children who are unforgettable and very much loved.

Although I leave much behind, I will be taking many things home with me: memories, new language and customs, new friendships, new thoughts and questions, new knowledge of myself and others, and a new capacity for coping, feeling and letting things be. I also take with me the newfound and no doubt temporary yoga ability to (on the second to last day of this sabbatical) get my leg over my shoulder (well close enough!) Wonders never cease to amaze. And of course, the final thing I will take home with me... shoes. No girl in their right mind leaves Bangkok without new shoes.

And so it was...

18 months after my adventure commenced, it now draws to a close. What lies beyond this adventure? What awaits me next? More aptly put, what dream do I feel compelled to turn into reality?

Signals keep coming, even before boarding the plane back home. It seems 2012 is already manifesting. Best we get some restful beauty sleep over the remaining months of 2011, because next year could be another twisting, turning year on this rollercoaster of life... but that is a whole other story.

For now, I long to go home and see my family. I long to cuddle Cash. I long to plant my spring garden.

I long to breathe the fresh air of Waiheke Island and to swim in the brisk waves at our local beach. These are the things I long for, for now...

Joy

In our biggest challenges, we get to see our deepest fears. In our deepest fears, we can uncover hidden truths about ourselves. These are the truths that shape our lives. Discover them, shed light on them, and you will have power over your life in a way you have never experienced before.

If you want to know what I think when I look back at the last 18 months and wonder how I ended up where I am, I will tell you that I don't think about it. I feel it. When I review this documented account and relive my experiences...

I remember the day that my younger self sat on the toilet in Charlotte's bathroom, crying, thinking my life was over, and hearing her words. I feel love and say, "I will never forget all you've done for me."

I remember when Jessie met me for coffee and encouraged me to see Augustus. I feel grateful and say, "Thank you."

I remember when we moved our life to Waiheke Island. I feel fulfilled and say, "Amazing."

I remember the moment I declared myself an author. I feel liberated and say, "Go me!"

I remember scrubbing dog poo off my carpet. I feel comical laughter rising and say, "Bahahahaha." (That's me laughing riotously!)

I remember the moment when the last brick wall crumbled before me, clearing the way for Project Thailand to happen, showing me the yellow brick road ahead. I feel excitement and say, "Awesome-er."

I remember Samui, gazing out of my writing room at the blue sky and coconut trees, seeing all I had dreamed about actually manifested as reality around me. I feel freedom and say, "Life cannot get any better than this... can it?"

I sit now in Thonburi, reflecting on how it has grounded me, and all it has taught me. I feel total gratitude of the type that I have never felt before and say, "Thank you for showing me the way home to my true self."

As I look at my life, present and future—Waiheke, Thailand, Author, Coach, Healer, Wife and Puppy Mummy—I feel deep down in my gut true blue joy and say, "PINCH ME!"

Life is an adventure, a spiritual seeking, a quest to know, be, do and have more, a melting pot of challenges, a catalogue of questions and a journey for answers. Take whatever analogy works for you— plunge into the river, turn on your tap, become a pear. Just grab the essentials for adventure (an open mind and trust), set out to see where it leads, and let the signals guide you.

Joy awaits you!

What Next?

Here is a taste of what is to come, post-Thailand statements heard directly from the horse's mouth. Not even B knows the answers to some of these questions...

"Quit completely? What about income? Do I have to?"

"But specifically which Hawaiian island?"

"Who the heck is Carol Daubney?"

After returning home to New Zealand and experiencing more twists and turns, B's next adventure out into the wild blue yonder started with the following entry in her new set of notebooks for 2012...

*****

Life has become a perpetual orienteering expedition, an adrenaline filled journey of discovery. I adjust my tap and set forth, ready for signals. What's around the corner? I can't wait to get out of bed today to see what is going to happen next!

That being said, the biggest, scariest leaps of faith are yet to come. When you are guided to let go of <u>all</u> your security and stability, and you've asked 20 times and had the same answer from upstairs, there is nothing more that you can do but trust. As you look over the edge, ready to jump into a total vacuum of nothingness, you can say one of two things and your answer will define your future...

You're completely crazy if you think I'm going to listen on this occasion. That vacuum of time and space is empty, dark, cold and scary, where unknown things lie, and if you think I'm going to give up my comforts and security to go there, then you're dreaming. How can that be good?

OR

Bring it on! That vacuum before me is an empty, mysterious, vast vortex of endless opportunity, where, if I surrender up any pre-conceived ideas of how my life is going to play out, then every possible thing in the world becomes a potential path for me. How can that be bad?

*****

I wonder which option she chose.

About the Author

Bernadette is an author and transformational coach.

She founded her business Pinch Me Living in 2011 to support others with creating life-affirming changes for themselves.

To connect with Bernadette, and for more information on private coaching, retreats, live events, as well as free resources, please visit **www.pinchmeliving.com**.

Also by the Author:
Going Out On A Limb
Unleash Your Life

References & Resources

1. Spirit Channeler definition sourced from www.wikipedia.org

2. Palmistry definition sourced from www.wikipedia.org

3. Reference to *The Secret* by Rhonda Byrne, 2006.

4. Quote from the Encyclopedia of Nursing & Allied Health, 2002, quote obtained from www.enotes.com

5. Quote from *A New Earth* by Eckhart Tolle, 2005.

6. Quote from *The Life You Were Born to Live* by Dan Millman, 1993.

7. Reference to Many Lives Many Masters by Dr. Brian Weiss, 1988.

8. Reference to *The Power of Now* by Eckhart Tolle, 1999.

9. Quote from *Animal Speak* by Ted Andrews, 1993.

10. Quote from *Animal Speak* by Ted Andrews, 1993.

11. Lyrics from *Up Where We Belong* by Joe Cocker & Jennifer Warnes, written by Will Jennings (source: www.wikipedia.org).

12. Quote from *Animal Speak* by Ted Andrews, 1993.

13. Energy Healing definition sourced from www.wikipedia.org

14. Reference to *The Reconnection* by Dr. Eric Pearl, 2001.

15. Quote from www.asara.com, website of Asara Lovejoy.

16. ThetaHealing™, ThetaHealer™, Basic DNA™, ThetaHealing Institute of Knowledge™, and Certified by Vianna™ are trademarks of Nature Path, Inc., Idaho, USA, and are used by permission.

17. Lyrics from *I Still Haven't Found What I'm Looking For* by U2.

18. Reference to *The Winner's Bible* by Dr. Kerry Spackman, 2009.

19. Quote from *The 4-Hour Workweek* by Timothy Ferriss, 2008 edition.

20. Quote from *Notes from the Universe* daily email quotes by Mike Dooley, www.tut.com

21. Reference to *Outliers* by Malcolm Gladwell, 2008.

22. Quote from *Medicine Cards* by Jamie Sams & David Carson, 1999.

23. Quote from *Medicine Cards* by Jamie Sams & David Carson, 1999.

24. Quote from *Medicine Cards* by Jamie Sams & David Carson, 1999.

25. Quote from the back cover review by Phil Carroll, from *Synchronicity: The Inner Path of Leadership* by Joseph Jaworski, 1998.

26. Reference to *Servant Leadership* by Robert K. Greenleaf, as noted within the Introduction by Peter Senge, from *Synchronicity: The Inner Path of Leadership* by Joseph Jaworski, 1998.

27. Quote from the Introduction by Peter Senge, from *Synchronicity: The Inner Path of Leadership* by Joseph Jaworski, 1998.

28. Quote from *The Serenity Prayer* by Reinhold Niebuhr.

29. Lyrics from *It's My Life* by Bon Jovi, written by Jon Bon Jovi, Richie Sambora and Max Martin (source: www.wikipedia.org).

30. Lyrics from *Venus* by The Feelers.

31. Quote from *The Shack* by William P Young, 2007.

32. Lyrics from *When Tomorrow Comes* by The Eurhythmics, written by Annie Lennox, David A. Stewart and Pat Seymour (source: www.wikipedia.org).

33. Lyrics from *Need You Now* by Lady Antebellum, written by Lady Antebellum and Josh Kear (source: www.wikipedia.org).

34. Quote from *A Return to Love* by Marianne Williamson, 1992.

35. Quote from *Eat Pray Love* by Elizabeth Gilbert, 2006.

36. Translation of English to Thai words and phrases quoted from www.thai2english.com

37. Lyrics from *More Than I Can Say* by Leo Sayer, written by Sonny Curtis and Jerry Allison (source: www.wikipedia.org).

38. Lyrics from *We Gotta Get Out of This Place* by The Animals, written by Barry Mann and Cynthia Weil (source: www.wikipedia.org).

39. Lyrics from *Big Girls Don't Cry* by Fergie, written by Fergie and Toby Gad (source: www.wikipedia.org).

40. Lyrics from *I Think We're Alone Now* by Tiffany, written by Ritchie Cordell (source: www.wikipedia.org).

41. Lyrics from *Bring Me to Life* by Evanescence, written by Amy Lee, David Hodges and Ben Moody (source: www.wikipedia.org).

42. Lyrics from *Crazy* by Gnarls Barkley, written by Danger Mouse and Cee Lo Green (source: www.wikipedia.org).

43. Lyrics from *Unforgettable* by Nat King Cole, written by Irving Gordon (source: www.wikipedia.org).

44. Lyrics from Que Sera Sera written by Jay Livingston and Ray Evans (source: www.wikipedia.org).

Reflections